Decisions about Decisions

Here is one of the most fundamental questions in human life: How do we decide how we decide? We make such decisions all the time. If you trust your doctor, you might decide to follow a simple rule for medical decisions: Do whatever your doctor suggests. If you like someone a lot, and maybe love them, but are not sure whether you want to marry them, you might do this: Live with them first. Some of these strategies are wise. They prevent error. They improve your emotional well-being. Some of these strategies are foolish. They lead you in the direction of terrible mistakes. They prevent you from learning. They might make you miserable. *Decisions about Decisions* explores how people do, and should, make decisions about decisions. It aims to see what such decisions are, to explore how they go right, and see where they go wrong.

Cass R. Sunstein is the Robert Walmsley University Professor at Harvard. He is the founder and director of the Program on Behavioral Economics and Public Policy at Harvard Law School. He is also a Distinguished Academic Visitor at Queen's College and an Honorary Fellow at Judd Business School, Cambridge University. In 2018, he received the Holberg Prize from the government of Norway.

Decisions about Decisions

Practical Reason in Ordinary Life

Cass R. Sunstein

Harvard University

CAMBRIDGE
UNIVERSITY PRESS

Shaftesbury Road, Cambridge CB2 8EA, United Kingdom

One Liberty Plaza, 20th Floor, New York, NY 10006, USA

477 Williamstown Road, Port Melbourne, VIC 3207, Australia

314–321, 3rd Floor, Plot 3, Splendor Forum, Jasola District Centre, New Delhi – 110025, India

103 Penang Road, #05–06/07, Visioncrest Commercial, Singapore 238467

Cambridge University Press is part of Cambridge University Press & Assessment, a department of the University of Cambridge.

We share the University's mission to contribute to society through the pursuit of education, learning and research at the highest international levels of excellence.

www.cambridge.org
Information on this title: www.cambridge.org/9781009400466

DOI: 10.1017/9781009400480

First published 2023

A catalogue record for this publication is available from the British Library

ISBN   978-1-009-40046-6   Hardback

Cambridge University Press & Assessment has no responsibility for the persistence or accuracy of URLs for external or third-party internet websites referred to in this publication and does not guarantee that any content on such websites is, or will remain, accurate or appropriate.

CONTENTS

TABLES

PREFACE

Frank Ramsey was a philosopher at the University of Cambridge who was also a member of the Apostles, an invitation-only group of the intellectual elite at Cambridge – the best of the best. Perhaps the greatest thinker of his generation, Ramsey died at twenty-six. When he was twenty-three, he gave an evening speech that was directed above all at Ludwig Wittgenstein, in some ways his mentor, who contended that on questions that did not involve facts, philosophy did not have a lot to say. Ramsey announced, "Humanity which fills the foreground of my picture I find interesting and on the whole admirable. I find, just now at least, the world a pleasant and exciting place."[1]

Squarely addressing Wittgenstein, Ramsey acknowledged, "You may find it depressing; I am sorry for you, and you despise me." But, Ramsey added, "I have reason and you have none; you would only have a reason for despising me if your feeling corresponded to the fact in a way mine didn't. But neither can correspond to the fact." Ramsey's crescendo: "The fact is not in itself good or bad; it is just that it thrills me but depresses you. On the other hand I pity you with reason because it is pleasanter to be thrilled than to be depressed, and not merely pleasanter but better for all one's activities."

A major goal of this book is to pause over Ramsey's crescendo. It is pleasanter to be thrilled than to be depressed, and that fact should inform our decisions, even when our eye is on some other ball. Before

---

[1] CHERYL MISAK, FRANK RAMSEY: A SHEER EXCESS OF POWERS 218–19 (Oxford University Press 2020).

this book was completed, I visited Cambridge University and was fortunate enough to see some of Ramsey's personal letters, including a number that he wrote to his wife, with whom he was enraptured. His exuberance – his delight about people, ideas, and life – shines through those letters. I hope that a little bit of Ramsey's spirit has made its way into these pages.

* * *

A few months ago, I rented a car for a period of two weeks in Ireland. I arrived at Shannon Airport after a five-hour flight from New York, and a nice person at the rental car counter asked me various questions. I was half-asleep, but I knew that some of those questions had to do with insurance. Long ago, a good friend of mine, a distinguished economist, told me always to decline insurance when renting a car, and that is what I did, I thought.

Two days later, I found myself in a rural area in Ireland, driving on the left-hand side of the street on an impossibly compressed road, without room for two-way traffic, even though there was a lot of two-way traffic. It was harrowing. I also got lost.

Amidst the fun, a friend called me. I picked up quickly and said, "I can't talk! The driving conditions are terrible, and if I talk, I'll probably get into an accident." I hung up. The friend immediately called back, and I pulled the car over to talk. You probably know what happened. SCREECH! The left-hand side of the car smashed into a gate, which was much closer than I imagined. No one was hurt, and the gate was fine, but the car suffered real damage.

I had the car for another ten days. On every one of those days, I felt that there was a dark cloud in the sky. How much would I have to pay? Nothing? A lot?

I looked at my rental car agreement. I didn't quite understand it, and didn't enjoy trying to figure it out. As best I could tell, I appeared, in my fog, not to have declined insurance altogether, but to have entered into an agreement to pay a maximum of $2,000 for any damage. That was a lot worse than $0 (which, I think, would have been the result if I had obtained insurance), but a lot better than $5,000 or $10,000.

The car didn't seem that horrifically damaged, and a $2,000 ceiling was not a nightmare. Still, I didn't know where I stood. That dark cloud was visible in the sky.

When I returned the car to the rental car company, I learned that in my fog, I had indeed arranged for an agreement with a $2,000 ceiling. I don't know exactly how or why I had done that. And not long after I received the bill for the rental, which included that amount.

Here is what I learned from that little episode: My economist friend might be wrong to advise people to decline car rental insurance. At least he's not right. True, declining insurance might be the right choice if your goal, over a lifetime, is to save money. But as they say, money isn't everything. There is also one's emotional state. For car renters to know that they won't have to pay anything if they have an accident – or to know that they won't have to pay more than a specified amount – is worth a lot. My time in Ireland was great, but it would definitely have been greater if I had known, for certain, that I would not have to pay more than $2,000 – and it would have been greater still if I had known that I would not have had to pay anything at all.

At this point, you might be thinking: What else is new? Insurance companies say that they sell "peace of mind." By promising to do that, they sometimes get a lot more money from consumers than they should. But there is a broader point. When we make decisions, material outcomes matter. Money matters; health matters; safety matters. But people's emotional experiences also matter, and when we make decisions, we ought to focus on that fact. Our actual and anticipated emotions can steer us right or steer us wrong. You might believe what you believe in part because you really like believing it. You might seek out information because you think it will make you smile; you might hide your head in the sand because you don't want bad news. You might make a choice because you think it's fun to make choices. You might refuse to make a choice because making choices makes you miserable.

How do we decide how we decide? We make such decisions all the time, whether or not we think much about them. If you trust your doctor, you might decide to follow a simple rule for medical decisions: *Do whatever your doctor suggests.* If you are interested in changing occupations but unsure whether you might be being reckless, you might take a small step: *Try a new job on a part-time basis.* If you like someone a lot, and maybe love them, but are not sure whether you want to marry them, you might do this: *Live with them first.* If you do not like reading menus at restaurants, and do not enjoy choosing among multiple options, you might do what I do: *Decide in favor of the first appealing item you see.*

Some of those decisions are rapid and intuitive; we do not formalize them in our minds. It is simply how we proceed. Some of those decisions are a product of experience or reflection. You might learn, over the years, that you cannot handle alcohol, and so you might adopt a firm rule: no alcohol, ever. Or you might have figured out, through long experience, that it rarely helps to get angry with people at work, so you might have decided that, if you are inclined to rage at someone, you will take a deep breath and turn the other cheek. Or you might know that you despise making certain choices, and you might find a way not to make them.

Some of these strategies are wise. They prevent error. They save time. They improve your emotional well-being; they help you to enjoy your minutes, your hours, your days, and your months. Some of these strategies are foolish. They lead you in the direction of terrible mistakes. They prevent you from learning. They might be too flexible. They might be too rigid. They might make you miserable. My main goal here is to understand decisions about decisions – to see what they are, to explore how they go right, and to see where they go wrong. Throughout we shall keep Ramsey's wisdom in mind: "[I]t is pleasanter to be thrilled than to be depressed, and not merely pleasanter but better for all one's activities." That principle applies not only when we are deciding what to do but also when we are deciding what to know and even when we are deciding what to believe.

* * *

I have been working on these subjects for about thirty years, and this book has emerged from a set of previously published essays, focused not on policy and law (my usual topics) but on practical reason in human life. Not long ago, it occurred to me that I had written something like a book on that topic without knowing it. To turn those essays into a book, I have made substantial revisions – in part because of what I have learned and in part in the interest of unity. If the seams occasionally show (and I know they do), I thank readers for their indulgence.

This book covers a great deal of territory. Most of the focus is on decisions about decisions, but (a confession) the lens will occasionally shift to decisions, period. We will attend, at essentially all points, to the emotional impact of decisions – to how it feels to make them; to whether claiming responsibility is pleasant or joyful or instead a burden or a source of terror; to whether a large-scale change seems like an opportunity and a world of fun, or a threat and a menace; to whether having a certain belief, or seeking new knowledge, induces a sense of security and hope or a sense of fear or despair.

For those who would like a brief overview: Chapter 1 offers general orientation. It explores second-order decisions in general, seeking to identify the specific strategies that we use to make life simpler and less stressful, and to explain when one or another such strategy makes sense.

Chapter 2 turns to decisions about the very largest matters, which might seem to defy ordinary rationality. The reason is that such decisions *change who we are and what we value.* Even there, I suggest, we can figure out how to decide.

Chapter 3 deals with the decision whether to know. Knowledge is power, as they say, but ignorance is bliss, as they also say. They are right on both counts. The challenge is to know whether we have a knowledge-is-power situation or an ignorance-is-bliss situation. My emphasis is on the fact that information can make us happy or sad; our anticipated emotional reaction to information is often the driver of our decision whether to seek or to avoid information. That is not exactly irrational, but sometimes we neglect our ability to adjust to bad news.

Chapters 4 and 5 deal with a closely related decision: the decision to believe. Chapter 4 explores the case of climate change. It offers evidence that on that question, people decide to believe what they want to believe – which helps explain the polarization we now observe in many nations, and which helps explain how we form beliefs in ordinary life. Broadening the viewscreen, Chapter 5 looks at beliefs in general. It suggests that beliefs are, in a sense, like goods, and we decide whether to "buy" them. We often make a rapid decision: If I believe *this*, will my life be better? How?

Note well: People might refuse to believe something even if it can help them live a little longer, if believing it will make them live a lot sadder.

Chapter 6 turns to the problem of inconsistency in decisions. With respect to jobs, laptops, cities, and romantic partners, people might decide in favor of A over B, but also decide in favor of B over A. How can that be? I emphasize what seems to me one of the deepest and most intriguing puzzles in all of modern social science: In separate evaluation, A might look a lot better than B, but in joint evaluation,

B might look a lot better than A. This is not a simple matter, but very briefly: The comparison set greatly matters, and if you are comparing a very nice house with a much nicer house, the very nice house might not look nice at all. This point matters to daily life, business, and politics.

Chapters 7 and 8 deal with consumption. The unifying claim is that people often decide to consume what others consume. They do so when they are choosing what might be called *solidarity goods*, as distinguished from *exclusivity goods*, which people choose because no one else seems to be choosing them. The existence of solidarity goods obviously bears on the success of social media platforms. Chapter 8 turns to those platforms in particular. Among other things, it finds that a lot of people would pay exactly *nothing* to be able to use them – and also that a lot of people are made less happy by them (but nonetheless keep using them). One lesson is that people do not care only about being made happy. They might want to know useful things, even if the knowledge makes them a little anxious or a little depressed. (There is an evident link here to Chapter 3.)

Chapter 9 explores a pressing current issue, which is when and whether people should rely on algorithms. The discussion tends to answer "yes," on the ground that algorithms can remove both bias (understood as systematic error) and noise (understood as unwanted variability). But I also emphasize the importance of knowing whether people like or do not like deciding in the particular circumstances. If people like deciding – perhaps because they enjoy it, perhaps because they want to claim responsibility – they will not like deciding by algorithm. It follows that in many cases, people will find deciding by algorithm a blessing, because deciding on one's own is anything but that. I also have something to say about what algorithms can and cannot do. A preview, potentially with general lessons: They do not seem to be very good at predicting when people will make a romantic connection.

Chapter 10 proposes a right not to be manipulated. It puts a spotlight on, and broadly endorses, a right to decisional autonomy. The Epilogue is called "Get Drunk!" That is more or less what it is about.

1 SECOND-ORDER DECISIONS

According to one picture of practical reasoning, people are decision-making animals, assessing the advantages and disadvantages of proposed courses of action and choosing in accordance with that assessment. This picture plays a familiar role in economics and decision theory; in various forms, it is central to leading descriptions of reasoning in law and politics. Even in psychology, where models of bounded rationality are pervasive and where it is common to speak of "satisficing" rather than optimizing, the deviations can be understood only against the background of this picture.

This understanding of practical reasoning is quite inadequate. An important problem is that it ignores the existence of simplifying strategies that people adopt well before on-the-spot decisions must be made.[1] People might not like making decisions; doing so might create anxiety and stress, and perhaps an unwelcome sense of responsibility. People also know that they might err. They seek to overcome their own shortcomings – calculative, moral, or otherwise – by making some meta-choice before the moment of ultimate decision. Ordinary people and social institutions are often reluctant to make on-the-spot decisions.

Second-order decisions involve the strategies that people use in order to avoid getting into an ordinary decision-making situation

[1] John Stuart Mill himself emphasized the point: *see* JOHN STUART MILL, *Utilitarianism, in* JOHN STUART MILL ON LIBERTY AND OTHER ESSAYS 131, 151–53 (John Gray ed., 1991).

in the first instance. There are important issues here about cognitive burdens and also about responsibility, equality, and fairness. In daily life, we might adopt a firm rule: Never lie or cheat, for example, or never drink alcohol before dinner. In law, some judges favor a second-order decision on behalf of rules, on the ground that rules promote predictability and minimize the burdens of subsequent decisions. In politics, legislatures often adopt a second-order decision in favor of a delegation to some third party, like an administrative agency. But there are many alternative strategies, and serious questions can be raised by rule-bound decisions (as opposed, for example, to small, reversible steps) and by delegations (as opposed, for example, to rebuttable presumptions).

People have diverse second-order strategies, and a main goal here is to identify them and to understand why one or another might be best. As we shall see, these strategies differ in the extent to which they produce mistakes and also in the extent to which they impose informational, moral, and other burdens on the agent and on others, either *before* the process of ultimate decision or *during* the process of ultimate decision. There are three especially interesting kinds of cases.

The first involves second-order decisions that greatly reduce the burdens of on-the-spot decisions, and that might even eliminate those burdens, but that require considerable thinking in advance. Consider a decision about how to handle a health problem – a decision that once made, requires few decisions, or even no decisions, in the future. Decisions of this kind, which we might call High-Low, may be difficult and not at all fun to make before the fact; the question is whether those burdens are worth incurring in light of the aggregate burdens – cognitive, moral, cognitive, and otherwise – of second-order and first-order decisions taken together.

The second are Low-Low. These second-order strategies impose little in the way of decisional burdens either before or during the ultimate decision. This is a great advantage. A major question is whether the strategy in question (consider a decision to flip a coin) produces too many mistakes or too much inconsistency or unfairness.

The third are Low-High. These second-order strategies involve low before-the-fact decisional burdens for the agents themselves, at the cost of imposing possibly high subsequent burdens on the agent's future self, or on someone else to whom the first-order decision is "exported." A delegation of power to some trusted associate, or to an authority, is the most obvious case.

An understanding of actual practices provides guidance for seeing when one or another strategy will be chosen, when one or another makes best sense, and how both rational and boundedly rational persons and institutions might go about making the relevant choices.[2] No particular strategy can be said to be better in the abstract; but it is possible to identify, in the abstract, the factors that argue in favor of one or another strategy, and also the contexts in which each approach makes sense. We shall see, for example, that a second-order decision in favor of firm rules (a form of High-Low) is appropriate when an agent faces a large number of decisions with similar features and when advance planning is especially important; in such cases, the crudeness of rules might be tolerated because of their overall advantages.

By contrast, a second-order decision in favor of small, reversible steps (a form of Low-Low) is preferable when the agent lacks reliable information and reasonably fears unanticipated bad consequences; this point helps explain the method that is often at work in both personal lives and common law courts (and argues against some of the critics of that method). A sensible agent will choose the alternative second-order strategy of delegating to another person or institution (a form of Low-High) when there is a special problem with assuming responsibility – informational, moral, or otherwise – and when an appropriate delegate, with sufficient time and expertise, turns out to be available; this point helps illuminate debates over delegations including those within families, the workplace, religious organizations, legislatures, administrative agencies, and other groups.[3] In the process it will be necessary to address a range of ethical, political, and legal issues that are raised by various second-order decisions.

---

[2] Of course, second-order decisions might operate as a rational response, by boundedly rational persons or institutions, to their own bounded rationality; but such decisions might also suffer from bounded rationality and go wrong because of cognitive or motivational problems.

[3] Of course, self-interested participants in politics will attempt to exploit arguments of this kind in order to produce their preferred outcome. An industry representation nervous about its chances of success in the legislature might argue strongly on behalf of a delegation, in the hopes that the delegate will be more receptive to its arguments (or more vulnerable to its influence).

Decisions and Mistakes

Strategies

The following catalogue captures the major second-order strategies. The taxonomy is intended to be exhaustive of the possibilities, but the various items should not be seen as exclusive of one another; there is some overlap between them.

Rules

People anticipating hard or repetitive decisions may do best to adopt a rule. A key feature of a rule is that it amounts to a full, or nearly full, ex ante specification of results in individual cases. People might decide, for example, that they will never park illegally, stay up after midnight, eat meat, or fail to meet a deadline. For individuals, an evident advantage of rules is that people do not have to spend time making decisions in individual cases; that might make life simpler and more pleasant. A legislature might provide that judges can never make exceptions to the speed limit law or the law banning dogs from restaurants, or that everyone who has been convicted of three felonies must be sentenced to life imprisonment.

Presumptions

Sometimes ordinary people and public institutions rely not on a rule but instead on a presumption, which can be rebutted. The result, it is hoped, is to make fewer mistakes while at the same time incurring reasonable decisional burdens.[4] People might decide, for example, that they will not park illegally unless the circumstances really require it. An

---

[4] It is important here to distinguish between a presumption and a rule with exceptions. A rule with exceptions has the following structure: "Do X – except in circumstances A, in which case you are exempt from doing X." For example, "observe the speed limit – except when you're driving a police car or an ambulance in an emergency, in which cases you may exceed it." By contrast, a typical presumption says something like: "Act on the assumption that P – unless and until circumstances A are shown to obtain, in which case, do something else." The two amount to the same thing when the agent knows whether or not circumstances A obtain. The two are quite different when the agent lacks that information. With a presumption, you can proceed without the information; with a rule with exceptions, you cannot proceed, that is, you are justified neither in doing X nor in not doing X. *See* Edna Ullmann-Margalit, *On Presumption*, 80 J. PHIL. 143, 143–62 (1983).

administrative agency might presume that no one may emit more than X tons of a certain pollutant, but the presumption can be rebutted by showing that further reductions are not feasible.

Standards

Rules are often contrasted with standards.[5] A ban on "excessive" speed on the highway is a standard; so is a requirement that pilots of airplanes be "competent," or that student behavior in the classroom be "reasonable." These might be compared with rules specifying a 55-mph speed limit, or a ban on pilots who are over the age of seventy, or a requirement that students sit in assigned seats. In daily life, we might adopt a standard. We will not eat or drink "too much," and we will not drive "too much."

Routines

Sometimes a reasonable way to deal with a decisional burden is to adopt a routine. This term is meant to refer to something similar to a habit, but more voluntary, more self-conscious, and without the pejorative connotations of some habits (like the habit of chewing one's fingernails). A forgetful person might adopt a routine of locking his door every time he leaves his office, even though sometimes he knows he will return in a few minutes; a commuter might adopt a particular route and follow it every day, even though on some days another route would be better; an employee might arrive at the office by a specified time every morning, even though he does not always need to be in that early.

Small steps

A possible way of simplifying a difficult situation at the time of choice is to make a small, incremental decision, and to leave other questions for another day. When a personal decision involves imponderable and apparently incommensurable elements, people often take

---

[5] *See, e.g.,* Louis Kaplow, *Rules versus Standards: An Economic Analysis,* 42 DUKE L.J. 557 (1992); Kathleen M. Sullivan, *Foreword: The Justices of Rules and Standards,* 106 HARV. L. REV. 22, 22–103 (1992).

small, reversible steps first.[6] For example, Jane may decide to live with Robert before she decides whether she wants to marry him; Marilyn may go to night school to see if she is really interested in law. A similar "small-steps" approach is the hallmark of Anglo-American common law.[7] Judges typically make narrow decisions, resolving little beyond the individual case; at least this is their preferred method of operation when they lack confidence about the larger issues, not only in the common law but in constitutional law too.[8]

Picking

Sometimes the difficulty of decision, or symmetry among the options, pushes people to decide on a random basis. They might, for example, flip a coin, decide in favor of the option they see first, or make some apparently irrelevant factor decisive ("it's a sunny day, so I'll take that job in Florida"). Thus they might "pick" rather than "choose" (taking the latter term to mean basing a decision on preference or by reference to reasons).[9] A legal system might use a lottery to decide who serves on juries or in the military. Indeed, lotteries are used in many domains where the burdens of individualized choice are high, and when there is some particular problem with deliberation about the grounds of choice, sometimes because of apparent symmetries among the candidates. In day-to-day life, we often decide by reference to something like a lottery, even if the decision to do that happens unconsciously and rapidly.

[6] See Edna Ullmann-Margalit, *Opting: The Case of 'Big' Decisions*, THE 1984–85 YEAR-BOOK OF THE WISSENSCHAFTSKOLLEG ZU BERLIN 441, 441–54 (1985).

[7] See EDWARD H. LEVI, AN INTRODUCTION TO LEGAL REASONING 3–15 (Univ. Chi. Press, 1949). In political science, see Charles E. Lindblom, *The Science of "Muddling Through,"* 19 PUB. ADMIN. REV. 79 (1959), which offers an influential and relevant argument about incrementalism. *See also* Charles E. Lindblom, *Still Muddling, Not Yet Through*, 39 PUB. ADMIN. REV. 517, 517–26 (1979). Lindblom's discussion is in the same general family as our exploration of small steps, though (oddly) Lindblom does not discuss the judiciary, and he does not explore when other second-order strategies might be preferable.

[8] Thus in cases involving the right to die, affirmative action, and sex equality, Justices Sandra Day O'Connor and Ruth Bader Ginsburg much favored small steps as the strategy of choice; this is the ground on which they tended to disagree with Justice Scalia, and in fact it counts as the leading jurisprudential dispute on the current Supreme Court. The tension between the rule of law and the common law method is the basic theme of ANTONIN SCALIA, A MATTER OF INTERPRETATION 5–15 (1997). For general discussion, see CASS R.SUNSTEIN, ONE CASE AT A TIME: JUDICIAL MINIMALISM ON THE SUPREME COURT (1999).

[9] See Edna Ullmann-Margalit & Sidney Morgenbesser, *Picking and Choosing*, 44 SOC. RSCH. 757, 757–83 (1977).

Delegation

A familiar way of handling decisional burdens is to delegate the decision to someone else. People might rely on a spouse, a lover, an expert, or a friend, or choose an institutional arrangement by which certain decisions are made by authorities established at the time or well in advance. Such arrangements can be more or less formal; they involve diverse mechanisms of control, or entirely relinquished control, by the person or people for whose benefit they have been created.

Heuristics

People often use heuristic devices, or mental shortcuts, as a way of bypassing the need for individualized choice. For example, it can be overwhelming to figure out for whom to vote in local elections; people may therefore use the heuristic of party affiliation. When meeting someone new, your behavior may be a result of heuristic devices specifying the appropriate type of behavior with a person falling in the general category in which the new person seems to fall. A great deal of attention has been given to heuristic devices said to produce departures from "rationality."[10] But often heuristic devices are fully rational, if understood as a way of producing pretty good outcomes, and perhaps excellent outcomes, while at the same time reducing cognitive overload or other decisional burdens.

Costs of Decisions and Costs of Errors

Under what circumstances will, or should, a person or institution make some second-order decisions rather than making an all-things-considered judgment on the spot? And under what circumstances will, or should, one or another strategy be chosen? Many people have emphasized the particular value of rules, which can overcome myopia or weakness of will;[11] but the problem is far more general, and rules are just one of many possible solutions.

---

[10] *See, e.g.,* John Conlisk, *Why Bounded Rationality?*, 34 J. ECON. LIT. 669, 669–98 (1996).

[11] For a discussion of precommitment, *see* JON ELSTER, ULYSSES AND THE SIRENS 36–47 (1979), and the treatment of "resolute choice" in EDWARD F. MCCLENNEN, RATIONALITY AND DYNAMIC CHOICE (1990).

Recall that second-order strategies differ in the extent to which they produce decisional burdens and mistakes. Those burdens might be emotional; it might be unpleasant to make decisions on the spot, and second-order strategies might reduce or eliminate that unpleasantness. Those burdens might be cognitive; it might take a lot of time and energy to make decisions on the spot, and second-order strategies might be a blessing. Second-order strategies should be chosen by attempting to minimize the sum of the costs of making decisions and the costs of error, where the costs of making decisions are the costs of coming to closure on some action or set of actions, and where the costs of error are assessed by examining the number, the magnitude, and the kinds of mistakes.[12]

"Errors" are understood as suboptimal outcomes, whatever the criteria for deciding what is optimal; both rules and delegations can produce errors (the rule may be crude; the delegate may be incompetent). If the emotional and cognitive costs of producing optimal decisions were zero, it would be best to make individual calculations in each case, for this approach would produce correct judgments without compromising accuracy or any other important value (bracketing the possibility that advance planning might be helpful or important). This would be true for individual agents and also for institutions. It is largely because people (including public officials) seek to reduce decisional burdens, and to minimize their own errors, that sometimes they would like not to have *options* and sometimes not to have *information*; and they may make second-order decisions to reduce either options or information (or both).[13]

Three additional points are necessary here. The first involves responsibility: People sometimes want to assume responsibility for

---

[12] Kaplow, *supra* note 5, illuminatingly uses a framework of this sort, but in a way that seems too reductionistic. FREDERICK SCHAUER, PLAYING BY THE RULES 196–206 (1991), recognizes that the case for rules depends on empirical considerations. The treatments of precommitment in ELSTER, *supra* note 11, and Thomas C. Schelling, *Enforcing Rules on Oneself*, 1 J.L. ECON. & ORG. 357 (1985), do not explore the circumstances in which a rule-bound strategy is preferable to some other (second-order) approach, nor do they explore the grounds for choice among the various second-order strategies discussed here. In general, existing treatments of precommitment tend to be ambiguous about whether the relevant strategy is a rule or something else. *See, e.g.,* ELSTER, *supra* note 11, at 37–40 (collecting heterogeneous illustrations).

[13] *See* Edna Ullmann-Margalit, *On Not Wanting To Know, in* REASONING PRACTICALLY 17 (Edna Ullmann-Margalit ed., 2000); Gerald Dworkin, *Is More Choice Better than Less?, in* THE THEORY AND PRACTICE OF AUTONOMY (1991).

certain decisions even if others would make those decisions better, and people sometimes want to relieve themselves of responsibility for certain decisions even if other people would make those decisions worse. These are familiar phenomena in daily life; you might want to be the person who decides what you will do for the next year, and you might not want to be the person who makes certain boring financial decisions. So too in business, politics, and law, where people with authority might gain a great deal from making the decisions themselves, or might gain a great deal for giving that responsibility to others. A failure of responsibility might be understood as a kind of "cost," but it is qualitatively different from the decision costs and error costs discussed thus far, and raises separate questions. Special issues are created by institutional arrangements that divide authority, such as the separation of powers; such arrangements might forbid people from assuming or delegating certain decisions, even if they would very much like to do so.

The second point comes from the fact that multiparty situations raise distinctive problems. Above all, public institutions (including legislatures, agencies, and courts) may seek to promote *planning* by setting down rules and presumptions in advance. The need for planning can argue strongly against on-the-spot decisions even if they would be both correct and costless to achieve. As we will see, the need for planning can lead in the direction of a particular kind of second-order strategy, one that makes on-the-spot decisions more or less mechanical.

The third and most important point is that a reference to a "sum" of decision costs and error costs should not be taken to suggest that a straightforward cost-benefit analysis is an adequate way to understand the choice among second-order strategies. There is no simple metric along which to align the various considerations. Important qualitative differences can be found between decision costs and error costs, among the various kinds of decision costs, and also among the various kinds of error costs. For any one of us, the costs of decision may include time, money, unpopularity, sadness, stress, anxiety, boredom, agitation, anticipated ex post regret or remorse, feelings of responsibility for harm done to self or others, injury to self-perception, guilt, or shame.

Things become differently complicated for multimember institutions, where these points also apply, but where interest-group pressures may be important, and where there is the special problem of reaching a degree of consensus. A legislature might find it especially difficult to specify the appropriate approach to climate change, given the problems posed by disagreement, varying intensity of preference, and aggregation issues; for similar reasons, a multimember court may have a hard time agreeing on how to handle an asserted right to physician-assisted suicide. The result may be strategies for delegation or for deferring decision, often via small steps.

An institution facing political pressures may have a distinctive reason to adopt a particular kind of second-order decision, one that will *deflect responsibility for choice*. Jean Bodin defended the creation of an independent judiciary, and thus provided an initial insight into a system of separated and divided powers, on just this ground; a monarch is relieved of responsibility for unpopular but indispensable decisions if he can point to a separate institution that has been charged with the relevant duty.[14] This is an important kind of *enabling constraint*, characteristic of good second-order decisions.

In many nations, the existence of an independent central bank is often justified on this ground. In the United States, the president has no authority over the money supply and indeed no authority over the Chair of the Federal Reserve Board, partly on the theory that it is advantageous to separate the president from necessary but unpopular decisions (such as refusing to increase the supply of money when unemployment seems too high); presidents might be reluctant to make such decisions, the fact that the Federal Reserve Board is unelected is an advantage here. There are analogues in business, in workplaces, and even in families, where a mother or father may be given the responsibility for making certain choices, partly in order to relieve the other of responsibility. Of course, this approach can cause problems of unfairness and inequality, and it might lead to mistakes.

Burdens Ex Ante and Burdens on the Spot

The inquiry into second-order strategies can be organized by noticing a simple point: Some such strategies require substantial thought in advance but little thought on the spot, whereas others require little thought before the situation of choice arises and also little thought on the spot. Still others involve little ex ante thought, which

---

[14] *See* STEPHEN HOLMES, PASSIONS AND CONSTRAINT (1995).

Table 1.1 Ex ante burdens and burdens on the spot

	Little ex ante thinking	Substantial ex ante thinking
Little on-the-spot thinking	Low-Low: picking; small steps; various heuristics; some standards (1)	High-Low: rules; presumptions; some standards; routines (2)
Substantial on-the-spot thinking	Low-High: delegation (3)	High-High: some characters in Henry James novels; anxious people; people who relish decisions; dysfunctional governments (4)

leads to imposing the possibly high decisional burdens on self or others. Thus there is a temporal difference in the imposition of the burdens of decision, which can be described with the terms "High-Low," "Low-Low," and "Low-High." To fill out the possibilities, we should add "High-High" as well. The term decision costs refers here to the overall costs, which may be borne by different people or agencies: The work done before the fact of choice may not be carried out by the same actors who will have to do the thinking during the ultimate choice. Consider Table 1.1.

Cell (1) captures strategies that promise to minimize the overall burdens of having to make decisions (whether or not they promote good overall decisions). These are cases in which agents do not invest a great deal of thought either before or at the time of decision. Picking is the most obvious case; consider the possibility of flipping a coin. Small steps are more demanding, since the agent does have to make some decisions, but because the steps are small, there need be comparatively little thought before or during the decision.

The most sharply contrasting set of cases is High-High, Cell (4). As this cell captures strategies that maximize overall decision costs, it ought for current purposes to remain empty, or at least nearly so. Fortunately, it seems to be represented only by a small minority of people in actual life; usually they are doing themselves no favors. Often those who fall in Cell (4) seem hopelessly indecisive, but it is possible to imagine people thinking that High-High represents a norm of moral responsibility, or that (as some people seem to think) incurring high burdens of decision is something to relish. It is also possible to urge High-High where the issue is extremely important and where there is no other way of ensuring accuracy; consider, for example, the decision whether to take a job, to leave a marriage, or to start a war, decisions that may reasonably call for a great deal of deliberation both before and during the period of choice.

Cell (2) captures a common aspiration for individuals and agents that prefer their lives to be rule-bound. Some institutions and agents spend a great deal of time choosing the appropriate rules; once the rules are in place, decisions become extremely simple, rigid, even mechanical. Everyone knows people of this sort; they can seem both noble and frustrating precisely because they follow rules to the letter. (No drinking, ever; no staying up late, ever; no fun, ever.) Legal formalism – the commitment to setting out clear rules in advance and mechanical decision afterwards, a commitment defended by US Supreme Court Justices Hugo Black and Antonin Scalia – is associated with cell (2).[15]

When planning is important and when a large number of decisions must be made, cell (2) is often the best approach. For each of us, rules are a blessing – and a great simplifier of life – even if it takes time and trouble to come up with them. Or consider the twentieth-century movement away from the common law and toward bureaucracy and simple rules. Individual cases of mistake, and individual cases of error or even unfairness, may be tolerable if the overall result is to prevent the system from being overwhelmed by decisional demands. Cell (2) is also likely to be the best approach when many people are involved and it is known in advance that the people who will have to carry out on-the-spot decisions constantly change. Consider institutions with many employees and a large turnover (the army, entry levels of large corporations, and so forth). The head of an organization may not want newly recruited, less-than-well-trained people to make decisions for the firm: Rules should be in place so as to ensure continuity and uniform level of performance.

On the other hand, the possibility that life will confound the rules often produces arguments for institutional reform in the form of granting power to administrators or employees to exercise "common sense" in the face of rules.[16] An intermediate case can be found with most standards; the creation of the standard may itself require substantial thinking, but

[15] See SCALIA, *supra* note 8, at 5–20.
[16] See PHILIP K. HOWARD, THE DEATH OF COMMON SENSE 12–51 (1995).

even when the standard is in place, agents may have to do some deliberating in order to reach closure.

Cell (3) suggests that institutions and individuals sometimes do little thinking in advance but may or may not minimize the aggregate costs of decision. The best case for this approach involves an agent who lacks much information or seeks for some other reason to avoid responsibility, and a delegate who promises to make good decisions relatively easily. As we have seen, delegations may require little advance thinking, at least on the substance of the issues to be decided; the burdens of decision will eventually be faced by the object of the delegation (who may be one's future self). While some delegations are almost automatic (say, in a family), some people think long and hard about whether and to whom to delegate. Also, some people who have been delegated power will proceed by rules, presumptions, standards, small steps, picking, or even subdelegations. Note that small steps might be seen as an effort to "export" the costs of decision to one's future self; this is important in ordinary life and related to an important theme in the common law, one that is highly valued by many judges.

It is an important social fact that many people are relieved of the burdens of decision through something other than their own explicit wishes. Consider young children and people with cognitive problems or mental health issues; in a range of cases, society or law makes a second-order decision on someone else's behalf, often without a clear or binding indication of that person's own desires. The displacement of another's decisions is typically based on a belief that the relevant other will systematically err. This is of course a form of paternalism, which can arises when there is delegation without consent.

In some cases, second-order decisions produce something best described as Medium-Medium, with imaginable extensions toward Moderately High-Moderately Low, and Moderately Low-Moderately High. Consider some standards, which, it will be recalled, structure first-order decisions but require a degree of work on the spot, with the degree depending on the nature of the particular standard. But after understanding the polar cases, analysis of these intermediate cases is straightforward.

Let us now turn to the contexts in which individuals and institutions will, or should, follow one or another of the basic second-order strategies.

Low-High (With Special Reference to Delegation)

Informal and Formal Delegations

I have lunch periodically with a good friend, who happens to be a behavioral economist. For years, I have asked him, in advance, where he would like to go. I thought that was a polite thing to do. On one of those occasions, he responded, "Why don't you decide?" Before I did, I asked him why he wanted me to be the decider. He replied, sweetly, "I never like deciding where to go for lunch. Actually I hate doing that."

Suppose that you do not like making some set of decisions; they are really not fun to make. Or suppose that you know that you are not good at making some set of decisions; you might get it badly wrong. You might direct, or ask, someone else to decide. As a first approximation, a delegation is a second-order strategy that exports decision-making burdens to someone else, in an effort to reduce the agent's burdens both before and at the time of making the ultimate decision. A typical case involves an agent who does not enjoy making the relevant decisions, who does not trust her own capacity to decide wisely, or who seeks to avoid responsibility (for some strategic or ethical reason, or because of a simple lack of information) – and who identifies an available delegate whom she trusts to make a good, right, or expert decision.

Informal delegations occur all the time. One spouse may delegate to another the decision about what the family will eat for dinner, what investments to choose, or what car to buy. Such delegations often occur because the burdens of decision are high for the agent but low for the delegate, who may have specialized information, who may lack relevant biases or motivational problems, or who may not mind (and who may even enjoy) taking responsibility for the decision in question. (These cases may then be more accurately captured as special cases of Low-Low.) The intrinsic burdens of having to make the decision are often counterbalanced by the benefits of having been asked to assume responsibility for it (though these may be costs rather than benefits in some cases). Some delegates are glad or even delighted to assume their role; this is relevant to some ethical issues involving delegation (consider the question of justice within the family; if a husband delegates too many decisions to his wife, we might have an issue of justice). And there is an uneasy line, raising knotty conceptual and empirical questions, between a delegation and a division of labor (consider the allocation of household duties). A key issue here is whether the recipient of the delegation has the authority to decline, or is essentially forced to say "yes!" or at least "okay!"

In business, delegations often occur for parallel reasons. One person in a company might delegate to another, with the delegator believing that she is busy with other matters or that she lacks relevant expertise. Someone within the company might have plenty of time to figure things out, or might be a specialist in the matter at hand. When I worked in the White House under President Barack Obama, I was part of a small team of officials working on financial regulatory reform under the leadership of Larry Summers, who was head of the National Economic Council. Summers would sometimes disagree with his team, and after a brief argument, he would occasionally say, "All right you geniuses, you figure it out."

Government itself is a large recipient of delegated decisions, at least if sovereignty is understood to lie in the citizenry. On this view, various public institutions – legislatures, courts, the executive branch – exercise explicitly or implicitly delegated authority, and there are numerous subdelegations, especially for the legislature, which must relieve itself of many decisional burdens. A legislature may delegate because it believes that it lacks information about, for example, environmental problems or changes in the telecommunications market; the result is an Environmental Protection Agency or a Federal Communications Commission. Or the legislature may have the information but find itself unable to forge a consensus on underlying values about, for example, the right approach to climate change, nuclear power, or age discrimination.

Often a legislature lacks the time and the organization to make the daily decisions that administrative agencies are asked to handle; consider the fact that legislatures that attempt to reconsider agency decisions often find themselves involved in weeks or even months of work, and fail to reach closure. Or the legislature may be aware that its vulnerability to interest-group pressures will lead it in bad directions, and it may hope and believe that the object of the delegation will be relatively immune. Interest-group pressures may themselves produce a delegation, as where powerful groups are unable to achieve a clear victory in a legislature but are able to obtain a grant of authority to an administrative agency over which they will have power. The legislature may even want to avoid responsibility for some hard choice, fearing that decisions will produce electoral reprisal. Self-interested representatives may well find it in their electoral self-interest to enact a vague or vacant standard ("the public interest," "reasonable accommodation" of the disabled, "reasonable regulation" of pesticides), and to delegate the task of specification to someone else, secure in the knowledge that the delegate will be blamed for problems in implementation. There are close parallels in companies and in daily life.

When to Delegate

Delegation deserves to be considered whenever an appropriate and trustworthy delegate is available and there is some sense in which it seems undesirable for the agent to be making the decision by himself. But obviously delegation can be a mistake – an abdication of responsibility; a source of unfairness; a recipe for more rather than fewer errors, and so for even higher (aggregate) costs of decision. And since delegation is only one of a number of second-order strategies, an agent might want to consider other possibilities before delegating.

Compared to a High-Low approach, a delegation will be desirable if the delegator does not want to face the burdens of decision or is unable to generate a workable rule or presumption (and if anything it could come up with would be costly to produce), and if a delegate would do well enough or better on the merits. This may be the case for an individual who just does not know how to make a decision (about, say, where to eat lunch, how to handle a difficult medical problem, or how to make investments). It may also be the case on a multimember body that is unable to reach agreement, or when an agent or institution faces a cognitive or motivational problem, such as weakness of will or susceptibility to outside influences. A delegation will also be favored over High-Low if the delegator seeks to avoid responsibility for the decision for political, social, or other reasons, though the effort to avoid responsibility may also create problems of legitimacy, as when a legislator relies on "experts" to make value judgments about environmental protection or disability discrimination.

As compared with small steps or picking, a delegation may or may not produce higher total decision costs (perhaps the delegate is slow or a procrastinator). Even if the delegation does produce higher total decision costs, it may also lead to more confidence in the eventual decisions, at least if reliable delegates are available. In private life, you might choose to rely on a financial advisor or a doctor, simply because you will trust the eventual decision. In the United States, the Federal Reserve Board has often had a high degree of public respect, which means that there is little pressure to eliminate or reduce the delegation. But a delegate – a friend, an expert, a spouse, the Environmental Protection Agency – may prove likely to err, and a rule, a presumption, or small steps may emerge instead. Special issues are raised in technical areas, which create strong arguments for delegation, but where the delegate's judgments may be hard to oversee (even if they conceal controversial judgments of value) return to the Environmental Protection Agency, which might be relied upon because of his expertise, but might be troublesome if it is seen as a free agent. Here again there are parallels in ordinary life, in which we might be tempted to rely on experts but are worried about their motivations and the risks that might arise if they are independent.

There is also the concern for fairness. In some circumstances, it is unfair to delegate to a friend or a spouse the power of decision, especially but not only because the delegate is not a specialist. People might hate the delegation; it might be a burden or a curse. Issues of gender equality arise when a husband delegates to his wife all decisions involving the household and the children, even if both husband and wife agree on the delegation. Apart from this issue, a delegation by one spouse to another may well seem inequitable if (say) it involves a child's problems with alcohol, because it is an abdication of responsibility, a way of transferring the burdens of decision to someone else who should not be forced to bear them alone.

In institutional settings, there is an analogous problem if the delegate (usually an administrative agency) lacks political accountability even if it has relevant expertise. The result is the continuing debate over the legitimacy of delegations to administrative agencies. Such delegations can be troublesome if they shift the burden of judgment from a democratically elected body to one that is insulated from political control. A legislature has plenty of alternatives to delegation. If it wants to avoid the degree of specificity entailed by rule-bound law, it might instead enact a presumption or take small steps (as, e.g., through an experimental pilot program). Related issues are raised by the possibly illegitimate abdication of authority when a judge delegates certain powers to law clerks (as is occasionally alleged about Supreme Court justices) or to special masters who are experts in complex questions of fact and law.

Three Complications

Three complications deserve comment. First, any delegate may itself resort to making second-order decisions, and it is familiar to find delegates undertaking each of the strategies described here. Sometimes delegates prefer High-Low and hence generate rules; this is the typical strategy of the tax authorities. Alternatively, delegates may use standards or proceed by small steps. Having been delegated certain decisions by a patient, a doctor might proceed incrementally, and refuse to do anything large or dramatic. In the United States, this has been the general approach of the National Labor Relations Board, which (strikingly) has tended to avoid rules, and prefers to proceed case-by-case. Or a delegate may undertake a subdelegation; confronted with a delegation from her husband, a wife may consult a sibling or a parent. Asked by Congress to make hard choices, the president may and frequently does subdelegate to some kind of commission, for some of the same reasons that spurred Congress to delegate in the first instance. Of course, a delegate may just pick.

The second complication is that the control of a delegate presents a potentially serious principal-agent problem. How can the person who has made the delegation ensure that the delegate will not make serious and numerous mistakes, or instead fritter away its time trying to decide how to decide? There are multiple possible mechanisms of control. Instead of giving final and irreversible powers of choice to the delegate, a person or institution might turn the delegate into a mere consultant or advice-giver. A wide range of intermediate relationships is possible. In the governmental setting, a legislature can influence the ultimate decision by voicing its concerns publicly if an administrative agency is heading in the wrong direction, and the legislature has the power to overturn an administrative agency if it can muster the will to do so.

Ultimately the delegator will usually retain the power to eliminate the delegation. To ensure against (what the delegator would consider to be) mistakes, it may be sufficient for the delegate to know this fact. In informal relations, involving friends, colleagues, and family members, there are various mechanisms for controlling any delegate. Some "delegates" know that they are only consultants; others know that they have the effective power of decision. All this happens through a range of cues, which may be subtle.

The third complication stems from the fact that at the outset, the burdens of a second-order decision of this kind may not be so low after all, since the person or institution must take the time to decide whether to delegate at all and if so, to whom to delegate. Complex issues may arise about the composition of any institution receiving the delegation; these burdens may be quite high and perhaps decisive against delegation altogether. A multimember institution often divides sharply on whether to delegate, and even after that decision is made, it may have trouble deciding on the recipient of the delegated authority.

Intrapersonal Delegations and Delegation to Chance

The focus thus far has been on cases in which the delegator exports the burdens of decision to some other person or party. What about the intrapersonal case? Can current John delegate decisions to future John?

On the one hand, there is no precise analogy between that problem and the cases under discussion. On the other hand, people confronted with hard choices can often be understood to have chosen to delegate the power of choice to their future selves. Consider, for example, such decisions as whether to buy a house, to have another child, to get married or divorced, or to move to a new city. In such cases, agents who procrastinate may understand themselves to have delegated the decision to their future selves.

There are two possible reasons for this kind of intrapersonal delegation, involving timing and content respectively. You may believe you know what the right decision is, but also believe it is not the right time to be making that decision, or at least not the right time to announce it publicly. It might not be the right time because you are in no mood to make it; making the decision would make you miserable. It might not be the right time because you may not know what the right decision is and believe that your future self will be in a better position to decide. You may think that your future self will have more information, enjoy making the decision more or hate making the decision less, suffer less or not at all from cognitive difficulties, bias, or motivational problems, or be in a better position to assume the relevant responsibility. Perhaps you are feeling under pressure, suffering from illness, or not sure of your judgment just yet. In such cases, the question of intrapersonal, intertemporal choice is not so far from the problem of delegation to others. It is even possible to see some over-lapping principal-agent problems with similar mechanisms of control, as people impose certain constraints on their future selves. There are close parallels for judges and legislators, who care a great deal about both timing and content, and who may wait for one or another reason.

From the standpoint of the agent, then, the strategy of small steps, like that of delay, can be seen as a form of delegation. Also, the strategy of delegation itself may turn into that of picking when the del-egate is a chance device. When I make my future decision depend on which card I draw from my deck of cards, I have delegated my decision to the random card-drawing mechanism, thereby effectively turning my decision from choosing to picking.

High-Low (With Special Reference to Rules and Presumptions)

We have seen that people often make second-order decisions that are themselves costly, simply in order to reduce the burdens of later decisions in particular cases. This is the most conventional kind of precommitment strategy. The most promising setting for rule-bound precommitment involves a large number of similar decisions and a need for advance planning (as opposed to improvisation). In such a setting, the occasional errors inevitably produced by rules are likely to be worth incurring. When this process is working well, there is much to do before the second-order decision has been made, but once the decision is in place, things are greatly simplified.[17]

Diverse Rules, Diverse Presumptions

We have seen that rules and presumptions belong to the High-Low category, and frequently this is true. But the point must be qualified; some rules and presumptions do not involve high burdens of decision before the fact. For example, a rule might be picked rather than chosen – drive on the right-hand side of the road, or spoons to the right, forks to the left. Especially when what it is important is to allow all actors to coordinate on a single course of conduct, there need be little investment

---

[17] See, e.g., JON ELSTER, SOLOMONIC JUDGMENTS 36–53 (1989), ELSTER, supra note 11, and Schelling, supra note 12.

in decisions about the content of the relevant rule. A rule might even be framed narrowly, so as to work as a kind of small step. Rules can embody small steps. The same points can be made about presumptions, which are sometimes picked rather than chosen and which might be quite narrow.

Let us focus on situations in which an institution or an agent is willing to deliberate a good deal to generate a rule or a presumption that, once in place, turns out greatly to simplify (without impairing and perhaps even improving) future decisions. This is a familiar aspiration in life, law, and politics. A family might adopt a presumption: We will take a vacation where we did last year, unless there is special reason to try something new. A legislature might decide in favor of a speed limit law, partly in order to ensure coordination among drivers, and partly as a result of a process of balancing various considerations about risks and benefits. People are especially willing to expend a great deal of effort to generate rules in two circumstances: (1) when planning and fair notice are important and (2) when a large number of decisions will be made.[18]

People do that consciously or unconsciously in daily life; habits are rules or presumptions. The conscious creation of habits, and the conscious or unconscious adherence to habits, make life a lot easier. In most well-functioning legal systems, it is clear what is and what is not a crime. People need to know when they may be subject to criminal punishment for what they do. In theory if not in practice, the American Constitution is taken to require a degree of clarity in the criminal law, and all would-be tyrants know that rules may be irritating constraints on their authority. So too, the law of contract and property is mostly defined by clear rules, simply because people could not otherwise plan, and in order for economic development to be possible they need to be in a position to do so.

When large numbers of decisions have to be made, there is a similar tendency to spend a great deal of time to clarify outcomes in advance. Doctors adopt a host of rules for treating cancer and heart disease. In the United States, the need to make a large number of decisions has pushed the legal system into the development of rules governing social security disability, workers' compensation, and criminal sentencing. The fact that these rules may produce a significant degree of error is not decisive; the sheer cost of administering the relevant systems, with so massive a number of decisions, makes a certain number of errors tolerable.

---

[18] See Kaplow, *supra* note 5.

Compared to rules, standards and "soft" presumptions serve to reduce the burdens of decision ex ante while increasing those burdens at the time of decision. This is both their virtue and their vice. In daily life, we might adopt standards and rebuttable presumptions for food and liquor consumption, or to help manage expenditures. Or consider the familiar strategy of enacting rigid, rule-like environmental regulations while at the same time allowing a "waiver" for special circumstances. The virtue of this approach is that the rigid rules will likely produce serious mistakes – high costs, low environmental benefits – in some cases; the waiver provision allows correction in the form of an individualized assessment of whether the statutory presumption should be rebutted. The potential vice of this approach is that it requires a fair degree of complexity in a number of individual cases. Whether the complexity is worthwhile turns on a comparative inquiry with genuine rules. How much error would be produced by the likely candidates? How expensive is it to correct those errors by turning the rules into presumptions?

Of Institutions, Planning, and Trust

Often institutions are faced with the decision whether to adopt a High-Low strategy or to delegate. We have seen contexts in which a delegation is better. But in three kinds of circumstances, the High-Low approach is to be preferred.

First, when planning is important, it is important to set out rules (or presumptions) in advance. The law of property is an example. Second, there is little reason to delegate when the agent or institution has a high degree of confidence that a rule (or presumption) can be generated at low enough cost, that the rule (or presumption) will be accurate, and that it will actually be followed. Third, and most obviously, High-Low is better when no trustworthy delegate is available, or when it seems unfair to ask another person or institution to make the relevant decision. If you do not trust anyone with whom you work, you might make relevant decisions yourself. And if you like making decisions, you might do the same thing.

Many nations take considerations of this kind as special reasons to justify rules in the context of criminal law. The law defining crimes is reasonably rule-like, partly because of the importance of citizen knowledge about what counts as a crime, partly because of a judgment that police officers and courts cannot be trusted to define the content of the law. Legislatures tend in the direction of rule-like judgment when they have little confidence in the executive; in the United States, important parts of the Clean Air Act are a prime example of a self-conscious choice of High-Low over delegation.

When would High-Low be favored over Low-Low (picking, small steps)? The interest in planning is highly relevant here and often pushes in the direction of substantial thinking in advance. If an individual or institution has faith in its ability to generate a good rule or presumption, it does not make much sense to proceed with a random choice or incrementally. Families adopt a host of rules, and so do investors. Legislatures have often displaced the common law approach of case-by-case judgment with clear rules set out in advance. In England and the United States, this was a great movement of the twentieth century, largely because of the interest in planning and decreased faith in the courts' ability to generate good outcomes through small steps. Mixed strategies are possible. An institution may produce a rule to cover certain cases but delegate decisions in other cases; a delegate may be disciplined by presumptions and standards; an area of law, or practical reason, may be covered by some combination of rule-bound judgment and small steps.

Private Decisions

We have said enough to show that in their individual capacity, people frequently adopt rules, presumptions, or self-conscious routines in order to guide decisions that they know might, in individual cases, be too costly to make or might be made incorrectly because of their own lack of information or motivational problems (including problems of self-control). Sarah might decide that she will turn down all invitations for out-of-town travel in the months of September or October, or John might adopt a presumption against going to any weddings or funerals unless they involve close family members, or Fred might make up his mind that at dinner parties, he will drink whatever the host is drinking. Rules, presumptions, and routines of this kind are an omnipresent feature of practical reason; sometimes they are chosen self-consciously and as an exercise of will, and often they are, or become, so familiar and simple that they appear to the agent not to be choices at all. Problems arise when a person finds that he cannot stick to his resolution, and thus High-Low may turn into High-High, and things may be as if the second-order decision had not been made at all.

Some especially important cases involve efforts to solve the kinds of intertemporal, intrapersonal problems that arise when isolated, small-step, first-order decisions are individually rational but produce harm to the individual when taken in the aggregate. These cases might be described as involving "intrapersonal collective action problems."[19] Consider, for example, the decision to smoke a cigarette (right now), or to have fudge brownies for dessert, or to have an alcoholic drink after dinner, or to gamble on weekends. Small steps, which may be rational choices when taken individually and which may produce net benefits when taken on their own, can lead to harm or even disaster when they accumulate. There is much room here for second-order decisions. As a self-control strategy, a person might adopt a rule: cigarettes only after dinner; no gambling, ever; fudge brownies only on holidays; alcohol only at parties when everyone else is drinking. But a presumption might work better – for example, a presumption against fudge brownies, with the possibility of rebuttal on special occasions, when celebration is in the air and the brownies look particularly amazing.

Well-known private agencies designed to help people with self-control problems (Alcoholics' Anonymous, Gamblers' Anonymous) have as their business the development of second-order strategies of this general kind. The most striking cases involve recovering addicts, but people who are not addicts, and who are not recovering from anything, often make similar second-order decisions. When self-control is particularly difficult to achieve, an agent may seek to delegate instead. Whether a delegation (Low-High) is preferable to a rule or presumption (High-Low) will depend in turn on the various considerations discussed earlier.

Low-Low (With Special Reference to Picking and Small Steps)

Equipoise, Responsibility, and Commitment

Why might an individual or institution pick rather than choose? When would small steps be best?

Suppose that you are at a restaurant, and there are thirty items on the menu, and you think you would like six of them. Should you

---

[19] Cf. Thomas C. Schelling, *Self-Command in Practice, in Policy, and in a Theory of Rational Choice*, 74 AM. ECON. REV. 1, 1–11 (1984).

focus on which of the six you would like most? Should you think about them at length and in detail? Should you interrogate the waiter? Maybe so, if you are the sort of person you likes that sort of thing. Maybe you greatly enjoy pondering what dinner choice would be best; maybe that improves your experience. But maybe you are at the restaurant to enjoy a night out with your partner or friend, and maybe you do not much care whether the meal is exceptional, very good, or good enough. If so, you will pick.

At the individual level, it can be obvious that when you do not enjoy choosing or when you are in equipoise, you might as well pick. It simply is not worthwhile to go through the process of choosing, with its high cognitive or emotional costs. As we have seen, the result can be picking in both low-stakes (cereal choices) and high-stakes (employment opportunities) settings. Picking can even be said to operate as a kind of delegation, where the object of the delegation is "fate," and the agent loses the sense of responsibility that might accompany an all-things-considered judgment. Thus some people sort out hard questions by resorting to a chance device (like flipping a coin).

Small steps, unlike a random process, are a form of choosing. Students in high schools tend to date in this spirit, at least most of the time; often adults do too. Newspapers and magazines offer trial subscriptions; the same is true for book clubs. Often advertisers (or for that matter prospective romantic partners) know that people prefer small steps, and they take advantage of that preference (no commitments).

In the first years of university, students are often told that they need not commit themselves to any particular course of study. They can take small steps in various directions, sampling as they choose. Typical situations for small steps thus involve a serious risk of unintended bad consequences because a large decision looms when people lack sufficient information; hence reversibility is especially important.

On the institutional side, consider lotteries for jury service. The appeal of a lottery for jury service stems from the relatively low costs of operating the system and the belief that any alternative device for allocation would produce more mistakes, because it would depend on a socially contentious judgment about who should be serving on juries, with possibly destructive results for the jury system itself. The key point is that the jury is supposed to be a cross-section of the community. A random process seems to be the best way of serving that goal (as well as the fairest way of apportioning what many people regard as a social burden). In light of the purposes of the jury system, alternative allocation methods might be thought to be worse; consider stated willingness to serve, an individualized inquiry into grounds for excuse, or financial payments (either to serve or not to serve).[20]

Change, Unintended Consequences, and Reversibility

Lotteries involve random processes; small steps do not. People often take small steps to minimize the burdens of decisions and the costs of error. Anglo-American judges often proceed case by case for the same reasons. Many legal cultures embed a kind of norm in favor of incremental movement. They do this partly because of the distinctive structure of adjudication and the limited information available to the judge: In any particular case, a judge will hear from the parties immediately affected, but little from others whose interests might be at stake. Hence, there is a second-order decision in favor of small steps.

Suppose, for example, that a court in a case involving the scope of freedom of speech by high-school students online finds that it has little information; if the court attempted to generate a rule that would cover all imaginable situations in which that freedom might be exercised, the case would take a very long time to decide. Perhaps the burdens of decision would be prohibitive. This might be so because of a sheer lack of information, or it might be because of the pressures imposed on a multimember court consisting of people who are unsure or in disagreement about a range of subjects. Such a court may have a great deal of difficulty in reaching closure on broad rules. Small steps are a natural result.

When judges proceed by small steps, they do so precisely because they know that their rulings create precedents; they want to narrow the scope of future applications of their rulings given the various problems described earlier, most importantly the lack of sufficient information about future problems. A distinctive problem involves the possibility of too *much* information. A particular case may have a surplus of apparently relevant details, and perhaps future cases will lack one or more of the relevant features, and this will be the source of the concern with creating wide precedents. The existence of (inter alia)

---

[20] On ethical and political issues associated with lotteries in general, *see* ELSTER, *supra* note 17, at 36–122.

features X or Y in case A, missing in case B, makes it hazardous to generate a rule in case A that would govern case B.

In ordinary life, small steps can also make special sense if circumstances are changing rapidly. Perhaps relevant facts and values will change in such a way as to make a rule quickly anachronistic even if it is well suited to present conditions. We can draw some lessons here from law. For example, any decision involving the application of the right of freedom of speech in the context of new communications technologies, including the Internet, might well be narrow, because a broad decision, rendered too early, would be so likely to go wrong. On this view, a small step is best because of the likelihood that a broad rule would be mistaken when applied to cases not before the court.

In an argument very much in this spirit, Joseph Raz has connected a kind of small step – the form usually produced by analogical reasoning – to the special problems created by one-shot interventions in complex systems.[21] In Raz's view, courts reason by analogy in order to prevent unintended side-effects from large disruptions. Similarly supportive of the small-step strategy, the German psychologist Dietrich Dorner has done some illuminating computer experiments designed to see whether people can engage in successful social engineering.[22] Participants are asked to solve problems faced by the inhabitants of some region of the world. Through the magic of the computer, many policy initiatives are available to solve the relevant problems (improved care of cattle, childhood immunization, drilling more wells). But most of the participants produce eventual calamities, because they do not see the complex, system-wide effects of particular interventions.

Only the rare participant is able to see a number of steps down the road – to understand the multiple effects of one-shot interventions on the system. The successful participants are alert to this risk and take small, reversible steps, allowing planning to occur over time. Hence Dorner, along with others focusing on the problems created by interventions into systems,[23] argues in favor of small steps. Many of us face similar problems, and incremental decisions are a good way of responding to the particular problem created by ignorance of possible adverse effects.

---

[21] JOSEPH RAZ, THE AUTHORITY OF LAW (2nd ed. 2009).
[22] DIETRICH DORNER, THE LOGIC OF FAILURE (1997).
[23] See JAMES C. SCOTT, SEEING LIKE A STATE (1998).

From these points we can see that small steps may be better than rules or delegation. Often an individual or institution lacks the information to generate a clear path for the future; often no appropriate delegate has that information. If circumstances are changing rapidly, any rule or presumption might be confounded by subsequent developments. What is especially important is that movement in any particular direction should be reversible if problems arise. On the other hand, a small-steps approach embodies a kind of big (if temporary) decision in favor of the status quo; in the legal context, a court that tries to handle a problem of discrimination incrementally may allow unjust practices to continue, and so too with a state that is trying to alleviate the problem of joblessness in poor areas. A small-steps approach might also undermine planning and fail to provide advance notice of the content of law or policy. It cannot be said that a small-steps approach is, in the abstract, the right approach to limited information or bounded rationality;[24] whether it is a (fully optimal) response or a (suboptimal) reflection of bounded rationality depends on the context.

The analysis is similar outside of the governmental setting. Agents might take small steps because they lack the information that would enable them to generate a rule or presumption, or because the decision they face is unique and not likely to be repeated, so that there is no reason for a rule or a presumption. Or small steps may follow from the likelihood of change over time, from the fact that a large decision might have unintended consequences, or from the wish to avoid or at least to defer the responsibility for large-scale change.

Second-Order Strategies

The discussion is summarized in Table 1.2. Recall that the terms "low" and "high" refer to the overall costs of the decision, which are not necessarily borne by the same agent: With Low-High the costs are split between delegator and delegate; with High-Low they may be split between an institution (which makes the rules, say) and an agent (who follows the rules).

There are two principal conclusions. The first is that no second-order strategy can reasonably be preferred in the abstract. The second is

---

[24] In one form or other, small steps are favored in *id.*, LEVI, *supra* note 7, and ALEXANDER M. BICKEL, THE LEAST DANGEROUS BRANCH (2nd ed. 1986).

Table 1.2 Second-order strategies

Strategies	Examples	Potential Advantages	Potential Disadvantages	Appropriate Context
1. Low-High: delegation	Relying on spouses, friends, experts, or one's future self; granting authority to administrative agencies	increased chance for good outcomes; relief from direct responsibility for ultimate decisions	possible high costs in deciding whether and to whom to delegate; problems relating to trust, fairness, and responsibility; distrust of one's future self	availability of appropriate and trustworthy delegate; an understanding that one's future self will be in a better position than one's current self
2. Low-Low: picking, small steps, various heuristics	Unimportant or trivial personal decisions; decisions with unforeseeable consequences; Anglo-American common law; lotteries	low overall costs; reversibility; coping with change and with unintended consequences	difficulty of planning; high aggregate decision costs; multiple mistakes	equipoise and symmetry of preferences or values; reasonable aversion to drastic changes; reasonable fear of unanticipated consequences
3. High-Low: rules, presumptions, routines	People with self-control problems; rigid people; speed limit laws; criminal law	low costs of numerous decisions once in place; easing life on-the-spot; uniformity; facilitates planning	difficulty of generating good rules or presumptions; mistakes once in place	Risk of error on-the-spot; sheer number of anticipated decisions; repetitive nature of future decisions; need for planning, confidence in ability to generate ex ante decisions
4. High-High	certain Henry James characters; dysfunctional governments	none (unless decision costs are actually pleasant to incur and decisions end up being good)	paralysis; unpopularity; individual or institutional collapse	agency or institution cannot do otherwise

that it is possible to identify the settings in which one or another is likely to make sense, and also the factors that argue in favor of, or against, any particular approach.

Making Second-Order Decisions

When do people, or institutions, actually make a self-conscious decision about which second-order strategy to favor, given the menu of possibilities? The simplest answer is: often. An employer might adopt a host of firm rules to simplify life for its employees. A family may choose, self-consciously, to proceed incrementally in terms of living arrangements (lease, don't buy); a legislature may deliberate and decide to delegate rather than to generate rules; having rejected the alternatives, a president may recommend a lottery system rather than other alternatives for admitting certain aliens to the country. An institution or a person will often make an all-things-considered decision in favor of one or another second-order strategy.

Sometimes, however, a rapid assessment of the situation takes place, rather than a full or deliberative weighing of alternative courses of action. This is often the case in private decisions, where judgments often seem immediate. Indeed, some second-order decisions might be too costly if they were a product of an optimizing strategy; so taken, they would present many of the problems of first-order decisions. As in the case of first-order decisions, it may make sense to proceed with what seems best, rather than to maximize in any systematic fashion, simply because the former way of proceeding is easier (and thus may maximize once we consider decision costs of various kinds). For both individuals and institutions, the salient features of the context often strongly suggest a particular kind of second-order strategy; there is no reason to think long and hard about the second-order decision.

These are intended as descriptive points about the operation of practical reason. But there is a normative issue here as well, for people's second-order decisions may go wrong. People tend to make mistakes when they choose strategies on the fly, and often they would do better to be self-conscious and reflective about the diverse possibilities. Pathologically rigid rules can be a serious problem for life, law, and policy. Sometimes delegation is a most unfortunate route to travel. At the political level, and occasionally at the individual level too, it would be much better to be more explicit and self-conscious about the various alternatives, so as to ensure that societies and institutions do not find themselves making bad second-order decisions, or choosing a second-order strategy without a sense of the candidates.

Rationality and Bounded Rationality

As we have seen, second-order strategies may solve the problems posed by unanticipated side-effects and the difficulty of obtaining knowledge about the future. They might be a response to anxiety or stress, or a recognition of the sheer unpleasantness of making certain kinds of decisions. Or they may respond to people's awareness that they are prone to err when a decision must be made on the spot. People might try, for example, to counteract their own tendencies toward impulsiveness, myopia, and unrealistic optimism. In these ways, second-order decisions can be seen as rational strategies by people making those decisions with full awareness of the costs of obtaining information and of their own propensities for error.

But a lack of information or bounded rationality can affect second-order decisions as well. A lack of information may press people and institutions in the direction of suboptimal second-order strategies. For example, an individual or an institution may choose small steps even though rules would be much better. The availability heuristic – by which people make probability judgments by asking if relevant events are cognitively "available" and hence come readily to mind – helps account for some erroneous judgments about appropriate second-order strategies. An impulsive or myopic person or institution may fail to see the extent to which rules will be confounded by subsequent developments; an unrealistically optimistic agent or institution may overestimate its capacity to take optimal small steps. People may choose second-order strategies that badly disserve their own goals.

Burdens and Benefits

Return to the major themes. Ordinary people and official institutions are often reluctant to make on-the-spot decisions; they respond with one or another second-order strategy. Some such strategies involve high initial burdens but make life much easier for the future. These strategies, generally taking the form of rules or presumptions, are best when the anticipated decisions are numerous and repetitive and when advance notice and planning are important. They might also be best when people face serious self-control problems. Other strategies involve both light initial burdens and light burdens at the time of making the ultimate decision. These approaches work well in diverse situations: when the stakes are low; when a first-order decision is simply too difficult to make (because of the cognitive or emotional burdens involved in the choice); when the first-order decision includes too many imponderables and a risk of large unintended consequences; and when a degree of randomization is appealing on normative grounds (perhaps because choices are otherwise in equipoise, or because no one should or will take responsibility for deliberate decision). A key point in favor of small steps involves reversibility.

Still other strategies involve low initial burdens but high exported burdens at the time of decision, as when a delegation is made to another person or institution, or to one's future self. Delegations take many different forms, with more or less control retained by the person or institution making the delegation. Strategies of delegation make sense when a delegate is available who has relevant expertise (perhaps because he is a specialist) or is otherwise trustworthy (perhaps because he does not suffer from bias or some other motivational problem), or when there are special political, strategic, or other advantages to placing the responsibility for decision on some other person or institution. Delegations can raise serious ethical or political issues and create problems of unfairness, as when delegates are burdened with tasks that they do not voluntarily assume, or would not assume under just conditions.

The final set of cases involves high burdens both before and at the time of decision, as in certain characters in novels and films, some people who are really struggling in life (and who may be crippled by anxiety), and highly dysfunctional governments. This strategy is usually a terrible idea. It can be considered reasonable only on the assumption that bearing high overall burdens of decision is something to relish (perhaps because it is actually pleasant) or an affirmative good (perhaps for moral reasons). This assumption is usually unrealistic. But it is not hard to identify situation in which people do incur high burdens well before they make decisions, and also at the time that they make decisions—behavior that often provides the motivation to consider the other, more promising second-order decisions discussed here.

2 DECIDING TO OPT

Some decisions are especially difficult for one reason: They involve some kind of upheaval. Those decisions might be exhilarating; they might be searing. For better or for worse, they put our values and preferences at risk. Such decisions raise a fundamental question: What should people try to promote or maximize? When we are deciding whether to "opt," we have to ask that question – but I am getting ahead of the story.

Psychological work on well-being has long emphasized two things that people might seek to maximize: (1) happiness, sometimes described as "pleasure" and (2) eudaimonia, sometimes described as "flourishing," and involving, as a constituent feature, a sense of "meaning." Some experiences are enjoyable, delightful, or comfortable, or all three at once; they are associated with happiness. Other experiences offer a sense of purpose; they are associated with a belief that one is living a meaningful life. Watching television, playing tennis, or going out to dinner with friends might be pleasurable, whether or not any of those activities is meaningful. Helping others, doing one's job well, or parenting might be meaningful, whether or not any of them is pleasant. People's experiences may or may not be pleasurable, and they may or may not be purposeful.[1] We might think that our lives are full of pleasure without being full of meaning; we might think that our lives

---

[1] *See* Paul Dolan, Happiness by Design (2014).

are full of meaning without being full of pleasure. Of course, the idea of eudaimonia might be taken to include both pleasure and meaning.

Psychological research has also explored the idea of "psychological richness," understood to include a diversity of experiences and perspectives, including experiences that challenge and alter one's preferences and values.[2] The basic idea is that people do not care only about pleasure and purpose. They might seek variety and change. They might want to be spontaneous. They might want a diversity of experiences. They might want something altogether new. Some of what they want may or may not be pleasant, and it may or may not be meaningful. A significant change might be both pleasant and meaningful, but the motivation for change might be psychological richness, not pleasure or purpose. People might even be willing to sacrifice pleasure or purpose for the sake of psychological richness (or vice versa). In fact, many people are willing to do exactly that.[3]

From all this we might be tempted to conclude that decisions reflect an effort to assess happiness, eudaimonia, and psychological richness, with appropriate weights. Some people will give particular weight to one factor; the context will greatly matter. And, of course, people do not care only about themselves. They might sacrifice their own well-being for others. Decisions about decisions are made accordingly.

Let us suppose that when people make decisions, including second-order decisions, they should calculate the probabilities of various outcomes, good and bad, and multiply those outcomes by the probabilities. Let us suppose that they care about pleasure, purpose, and psychological richness, in some combination. To be sure, they might lack necessary information. They might not know the probabilities of various outcomes. They might not even know the various outcomes. John Maynard Keynes drew attention to cases in which "there is no scientific basis on which to form any calculable probability whatever. We simply do not know."[4] Lacking information, they might use rules of thumb. Apart from the epistemic challenge, people might be risk-averse. If an option carries with it a small chance of catastrophe, for example, people might give that option more weight

[2] *See* Shigehiro Oishi & Erin C. Westgate, *A Psychologically Rich Life: Beyond Happiness and Meaning*, 129 PSYCH. REV. 790 (2022).

[3] *Id.*

[4] John Maynard Keynes, *The General Theory of Employment*, 51 Q.J. ECON. 212, 213 (1937).

than its expected value; people buy insurance for that reason, and they might also favor pleasure (including comfort) over psychological richness for that reason. People might also give particular weight to an option that carries with it a small chance of a miracle; you might gamble (say, on psychological richness) for that reason.

My focus in this chapter is on another kind of problem. It arises when people are at a crossroads. They are keenly aware, or should be keenly aware, that if they select one option, their preferences and values, and in a sense their identity and their self-understanding, will be different from what they would otherwise be. Some people are intrigued with the problem of "counterfactual history," which might involve a world in which Adolf Hitler never gained power, in which John F. Kennedy was not assassinated, or in which Donald Trump chose never to run for president. Might history take a fundamentally different course? Smaller-scale tales involve "sliding doors," in which the protagonists make a choice that turns them, in a sense, into different people – a lawyer rather than a doctor, a soldier rather than a civilian, married with children rather than not. Some of the most intriguing such tales depict both "versions" of the protagonist, and pose hard questions about whether the identity-altering choice was the right one.

Consider in this regard four cases:

1. Margaret is a single woman in her thirties. She is unsure whether to have a child. Her friends strongly encourage her to do so. She has a great deal of trepidation about being a mother, and especially about doing so without a partner, but she goes ahead with it. It is an understatement to say that she is happy that she did. Her child is the most important thing in her life; to her surprise, she identifies herself, first and foremost, as a mother.

2. Susan is a successful lawyer. She enjoys her job. At the same time, she has always loved writing fiction, which she does in her spare time. Her best friend, Carl, strongly encourages her to leave her law practice and to become a full-time writer. After years of hesitation, she does exactly that. She is now a writer. While she is not making much money, she loves what she does, and she cannot imagine going back to the practice of law.

3. Frank was born and raised in the United States. He has long identified as American. In recent years, he has started to question the direction of his country. He decides to spend time in Norway, where he forms

close friendships. His loyalties and values begin to change. He is full of admiration for Norwegians. After repeated urging by his friends, he moves to Oslo, and he is glad that did. Though he feels close to the nation in which he was born and raised, he can no longer imagine thinking of himself as American.

4. Larry is married – happily, or happily enough. For fifteen years, he has been faithful to his wife. At a large meeting, he encounters a woman to whom he is deeply attracted. They end up having an affair. For his marriage and his life, the affair is a serious problem and a source of constant stress. But he does not wish that he were not having an affair. It is one of the best and most important things in his life – in some ways, the best and the most important.

In these cases, our choices are *transformative*, in the sense that they alter our core values, our sense of self, and our preferences – what we care most about. Such decisions may or may not increase pleasure or purpose; they might well increase psychological richness. In recent years, transformative choices have received a great deal of attention.[5] Edna Ullmann-Margalit refers to these as "big decisions,"[6] which she defines as having four characteristics:

1. They are "transformative, or 'core affecting'";
2. They are irrevocable;
3. They are "undertaken in full awareness"; and
4. After they are made, "the choice not made casts a lingering shadow."

Ullmann-Margalit urges that a big decision "is likely to transform one's future self in a significant way." Such decisions involve "a critical juncture in one's life." They "call for leaping across an abyss." That sense of "leaping" is recognizable to most people, even if they feel it infrequently. At life's crossroads, people do not choose so much as "opt," and in Ullmann-Margalit's account, big decisions are cases of "opting." If you opt, you will emerge as in some sense a different person. The shift can be thought of as a process by which one's old self, defined by one's old values and preferences, is replaced by one's new self, defined by new values and preferences.

---

[5] *See* RICHARD PETTIGREW, CHOOSING FOR CHANGING SELVES (2019); L.A. PAUL, TRANSFORMATIVE EXPERIENCE (2014).

[6] *See* EDNA ULLMANN-MARGALIT, BIG DECISIONS: OPTING, DRIFTING, CONVERTING, 58 ROYAL INSTITUTE OF PHILOSOPHY SUPPLEMENT 157 (2006).

It is useful to distinguish between unquestionably big decisions, as Ullmann-Margalit understands them, and what we might see as little big decisions, which do not have the same transformative effects, but which are nonetheless transformative in certain respects, and which might affect one's core. A family might decide to spend the summer in Japan. A college student might decide to take a year abroad. A university professor might decide to spend two years working in the government. These decisions might add psychological richness to the relevant lives, and they might also add to both pleasure and purpose (or subtract from them). In particular, people might make such decisions because they care about psychological richness. But they are most unlikely to be "big" in Ullmann-Margalit's sense; they need not be "core affecting" and they are not irrevocable.

For big decisions, it may or may not be clear that the relevant agent actually is choosing or deciding. In the cases I have given, the relevant people are doing exactly that. But we could also imagine cases of "drifting," in which people end up, step by step, turning in a new direction.[7] That can certainly be true with a shift in occupations or a love affair. In some such cases, people might not be at all clear that they are making some kind of decision, or at least that they are making a large one. (They might be fooling themselves.) In other cases, agents might have the experience of something happening "to them." That might be true of a divorce, for example, if a spouse simply insists on it. It might also seem true of a divorce if a husband or wife finds, very much against his or her will, that "there is no alternative" to severing the marriage. But my focus is on cases in which a decision is being self-consciously made.

Ullmann-Margalit is at pains to distinguish among opting, choosing, and picking.[8] Choosing is the standard situation; we choose for reasons, and maximizing expected utility, however we understand it, is the coin of the realm. Recall from Chapter 1 that picking is akin to flipping a coin: In relative equipoise, and not enjoying the burdens of decision, we might pick. At first glance, opting and picking seem at opposite ends of a spectrum. Opting involves the largest choices; picking tends to the involve the smallest.

---

[7] See id.
[8] See Edna Ullmann-Margalit, *Picking and Choosing, in* NORMAL RATIONALITY 3 (Avishai Margalit & Cass R. Sunstein eds., 2017).

One of the noteworthy, and puzzling, features of an opting situation is that we can readily imagine that the agent *would be very glad about the outcome either way*. As I have described their situations, Margaret, Susan, Frank, and Larry have psychologically richer lives, and that may be one reason that they are glad to have opted. But if Margaret, Susan, Frank, and Larry had chosen to stick with the status quo, they might have been happy and relieved that they did. In fact they might have judged their decision to be right, whatever they decided. Consider Margaret: She decided to have a child, and through this process, she formed a strong preference to have her baby; she cannot even imagine what it would be like not to be a mother. The very thought makes her shudder. But if she had decided not to have a child, she could have formed an equally strong preference to live a child-free life, in part as a result of the numerous follow-up choices that she would have made. Perhaps she loves her freedom and shudders to imagine life without it. Perhaps she loves her career. Perhaps she thinks of motherhood as deadening and stultifying – with much less in the way of pleasure, with incalculably less in the way of purpose, and without psychological richness.

So too for Susan. If she had continued to be a lawyer, and not decided (opted) to become a writer, she might be so pleased and relieved. She might ask: "What on earth was I thinking?" As a lawyer, she might cherish the energy and dynamism of her days, her colleagues, and her clients, and she might treasure her security. The very idea of becoming a writer might seem to be a reckless dream, a foolish fantasy. She might agree that such a life could be psychologically richer, but at what price?

If Frank had stayed in the United States, he might have, at once, a sense of home, ease, and comfort, and a sense of commitment, meaning, and determination. Of his plan to move to Norway, he might then think: "What a wild and reckless thought that was!" In the United States, he might think that there are challenges and frustrations, not least because of what he sees as a dysfunctional political system. But every day, he might think: "It's home."

As I have described things, Larry is very glad (if ambivalently glad) that he chose to have an affair, but if he had decided not to do that, he might have been very glad that he did. He might have thought that he had dodged a bullet, involving both happiness and meaning, and avoided a course of action that would have torn up everything that mattered most to him. He might think of the almost-affair as a kind of madness. He might well think, with some relief, that at a crucial moment, he thought better of it. Psychological richness, of a certain sort, would have been far too costly (he thinks).

It would be most valuable to have data on this kind of question – to know whether those who opt, or those who do not opt, are generally glad that they did, or instead feel some form of regret. Existing evidence is supportive of a simple and striking conclusion: People benefit from making large life changes, and they are significantly more likely to show regret, and to be unhappy, if they stick with the status quo.[9] For ending a relationship or quitting a job, for example, the clear implication is that *people are more likely to err if they decide to be cautious than if they decide to take some kind of plunge.*[10] The challenge for individuals, of course, is that statistical generalizations cannot resolve hard questions.

In the case of big decisions, choosers will foresee situations with a person and a counterfactual person, where the latter walks on the road not taken (and hence the choice not made indeed casts a lingering shadow). What should we conclude about the possible fact that both the person and the counterfactual person would be very glad to have taken the road they did take? What criteria should we use to select the right decision in situations of opting? When does a rational person, or a reasonable person, opt?

Ullmann-Margalit offers a striking answer. In her view, we ordinarily choose for reasons, but sometimes we run out of them. Picking, involving small decisions, is one example; opting, involving big decisions, is another. If you decide in favor of A, you do so because of B, and you rely on B because of C, which is in turn justified by reference to D, and ultimately there is a P, a Q, or an R, which you cannot justify – what Ullmann-Margalit calls "the substratum of all your reasons." For example, the choice to be moral cannot be justified by reference to morality. The most fundamental choices of all, in Ullmann-Margalit's account, "cannot really be choices," in the particular sense that they are justifiable by reference to reasons. Pointing to existentialism, she urges that "we make our most fundamental choices of the canons of

---

[9] Steven D. Levitt, *Heads or Tails: The Impact of a Coin Toss on Major Life Decisions and Subsequent Happiness*, 88 REV. ECON. STUD. 378 (2021).

[10] *Id.*

morality, logic and rationality in total freedom and without appeal to reasons."[11]

Perhaps. (Would it be lovely to think so?) But consider another answer, even for big decisions: To make the right choice, the chooser must think hard about the effects of the choice on the chooser's welfare. For opting, people must ask: What would make their lives better? Of course, that question immediately leads to another one: What is the proper conception of welfare? Pleasure and purpose are relevant here, and psychological richness has its claims. Rational and reasonable people can make different decisions about the right amount of each. Some people focus on pleasure and purpose, and give less or little weight to psychological richness; other people give psychological richness pride of place, and might not much care about pleasure and purpose. We could imagine cases in which people have made self-evidently unreasonable decisions, because they have sacrificed their own welfare in a way that is impossible to defend. The only point is that the welfare question is the right one, even if different people can reasonably answer it in different ways.

It should be immediately apparent that I am bracketing an important and possibly decisive factor, which is that for transformative decisions, as for little big decisions and for decisions of all kinds, the welfare of other people, and moral considerations of multiple kinds, might be at stake. Susan might be a lawyer for causes that she really cares about; she might not much enjoy her work, but she is helping others. That might much matter to her, and it should matter to her. For example, Susan might be a government lawyer, helping to deliver economic help to people in need, working to reduce deaths on the highways, or seeking to figure out the best ways to combat a pandemic. Susan's decision whether to remain in the status quo or to transform her situation might be driven by this question: What is best for relevant others? John Stuart Mill said this:

> I must again repeat, what the assailants of utilitarianism seldom have the justice to acknowledge, that the happiness which forms the utilitarian standard of what is right in conduct, is not the agent's own happiness, but that of all concerned. As between his own happiness and that of others, utilitarianism requires him to be as strictly impartial as a disinterested and

benevolent spectator. In the golden rule of Jesus of Nazareth, we read the complete spirit of the ethics of utility. To do as you would be done by, and to love your neighbour as yourself, constitute the ideal perfection of utilitarian morality.[12]

To know what to do, the welfare of "all concerned" unquestionably matters. But for simplicity, let us assume that it is not clear which of the available paths helps others most, and that for Margaret, Susan, Frank, and Larry, their own welfare is the central consideration, or at least an important part of picture.

The writer Beatrice Kaufman said this: "I've been rich and I've been poor, and believe me, rich is better."[13] Fair enough. For big decisions, we might want people to make predictions of their subjective experience – of how they will likely experience their lives. With the assistance of available data, it is possible that we could measure that, or at least come relatively close. We should care about people's happiness or pleasure; we should care about their sense of purpose of meaning; we should also care about psychological richness. Existing tools are available to make at least rough assessments and they will inevitably get better.[14] But what, exactly, are we measuring?

The answer might be subjective happiness: Are people happy or are they miserable? Alternatively, the answer might be, or might include, a sense of purpose or meaning, which might also be measurable.[15] People could be happy, in the sense of smiling and content, without having much of a sense of purposefulness; perhaps they consider most of their days fun but trivial. Or people could have a sense of purposefulness without smiling much or being content; perhaps they are devoting themselves to good works, and perhaps their days are arduous. Still, it is important to ask: Do people have a sense that their life is meaningful and full of purpose? Or not so much? And we might ask about the richness of people's lives. If they did not opt, would they have a sense of regret? How dark is the lingering shadow? Would their lives be less eventful, or uneventful?

We could easily imagine answers to such questions that would help people like Margaret, Larry, Susan, and Frank to decide

---

[12] John Stuart Mill, Utilitarianism 17 (George Sher ed.) (Hackett Pub. 2002), 17 (1861).
[13] See Fred R. Shapiro, The Yale Book of Quotations (2006).
[14] See Dolan, supra note 1; see also Oishi & Westgate, supra note 2.
[15] See Dolan, supra note 17.

(reasonably and rationally) what to do. Margaret's life as a mother might have much more of a sense of meaning, and much more of a sense of joy, than Margaret's childless life. Susan might have been happy as a lawyer, and perhaps more relaxed about money and the like, but as a writer, she might well have ended up with a far greater sense of purpose, freedom, and play, and her life might have more in the way of psychological richness. Frank might be happy enough in Norway, but his life might well have been better, all things considered, if he had stayed in the United States. These are simply examples; we could imagine a wide range of variations.

Of course, subjective experience is not all that matters. Suppose that someone decides to leave a life of ease and contentment for one of challenge, difficulty, and strife, in which she learns a great deal, expands her horizons, and often fails. That idea is connected with the notion of psychological richness. Consider the famous words of Theodore Roosevelt, which can be seen as a plea for a sense of purpose, and also for a life of richness:

> It is not the critic who counts; not the man who points out how the strong man stumbles, or where the doer of deeds could have done them better. The credit belongs to the man who is actually in the arena, whose face is marred by dust and sweat and blood; who strives valiantly; who errs, who comes short again and again, because there is no effort without error and shortcoming; but who does actually strive to do the deeds; who knows great enthusiasms, the great devotions; who spends himself in a worthy cause; who at the best knows in the end the triumph of high achievement, and who at the worst, if he fails, at least fails while daring greatly, so that his place shall never be with those cold and timid souls who neither know victory nor defeat.[16]

These words are too grandiose for my taste, and also too self-congratulatory, but it is important to say that Roosevelt was not speaking of subjective experience, even if we include a sense of meaning. He was offering an account of what makes life good. Those who are deciding whether and how to opt would do well to consider their own account (even as they know that their account might shift after they opt).[17]

---

[16] Theodore Roosevelt, Citizenship in a Republic: Speech at the Sorbonne (Apr. 23, 1910).

[17] After opting, for example, a person might care more or less about psychological richness; pleasure may or may not loom very large. From the standpoint of a third party, trying to

Without knowing much more, we cannot say a lot about Larry's case. It is certainly a romance. It could also be a tragedy. It could be a comedy. The best treatment of a case like it, and perhaps the best and most searing treatment of big decisions in the English language, is *Possession*, by A.S. Byatt.[18] The novel involves a love affair (and an illicit one) between two poets: Randolph Ash (who was married) and Christabel LaMotte. Byatt offers this description of what sometimes happens after opting:

> In the morning, the whole world had a strange new smell. It was the smell of the aftermath, a green smell, a smell of shredded leaves and oozing resin, of crushed wood and splashed sap, a tart smell, which bore some relation to the smell of bitten apples. It was the smell of death and destruction, and it smelled fresh and lively and hopeful.[19]

LaMotte's final letter to the dying Ash captures something of the complexity of opting: "I would rather have lived alone, so, if you would have the truth. But since that might not be – and is granted to almost none – I thank God for you – if there must be a Dragon – that He was You ...."[20]

Would LaMotte really prefer to have lived alone? Perhaps. But perhaps not. She was ironic and she was playful; she was grateful for her Dragon. She can be read to have said, to her former lover, that she was willing to sacrifice something in the way of happiness (and comfort) in favor of a great deal in the way of meaning and psychological richness. As we have seen, reasonable people, confronted with a big decision, can assess the relevant goods in diverse ways. Sometimes the decision to opt, and to leap over a very large abyss, makes one's life go better, all things considered. Will it do that? That is a crucial question to ask when making big decisions.

---

figure out what an agent should do, there is no escaping an assessment of the welfare issue. From the standpoint of an agent, trying to figure out what to do, there is also no escaping an assessment of that issue, which means that the agent has to consider, right now, what she most values, even as she knows that if she opts, what she values might change.

[18]   A. S. Byatt, Possession (1990).

[19]   *Id.*, 549.

[20]   *Id.*, 544.

3 DECIDING TO KNOW

It is self-evident that to make a decision about a decision –
whether to delegate, whether to take a small step, whether to pick,
whether to opt – people need information. They may not be able to
obtain the information they need, which is one reason that they might
make a second-order decision (e.g. to delegate or to take small steps).
But they do need to know *something*, which makes it natural to assume
that it is always good to obtain information. But that conclusion is
too categorical. Sometimes we do not want to know. When, exactly, is
information good to have? And exactly how good is it? How do people
decide whether to seek or to avoid information? Information avoidance
is a central feature of human life. Sometimes we take active steps to
avoid information (deliberate ignorance). Sometimes we try to forget
what we know.

We need to distinguish here between *not wanting to know* and
wanting not to know. There is a great deal of information that people
have no interest in receiving. It has no value for them. It clutters the
mind. It is boring. In addition, there a great deal of information that
people want *not* to receive. It is unpleasant. It is painful. In some cases,
people do not *want* to know, in the sense that they have no particular
motivation to find out.[1] They will not take active steps to learn. In

---

[1] *See* Edna Ullmann-Margalit, *On Not Wanting to Know, in* NORMAL RATIONALITY 80
(Avishai Margalit & Cass R. Sunstein eds., 2017).

others, they want *not* to know, in the sense that they have a particular motivation not to find out. They decide to avoid learning, and they take active steps to avoid that.

You might not much care to learn the number of hairs on the heads of people sitting at the next table at a restaurant, or the precise metals that were used to make your automobile, or whether the coffee beans at the local store came from Brazil, Colombia, Vietnam, or somewhere else. You might not want to know whether you will get Alzheimer's disease, whether you have a genetic susceptibility to cancer and heart disease, what all of your colleagues really think about you, and the year of your likely death. You might not want to know about the health risks associated with consumption of beer, coffee, pizza, and ice cream – products that offer immediate pleasure but may create future harm. If your mind is full of those risks, consumption might produce fear, guilt, or shame. Ignorance might be bliss. (This very morning, I weighed myself. Doing that was not good for my mood.)

The general phenomenon of "information avoidance" suggests that people often prefer not to know and will actually take active steps to avoid information.[2] But what steps? And at what cost? The most fundamental question is whether receiving information increases people's well-being. That proposition argues in favor of a case-by-case approach, asking whether information would have that effect for the relevant population (even if it is a population of just one).[3] But what does well-being mean? And how would we measure it? Economists like to work with the idea of willingness to pay (WTP), insisting that it is the best measure we have of whether people will gain or lose from obtaining things – clothing, food, sporting goods, laptops, automobiles, or information. But WTP is hardly a perfect method for capturing well-being. An obvious problem is that if people lack money, they will not be willing to pay much for that reason. But let's bracket that point and work with WTP for now, seeing it as a way of testing whether people really do want something and how much. One of its advantages is that at least in principle, it should capture everything that human beings care about – everything that matters to them. In some cases, people are willing to pay a lot for information. In other cases, people are willing

---

[2] Russell Golman et al., *Information Avoidance*, 55 J. Econ. Literature 96 (2017); Ralph Hertwig & Christoph Engel, *Homo Ignorans: Deliberately Choosing Not to Know*, 11 Persps. on Psych. Sci. 359 (2016).

[3] *See* Ullmann-Margalit, *supra* note 1.

to pay exactly nothing for information. In other cases, they are willing to pay *not* to receive information.[4]

As we shall see, it is important to ask whether people's WTP, or not, is informed and rational. Crucially, people might lack the information to decide how much they are willing to pay for information. If so, their WTP might depend on an absence of information about the importance of that information. People's WTP might also depend on deprivation and injustice, leading them to lack interest in information that could greatly improve their lives. People who do not know how much they might gain from learning about (say) how to save money might have no interest in obtaining that information. People's WTP might also depend on some kind of cognitive bias, such as present bias (focusing on today and not tomorrow) or availability bias (making some bad outcomes, and not others appear likely to come to fruition).

WTP might depend on a rational desire to avoid distress – or to preserve the capacity for surprise. We want information when we want it, not before and not after. A surprise party isn't much fun if it isn't a surprise, and a mystery novel needs to maintain its secrets. At the same time, people might underestimate their ability to adapt. They might avoid potentially distressing information about their health, even though the distress might turn out to be short-term (and medical help might be on the way).

Nonetheless, the fact that people are willing to pay a lot for some information but nothing for other information tells us something important. It is even more interesting that people are sometimes willing to pay real money to avoid information.

Wanting to Know

When people want to know, it is often for one of two reasons.[5] First, the information might have *instrumental value*. It might enable

---

[4] For valuable discussions, *see* Linda Thunström et al., *Strategic Self-Ignorance*, 52 J. Risk & Uncertainty 117 (2016); Jonas Nordström et al., Strategic Self-Ignorance Negates the Effect of Risk Information (August 22, 2016) (unpublished European Economic Association paper) (available at https://editorialexpress.com/cgi-bin/conference/download .cgi?db_name=EEAESEM2016&paper_id=1949); Golman et al., *supra* note 2; Hertwig & Engel, *supra* note 2; Caroline J. Charpentier et al., *Valuation of Knowledge and Ignorance in Mesolimbic Reward Circuitry*, 115 Proc. Nat'l Acad. Sci. 7255 (2018).

[5] *See* Tali Sharot & Cass R. Sunstein, *How People Decide What They Want to Know*, 4 Nature Hum. Behav. 14 (2020).

us to do what we want to do, to go where we want to go, to choose what we want to choose, or to avoid what we want to avoid. Second, the information might produce *positive feelings*. It might provide joy, delight, amazement, or relief.

It follows that even if the information is not useful, people might want it because it makes them feel great. If people learn that they will never get cancer or that they are especially intelligent and good-looking, they are likely to be pleased, whether or not their behavior is altered. Information can create positive feelings of diverse kinds: joy, pride, satisfaction, contentment, relief, gratitude. In many cases, it is true and important to say that information has hedonic value – that is, it provides pleasure. Still, it is inadequate to describe the relevant feelings as narrowly hedonic. They might have little or nothing to do with pleasure; they involve welfare in a much broader sense. They might produce a sense that life has meaning. We can use the term *affective value* to describe positive feelings of these different kinds.

The instrumental value of information is captured in the idea that knowledge is power. If people find out that their boss thinks that they are underperforming, they might be able to do better. If people learn that the stock market will probably go up in the next few months, they will have an opportunity to invest and to make money. If teachers learn that their students did not enjoy their course, they can try to teach better. If people learn that they are at risk of diabetes, they might take steps to reduce that risk. If people learn that their car is not fuel-efficient, they can buy a new and more fuel-efficient one. Often people act differently, and do better, once they know. Information can save money and lives.

Note here that the instrumental value might involve one's own well-being or instead the well-being of others. Consumers might want information about certain products so that they can increase social benefits or reduce social harms. Public officials might require disclosure of such information not because consumers are demanding it, but to trigger their attention, conscience, and concern and in that way affect social norms and promote social goals. Consider animal welfare and climate change.

People might also want to know about their country, their planet, and their universe, even if the information does not especially please them and even if they cannot do anything with it. They might want to know about life in other nations and about the history of the world's religions for reasons that have nothing to do with what they can do with that information or whether they will be pleased by what they learn. They might be curious, or they might think that they have a moral obligation to know certain things. If people are suffering in their city or their country, or if there is a mass atrocity somewhere in the world, they might want to know about it.

More broadly still, people might think that certain kinds of knowledge make for a better or fuller or richer life, even if lacks instrumental or affective value. People might want to know something about their friends and family, even if that something does not make them happy and even if it cannot be used, because of their views about what makes a human life good or right. They might want to know about the life of William Shakespeare, the origins of Earth, the relationship between dogs and wolves, or the history of India, even if they are not rooting for a particular answer and regardless of whether or not they can use that information.

The Dark Side of Information

Much information does not enable people to do anything at all. If people learn the height of everyone born in Paris in 1920, the weather next week in a foreign city that they will not be visiting, or the words to twenty songs in a language that they do not understand, they are unlikely to live their lives differently. Finding out about those heights, that weather, or those words may not induce positive feelings. It might be tedious as well as useless.

Some information induces negative feelings. Do you want to know the year of your spouse's death? The year of your son's death? The results of a battery of medical tests? Whether the people who made your clothing were paid a decent wage? If the news could be bad or sad, people might want to avoid it for that very reason. And even if the news is likely to be relatively good, people might not want to take their chances on such questions. They might prefer a big question mark – or not to think about the matter. Information can produce distress, frustration, grief, rage, or despair. (Confession: It wasn't so bad, but I kind of wish I had not weighed myself this morning.)

Here is striking evidence. Sometimes people really do not want to know how much goods cost, and they will avoid information about price – *intentionally*.[6] Price, too, can ruin popcorn, and people know that. More specifically, Linda Thunström and Chian Jones Ritten find that some people are "spendthrifts" by their own lights, in the sense that they agree that they spend too much for their own good. Thunström and Ritten find that spendthrifts tend to be inaccurate in their judgments about the costs of their own recent purchases. They also find that spendthrifts tend to agree with this statement: "When I engage in an enjoyable activity, I prefer not to think of the cost of that activity." Their evidence strongly suggests that spendthrifts take steps to reduce their knowledge of and attention to cost. To be sure, it may not be easy to ignore price entirely. But consumers can focus less on price, so that it is not so visibly on their viewscreen and so that they think and know less about it. Thunström and Jones Ritten conclude that willful inattention to price can provide a justification for laws and policies that make prices transparent and salient.

Some information has *negative* instrumental value.[7] Suppose that you are a lawyer, representing a client accused of murder. Suppose that the evidence leaves significant doubt about whether your client is guilty or whether the police violated your client's constitutional rights. You might do a better job if you never know, for sure, whether your client is a murderer. Or suppose that you are fighting a serious illness. Your chances of success, and of a long life, might depend on not knowing the odds. (As Han Solo, the daredevil pilot in *Star Wars*, liked to say, "Never tell me the odds!") Or suppose that you are on a tennis team consisting of nine players, and the first team to win five matches wins the entire match. If you learn that four of your teammates are way ahead, you might not try so hard. You might be better off not knowing. Or suppose that you do not want to discriminate on certain grounds – sex, religion, age, race. You might fear that if you receive demographic information about a job applicant, you might discriminate. To avoid that risk, you might try not to know.

Some information has instrumental value but also induces negative feelings. If you learn that you are obese or that you suffer from high blood pressure, you are likely to be upset, but you can probably do something about it (which should reduce the negative affect). If

---

[6] *See* Linda Thunström & Chian Jones Ritten, *Endogenous Attention to Costs*, 59 J. RISK & UNCERTAINTY 1 (2019).

[7] Chip Heath & Dan Heath, *The Curse of Knowledge*, HARV. BUS. REV. MAG., Dec. 2006.

Table 3.1 Feelings and values

	Instrumental Value		
Feelings	Positive	Negative	None
Positive	(1)	(2)	(3)
Negative	(4)	(5)	(6)
None	(7)	(8)	(9)

you learn that your boss thinks that you could do a much better job, you might be hurt and angry, but you might be able to take steps to improve your performance. If you find out that your spouse is upset with you, you will not be happy about it, but perhaps you can improve the relationship.

Some information has negative instrumental value but also induces positive feelings. If a high-school student learns that she has gotten into the university of her choice, she might not work so hard during her last semester. If a football team learns that it has made the playoffs because its principal competitor has lost, it might not try so hard to win its next game. People might want to put off good news simply because it will adversely affect their performance.

For orientation, consider Table 3.1.

For different people, different information will occupy different cells. What is Cell (1) for some people will be Cell (7) for others, and what is Cell (5) for some people will be Cell (4) for others.

A number of years ago, I had an endless series of medical tests for what was almost certainly a nonissue. It was a bit of a nightmare. In the tenth round, the kindly doctor said, "I think you are fine. But a lot of people can't sleep at night unless they have all relevant tests. I would decide not to get this test if I were you, but the decision is yours." He thought that for me, this might have been a case of Cell (3) (no instrumental value, positive feelings about being being tested), but he was wrong; I found it a case of (6) (no instrumental value, negative feelings about yet another test). The key point is that the value of information and the feelings that emerge as a result of that information can be positive, negative, or neutral and that positive (or negative) value does not necessarily cause positive (or negative) feelings. Feelings and values can be mixed and matched in multiple ways.

A Bet

These are points about the effects of obtaining information, but when people say that they do or do not want to know, they will not know, in advance, what they will learn. They are making a kind of bet. The question is often to know *whether*, not to know *that*.

People might ask some question with a "yes" or "no" answer; a "yes" could induce positive affect and a "no" could produce misery. ("Does she love me? Even a little bit?") Or people might ask some question with ten, twenty, or a hundred possible answers ("What was my score on that test?" or "How much money will I be earning in ten years?"). Some of those answers will produce information that people could actually use, whereas others will not. It follows that when people are thinking about whether they want to know, they need to know both about expected outcomes and about the probability that these outcomes will occur. They will be interested above all in the probability that what they learn will induce positive feelings or will be useful. If the probability is very high (say, 90 percent), they might be more inclined to want to know than if the probability is very low (say, 10 percent). If people are confident that they will never get cancer – but are not quite sure – they might be interested in getting that information, simply because the odds seem to be in their favor. If a bad outcome is very bad, or if a good outcome is very good, their judgment will be affected, and this is true both for instrumental value and for hedonic value. Rational choosers, deciding whether to acquire or avoid information, would try to estimate some numbers.

Ideally, the decision whether to know would turn on a rational assessment of everything that matters: People would figure out what they care about (peace of mind, longevity, money, cordial relations with others), and their decisions to acquire information would reflect that assessment.[8] But unjust background conditions or injustice can infect people's decisions about what information to acquire.[9] Under circumstances of poverty, deprivation, or discrimination, people might not have an interest in obtaining important information, and they might not have the capacity to get it even if they do have an interest. In the worst cases, people's very preferences are adaptive to, or a product

---

[8] For relevant discussion, *see* Sharot & Sunstein, *supra* note 5.

[9] *See* JON ELSTER, SOUR GRAPES (1st ed. 1983).

of, the injustice to which they are subject. If so, they might not seek information of immense importance.

Behavioral scientists have also shown that our decisions are not always entirely rational. People use heuristics, or mental short-cuts, which may lead them in unfortunate directions, and they are also biased in various ways. When people decide whether to obtain information, heuristics and biases matter as well. Of special importance is *present bias*, which means that people often focus on today and tomorrow, while neglecting the long-term.[10] Suppose that the question is whether to seek information from which you might suffer today, but which might be of great value over the long-term. You should seek that information. But you might not. The short-term distress might prove decisive. You might not want to know. (You might not weigh yourself. You might skip that annual appointment with your doctor, which might be especially foolish because the more you delay, the more fearful you might be.)

Some of the most illuminating work on information-seeking emphasizes "strategic self-ignorance," understood as "the use of ignorance as an excuse to over-indulge in pleasurable activities that may be harmful to one's future self."[11] The idea here is that if people are present-biased, they might avoid information that would make current activities less attractive – perhaps because it would produce guilt or shame, perhaps because it would suggest an aggregate trade-off that would counsel against engaging in such activities. St. Augustine famously said, "God give me chastity – tomorrow." Present-biased agents think: "Please let me know the risks – tomorrow." Whenever people are thinking about engaging in an activity with short-term benefits but long-term costs, they might prefer to defer receipt of important information.[12] The same point might hold about information that might make people sad or mad: "Please tell me what I need to know – tomorrow."

Behavioral scientists have also emphasized *loss aversion*, which means that people particularly dislike losses; in fact, they dislike losses much more than they like equivalent gains.[13] If people are loss averse,

---

[10] *See* Thunström et al., *supra* note 4.
[11] *Id.*
[12] *Id.; see also* Nordström et al., *supra* note 4.
[13] Daniel Kahneman et al., *Experimental Tests of the Endowment Effect and the Coase Theorem*, 98 J. POL. ECON. 1325 (1990).

they might be especially reluctant to get information if they think that the news might well be bad. If the news involves a potential cancer diagnosis, for example, they might think: "I feel fine now. I think that I will continue to be fine. If I get tested, I might get bad news. Why should I get tested?" It should be clear that present bias and loss aversion can be a potent combination, producing high levels of information avoidance. When people mistakenly avoid information, or do not seek information, it is often because of that potent combination.

An important finding here is that when people receive bad news – involving, say, a higher-than-expected risk of health problems – *their initial level of distress is high, but they recover quite quickly.*[14] If people anticipate the distress but not the recovery, they will avoid information that might save their lives and that might not have a terribly adverse effect on their feelings over time. An extensive review of fifteen studies about people's responses to predictive genetic testing shows something similar: If anything, it finds that people do not feel significant distress at all in response to predictive genetic testing.[15] The studies focused on such testing for a variety of conditions: hereditary breast and ovarian cancer, Huntington's disease, familial adenomatous polyposis, and spinocerebellar ataxia. Almost all involved adults (only one involved children). The general pattern was that during the twelve months after testing, neither carriers nor noncarriers were likely to showed increased distress (understood as general and situational distress, anxiety, and depression). In only two of the studies did the outcome of the test predict distress more than a month after the test result. The authors conclude that that "those undergoing predictive genetic testing do not experience adverse psychological consequences," while also noting that the studies involve "self-selected populations who have agreed to participate in psychological studies."[16]

Even with that important qualification, I speculate that many people, in general and before undergoing genetic testing, would be

---

[14] Jada G. Hamilton et al., *Emotional Distress Following Genetic Testing for Hereditary Breast and Ovarian Cancer: A Meta-Analytic Review*, 28 HEALTH PSYCH. 510 (2009).

[15] *See* Marita Broadstock et al., *Psychological Consequences of Predictive Genetic Testing: A Systematic Review*, 8 EUR. J. HUM. GENETICS 731 (2000).

[16] *Id.* at 731. Valuable in this regard is research on "emotional self-regulation." *See, e.g.,* Charles S. Carver & Michael F. Scheier, *Cybernetic Control Processes and the Self-Regulation of Behavior*, in OXFORD HANDBOOK HUM. MOTIVATION 28 (Richard Ryan ed., 2012).

surprised to learn of these findings – which suggests a plausible hypothesis, to the effect that people overstate their likely reaction to unwelcome results from predictive testing. Apart from present bias and loss aversion, an inaccurate prediction might also be a product of the *focusing illusion*.[17] People often overestimate the effect of a particular event on their overall well-being, simply because they focus on it. As Daniel Kahneman and David Schkade have put it, "Nothing that you focus on will make as much difference as you think."[18] A cold rainy day, a shiny new car, an increase in salary, or even a serious illness might be anticipated to have a major impact, even though it quickly becomes part of the background, something like life's furniture. For that reason, people might exaggerate the welfare effect of bad news – and choose not to get it.

At the same time, the desire to obtain information will also be affected by optimistic bias. If people think that they are likely to receive good news, they are more likely to want to know "whether." And indeed, most people do show unrealistic optimism, at least in the sense that they think that their personal prospects (with respect to health, safety, and other things) are better than average – and in fact better than statistical reality warrants.[19] Unrealistic optimism can counteract loss aversion and lead people to get information that might turn out to be exceedingly useful.

In assessing probability, people use the *availability heuristic*, which means that they ask whether relevant examples come to mind. How likely is a flood, an airplane crash, a traffic jam, a terrorist attack, or a disaster at a nuclear power plant? Lacking statistical knowledge, people try to think of illustrations. Thus, "a class whose instances are easily retrieved will appear more numerous than a class of equal frequency whose instances are less retrievable."[20] If people are aware of cases in which others received bad news, their probability judgments will be inflated accordingly. A set of cases of good news will have corresponding effects.

---

[17] *See* Cass R. Sunstein, *Illusory Losses*, 37 J. LEGAL STUD. S157 (2008).
[18] David A. Schkade & Daniel Kahneman, *Does Living in California Make People Happy? A Focusing Illusion in Judgments of Life Satisfaction*, 9 PSYCH. SCI. 340, 346 (1998).
[19] TALI SHAROT, THE OPTIMISM BIAS: A TOUR OF THE IRRATIONALLY POSITIVE BRAIN (2011).
[20] Amos Tversky & Daniel Kahneman, *Judgment under Uncertainty: Heuristics and Biases*, 185 SCIENCE 1124, 1127 (1974).

In any population, there is likely to be a great deal of heterogeneity. Some people will be in a position to gain a great deal in instrumental terms from obtaining information about X, whereas other people will be in a position to gain only a little, and still others will gain nothing at all. Some people would be deeply alarmed at bad news, if it comes to that, whereas others would be mildly discomfited, and others would take it in stride. Many people are not resilient; many people are. Some people get hysterical; others get practical. A rational agent, deciding whether to seek information, would weigh both instrumental and affective values, and different rational agents, given their situations and sensibilities, would make different rational choices. Heterogeneity is greatly compounded in light of the fact that some people are more present-biased than others, more loss averse than others, and more optimistic than others. The availability heuristic will lead some people to anticipate good news and others to anticipate bad news. For different people, different outcomes and events will be cognitively available.

In light of these considerations, it should be no wonder that some people want to get a lot of medical tests, while other people want to get exactly none. Nor should it be surprising that some consumers are keenly interested in energy efficiency and in learning about fuel economy, whereas others are indifferent or would prefer not to know. Nor should it be surprising that some people care about and benefit from calorie labels, whereas other people (including people with little money or education) might neither care nor benefit, and might even think, "the more calories, the better." Of course, people have different moral convictions, and so some will want information relating to (say) animal welfare when others have no interest.

Clues

I have conducted a series of studies of these issues, using nationally representative populations from many nations.[21] Remarkably, the results are broadly similar across nations. I present here the results of a study using Amazon Mechanical Turk, in which I asked about 400 Americans whether they want information of diverse kinds and how much they would be willing to pay for that information. Though the

[21] Lucia Reisch, Cass R. Sunstein, and Micha Kaiser, *What Do People Want to Know? Information Avoidance and Food Policy Implications*, 102 FOOD POLICY, 102076 (2021).

sample is not nationally representative, the results are similar to those found with a nationally representative sample in the United States, and because it has a high level of detail, I use that study here. In brief, I hypothesized that I would find clear and clean evidence in favor of four simple propositions: (1) People want information if it would either be useful or produce positive affect; (2) people's WTP for information would depend on (a) how useful it would be or (b) how happy it would make them; (3) when information would not be useful or would make people sad, they would be far less likely to want it; and (4) there would be a great deal of heterogeneity in people's answers.

I believe that all of these propositions are correct. I was hopeful of obtaining such evidence, because a growing body of research tends to support all four propositions. For example:

1. People are more likely to check their investment portfolios and to learn whether they are gaining or losing money during periods when the stock market is going up than during periods when it is going down – a clear demonstration of the "ostrich effect."[22] When the hedonic value of receiving information is likely to be negative, people are more likely not to seek information.

2. People want to see political views that align with their own, partly because they believe that seeing opposing views will make them sad or mad.[23] Here again, people anticipate that the information will create negative feelings, and so they are less likely to want to receive it. Interestingly, people make mistakes on this count; they overestimate the extent to which seeing opposing views will make them feel bad. On this count, people make an "affective forecasting error"; they do not accurately predict how information will make them feel. There is a large lesson here, bearing on health-related information in particular.

3. People are more likely to favor calorie labels, and to be willing to pay for them, if they do not suffer from self-control problems and hence are likely to be in a position to benefit from those labels.[24] Such people believe that they can use such labels, and they might

---

[22] Niklas Karlsson et al., *The Ostrich Effect: Selective Attention to Information*, 38 J. RISK & UNCERTAINTY 95 (2009).

[23] *See* Charles A. Dorison et al., *Selective Exposure Partly Relies on Faulty Affective Forecasts*, 188 COGNITION 98 (2019).

[24] Linda Thunström, *Welfare Effects of Nudges: The Emotional Tax of Calorie Menu Labeling*, 14 JUDGMENT & DECISION MAKING 11 (2019).

even enjoy seeing them. By contrast, people who suffer from self-control problems are more willing to pay *not* to see them. Apparently, they believe that such labels will not help them and will just make them sad or upset.[25] (And, indeed, calorie labels seem to have exactly that effect on people with self-control problems.) The conclusion is that making calories salient "positively affects consumer welfare, although heterogeneity over consumers is substantial – the consumer value ranges from positive to negative."[26] In particular, those "with low self-control both experience a (higher) emotional cost from the nudge and no (or, at best, few) benefits from consumption adjustments, compared to higher level self-control consumers."[27]

4. Overwhelming majorities of people say that they do not want to know when their partner will die or the cause of their partner's death.[28] They also do not want to know when they themselves will die or the cause of their own death.

5. With respect to their own performance on a task, people are more likely to want information and to be willing to pay for it if they think the news will be good – that is, if they will learn that they performed well.[29] They are significantly less likely to want information and more likely to be willing to pay not to receive it if they think that they performed poorly. The relevant research studied not only behavior but also brain regions. It found that those regions of the brain that are associated with positive emotions are activated by good news – strongly suggesting that affective reactions help account for people's decision about whether to seek information.

In these particular cases, hedonic value seems dominant in determining whether people want to know. There is no more reason to check your portfolio when its value is growing than when its value is shrinking, though the latter is a lot less fun. But instrumental value unquestionably matters as well. With respect to calorie labels, it is reasonable to think that people's judgments are partly an answer to the question: Would I benefit from this information? People with high levels of self-control

---

25   *Id. See also* Nordström et al., *supra* note 4.
26   *See* Thunström, *supra* note 24, at 11.
27   *Id.* at 17.
28   Gerd Gigerenzer & Rocio Garcia-Retamero, *Cassandra's Regret: The Psychology of Not Wanting to Know*, 124 Psych. Rev. 179 (2017).
29   Charpentier et al., *supra* note 4.

would be more likely to answer "yes" and so they would be more likely to pay for the information. Similarly, people would undoubtedly be more likely to want to know about the cause of a partner's death if they thought that they could do something about it – and eliminate that cause.

There are actually two separate questions here. The first is: Would I benefit? The second is: Can I change the outcome if I don't like it? The questions are closely related, but the second puts a spotlight on people's sense of agency. The capacity for control generates positive feelings in itself. It can produce a benefit, in terms of (say) health or economics, but it has independent value.

We could easily design cases for which instrumental value, understood in terms of both questions, would be dominant. For example, we might ask people whether they want to know what the weather will be for every day of the next year, what their bosses most like in their employees, or whether the stock market will go up or down next month.

My own evidence attests to the importance of both hedonic and instrumental value. A solid majority of participants – about 60 percent – said that they want to know the annual cost of operating the appliances in their home. We could speculate that most people want that information so that they can save money. A solid majority – 59 percent – also said that they would like to know how to fix their cell phones if they failed to connect to the Internet. That would be handy information to have. About 58 percent wanted to know if a person for whom they have strong romantic feelings shares those feelings. In all of these cases, and perhaps especially the third, the relevant information is pretty useful.

It remains, of course, to explain why substantial minorities, in all three cases, are not interested in apparently useful information. The most plausible answers point to the word *apparently* – and also emphasize the importance of affect. In these cases, heterogeneity ought to be expected. Many people undoubtedly think that learning the annual cost of operating appliances is pretty dull stuff and that it would not do them a whole lot of good. Many others already have that information, or think they do, and so would not pay for it. Many others think, reasonably enough, that cell phones ordinarily connect to the Internet, and if theirs do not, well, chances are that the problem will resolve itself. Many people fear that people toward whom they have romantic feelings probably don't share those feelings, which means that they would get bad news. Many others think that good news might be a bit dangerous. (By the way, I asked a group of about forty people in their twenties the same question – and all but one wanted to know!)

I asked several questions involving serious health conditions, and on those participants were almost evenly divided. For example, most people (53 percent) said that they did not want to know if they would get Alzheimer's disease. Half said that they wanted to know if they were at serious risk of getting diabetes. Slightly more (58 percent) said that they wanted to know whether they had a genetic disposition to cancer or heart disease.[30] The large percentages in favor of ignorance undoubtedly stemmed in large part from the negative emotions that bad news would induce. But while the answers to such questions could be alarming, many people evidently thought that forewarned is forearmed. Perhaps they could do something to reduce the risk of getting diabetes, cancer, or heart disease. Perhaps they could arrange their life a bit differently, or a lot differently, if they learned that they would get Alzheimer's disease.

I also asked questions about information of diverse kinds. About 57 percent would like to know whether their partner or spouse ever cheats on them. Only 42 percent would like to know what their friends and family members really think about them! About 42 percent want to know how much warmer the planet will be in 2100. Only 27 percent said that they wanted to know the year of their likely death. Amazingly, just 54 percent want to know how the stock market would be doing on a specified date in the future. (Apparently, people did not think, as they should: If I receive that information, I can make essentially all the money I want.)

Strikingly, 71 percent want to know if there is life on other planets. Perhaps surprisingly, only a bare majority (53 percent) want to know if heaven really exists. Those who did not want to know probably fell within various categories: (1) those who are sure that heaven does exist, so the information would be worthless; (2) those who are sure that heaven does not exist, so the information would be worthless; (3) those

---

[30] For relevant data, *see* Yumi Iwamitsu et al., *Anxiety, Emotional Suppression, and Psychological Distress Before and After Breast Cancer Diagnosis*, 46 PSYCHOSOMATICS 19 (2005); Theresa M. Marteau & John Weinman, *Self-Regulation and the Behavioural Response to DNA Risk Information: A Theoretical Analysis and Framework for Future Research*, 62 SOC. SCI. & MED. 1360 (2006); Jada Hamilton et al., *supra* note 14.

who think that they will not get into heaven, so learning of its existence could only make them sad or upset; or (4) those who think that it is best to have a degree of uncertainty. A smaller number (44 percent) want to know if hell exists – which is probably testimony to the fact that if hell exists, a lot of people think that they will be in big trouble.

With respect to information that bears on consumption choices, only 43 percent said that they wanted to see calorie labels at restaurants. Their WTP for that information was modest: The median was just $15 annually, and the mean was just $48.61. For information about the annual cost of operating appliances in the home, WTP was comparable: a median of $15 and a mean of $43.71. These findings are of particular interest in light of evidence that an overwhelming majority of Americans favor a federal mandate requiring restaurants to disclose the calories associated with their offerings.[31] Many people who favor a federal mandate apparently believe that they themselves will not benefit from the information – and may even be harmed by it.[32] They want their government to require disclosure of information in which they have no interest (or which they would prefer not to get at all).

There is an evident paradox here: Why would people not want to see calorie labels – but nonetheless believe that the federal government should require restaurants to display them? It is reasonable to speculate that people believe that *other people* would benefit from that information. It is also possible that if people are asked whether companies should do something, they are willing to answer "yes," even if they would not benefit personally from that action.

WTP was somewhat higher for other kinds of information. For how the stock market will be doing on January 1, 2020, the median was $100 and the mean was $165.93. (Recall that that's wildly low, because you can make a ton of money with that information.) The median WTP of those who wanted to know whether they had a genetic predisposition to cancer was $79, with a mean of $115. For Alzheimer's, the corresponding numbers were $59 and $106.98; for the likely year of death, they were $93 and $154.44; for whether their partner or spouse ever cheats, they were $74.50 and $120.67. For the global temperature in 2100, the numbers were markedly lower: $19 and $59.37.

Table 3.2 presents the key results.

---

[31] See CASS R. SUNSTEIN, THE ETHICS OF INFLUENCE (2016).
[32] Thunström et al., *supra* note 4.

Table 3.2 Disclosure of potentially important information

Information offered	Want information	Annual WTP Median ($)	Mean ($)
Whether participant will get Alzheimer's disease	47%	59	106.98
Stock market performance on January 1, 2020	54%	100	165.93
The weather for every day of the remainder of the year	55%	70	121
Genetic predisposition to cancer or heart disease	58%	79	115
At serious risk of getting diabetes	50%	52	116
Whether participant's partner or spouse ever cheats	57%	74.50	129.67
Whether heaven exists	53%	200	221
Whether hell exists	44%	148	210
Whether ever get cancer	52%	26	101
Capitals of all the nations in Africa	20%	18	122
Winner of baseball's next World Series	42%	105	187
How to fix cell phone if it is not connecting to provider	59%	11	61
Whether there is life on other planets	71%	51	125
Whether person for whom you have strong romantic feelings shares those feelings	58%	67	114
The number of nations in the United Nations	30%	10	97
All of the terms and conditions, including possible late fees, associated with credit card	56%	1	60
The year of your spouse's death	26%	167	198
What your friends and family members really think about you	42%	88	130
Annual cost of operating the appliances in participant's home	60%	15	43.71
Global temperature in 2100	42%	19	59.37
Likely year of death	27%	93	154.44
Calorie labels at restaurants	43%	15	48.61

Do Consumers Want to Be Informed?

I conducted a similar study, again using Amazon Mechanical Turk and 400 Americans, exclusively involving information that might benefit consumers. All of that information would appear to be at least somewhat useful, though more so for some people than for others. Some of that information might not be a lot of fun to receive, though less so for some than for others.

Here, too, there was a great deal of heterogeneity, and many people showed no interest in receiving the relevant information. Only 62 percent of respondents wanted information about the standard fee for a late payment of their credit card bill. The remaining 38 percent might pay their bills on time or might not care about late fees. Only 60 percent wanted to know whether their food contained genetically modified organisms. Perhaps 40 percent already know or simply do not care.

Only 64 percent wanted to know about the amount of over-use charges for their cell phone. About 67 percent wanted information about the safety ratings for their tires. (This is relatively high; the word "safety" might be a trigger.) About 65 percent wanted information about the potential side-effects of pain relievers (such as Advil and Tylenol). About 55 percent wanted information about whether the products they bought contained conflict minerals (defined as minerals from Congo used to finance mass atrocities). It is reasonable to speculate that some people really care about that issue and would use the information in their consumption choices, while others just do not.

The median WTP, in all of these cases, was pretty small: $8 for late payments ($103 mean); $24 for genetically modified organisms ($101 mean); $10 for overuse charges ($95 mean); $16 for safety ratings ($101 mean); $9 for side-effects of pain relievers ($85 mean); and $26.50 for conflict minerals ($109 mean).

Table 3.3 presents the results.

It is safe to conclude that many people do not want to receive some information even if it seems relevant to their choices – and that when they do want that information, they often do not place an especially high value on it. Many people must think that the information would not affect their choices or that it would be unpleasant to receive it.

With respect to public policy, we should not take people's answers as authoritative. One more time: They might reflect an absence

Table 3.3 Consumer disclosure

Information offered	Annual WTP		
	Want information	Median ($)	Mean ($)
Standard fee for late payment of participant's credit card bill	62%	8	103
Food contains genetically modified organisms	60%	24	101
Amount of overuse charges for participant's cell phone	64%	10	95
Safety ratings for participant's tires	67%	16	101
Potential side-effects of pain relievers	65%	9	85
Products contain conflict minerals	55%	26.50	109

of information, unjust background conditions, or some kind of behavioral bias. But in light of these findings, we have some reason for personalized disclosure, giving information only to those who actually want it (assuming, perhaps inaccurately, that those who want it, and those who do not, do not suffer from a relevant informational problem, background injustice, or behavioral bias). Unfortunately, personalization is often infeasible. Information may be a public good, in the sense that if one person receives it, others do as well. Consider the case of calorie labels. But there is good news. In the future, new technologies will make personalized or targeted disclosure more feasible than it has ever been before.

For the moment, let us step back from the details. When people decide to seek information, it is usually because it is useful to have, because it is pleasant to have, or both. In cases that are both common and hard, information is useful to have but unpleasant to have. (Welcome to the human condition.) In rare cases, information is pleasant to have but harmful to have. In many cases, the decision whether to seek information or instead to avoid it depends on a kind of bet. People are playing something like high-stakes poker. If they are optimistic, they might seek information even if it could make them feel terrible. If they are especially averse of short-term losses, they might avoid information even if it could ultimately save their lives. To say the least, that is a problem.

4 DECIDING TO BELIEVE, 1
The Case of Climate Change

Obtaining information is one thing; adopting some kind of belief is another. You might decide to avoid information because of what you want to believe, or because of what you want to do. Beliefs typically depend on information, but not always. You might ignore information. You might decide not to find it credible. You might dismiss it, either because you really should (it is not, in fact, credible) or because you want to do that (it is credible, but it is not a lot of fun to believe it).

How do people decide what to believe? In a way, the very question is confusing. You do not decide to believe that dropped objects fall; you just believe that dropped objects fall. Seeing is believing, as they say, and you believe what you see. In believing what you see, maybe you don't decide much of anything. But in countless cases, we don't really see anything. Even so, it is not clear that you *decided* to believe that the Earth goes around the Sun, that Charles Darwin was mostly right, that dinosaurs once existed, that Hitler was evil, or that the person with whom you are in love is the person with whom you ought to be in love.

The relation between volition and belief is a complicated matter. Nonetheless, there are decision points. You have to decide, even if very rapidly, what you take to be credible or to count as evidence, even if that decision does not feel like a decision at all. Many of your beliefs are based on your decisions, and also on your decisions about your decisions.

Pascal famously argued that you should *decide* to believe in God. Here is his wager, in brief: "Let us weigh the gain and the loss involved in wagering that God exists. Let us estimate these two probabilities; if you win, you win all; if you lose, you lose nothing. Wager then, without hesitation, that He does exist." On Pascal's view, you might decide to believe something because you have far more to gain than to lose from believing it. In fact, that will be one of my central themes here: We do indeed believe many things because the benefits of believing those things exceed the costs. But many people, including Pascal, have rightly worried about the psychological realism of Pascal's wager. It is easy to believe something because it seems to be true; it is harder to believe something because one would benefit, in some sense, from believing that it is true. True, you could decide to *act* to reduce the risks of climate change on the basis of something like Pascal's logic. But could you decide to *believe* in climate change on the basis of that logic?

Still, there is no question that people do believe many things in part because they like believing them. We might be inclined to believe nice things about ourselves – our character, our competence, our judgment, our looks, our rectitude – because it is pleasant to believe those things. We might refuse to believe bad things about ourselves because it is unpleasant to believe those things. We might be inclined to have certain beliefs about the world for the same reason.

It is true that in adopting beliefs about facts, we may or may not have the experience of making a *decision*. It might seem instead that we are making an *assessment*. That is fair. I believe that Finley, my dog, is both intelligent and well-behaved, and I believe that Franklin Delano Roosevelt was a great president, and I believe that John Rawls was a great philosopher. I also believe that the Supreme Court was right to require school desegregation in 1954. Did I decide to believe those things? That is not a simple matter. Even if I did not, an assessment will be based on an assortment of decisions. Among other things, we have to decide what to credit and what to dismiss. How do we do that?

We Have a Problem

With respect to climate change, people are presented with a great deal of information, and it is highly variable. Some of the projections about the likely impacts of climate change give reason for pessimism and perhaps even despair; some of the projections give reason for optimism and hope. There is a great deal of bad news, and there is some good news. There are also wide ranges. Within the United States, the Environmental Protection Agency once stated, "Increases in average global temperatures are expected to be within the range of 0.5°F to 8.6°F by 2100, with a likely increase of at least 2.7°F for all scenarios except the one representing the most aggressive mitigation of greenhouse gas emissions."[1] That range is extremely wide: 0.5°F is quite modest, whereas 8.6° F would be catastrophic. It is easy to find projections near the lower end of the range, and it is even easier to find projections near the highest end, or even above it.

Moreover, projections of anticipated warming have changed significantly over time. From reputable sources, with a great deal of expertise, the projections in one month might well be different from the projections three months later. To know how much warming there will be, we need to know the "climate sensitivity": For a given increase in emissions, how much warmer will it get? There are also sharp disagreements about the likely effects of different levels of warming. To resolve those disagreements, we need to specify a "damage function." To do that, we also need to incorporate adaptation: How, exactly, will the nations of the world adapt to different temperatures? It should be no wonder that the integrated assessment models, used by various governments to project the social cost of carbon, offer dramatically different estimates of those effects, and they too change over time.[2] Some people believe that those projections greatly understate the level of uncertainty and are therefore essentially worthless.[3] In their view, exceptionally wide ranges are the best that can be done with respect to likely warming, and for damages, the ranges are too wide to be useful. Some people say that with respect to the harmful effects of climate change, the best view is: "We simply do not know."

Let us put that provocative claim to one side. The aim of this chapter is to investigate two simple questions:

1. How do people update their beliefs when they receive new information about likely warming?
2. How do people's prior beliefs affect their response to such information?

---

[1] *Future of Climate Change*, Environmental Protection Agency, https://climatechange.chicago .gov/climate-change-science/future-climate-change#ref2 (last visited October 20, 2022).
[2] *See* Michael Greenstone et al., *Developing a Social Cost of Carbon for U.S. Regulatory Analysis: A Methodology and Interpretation*, 7 REV. ENV'T ECON. & POL'Y 23 (2013).
[3] *See* Robert S. Pindyck, *Climate Change Policy: What Do the Models Tell Us?* (Nat'l Bureau of Econ. Rsch., Working Paper No. 19244, 2013).

The answers to these questions are valuable in themselves, because they show how different groups, with different initial views about climate change, will respond to new information. Simple though they are, the answers also offer more general lessons about how people will update their beliefs in their daily lives. We should think of the answers as telling us something concrete about how people decide what to believe, and even how they decide how they decide what to believe.

There are three central findings:

1. People who strongly believe that man-made climate change is occurring, and who strongly favor an international agreement to reduce greenhouse gas emissions, show a form of *asymmetrical updating*: They change their beliefs far more in response to unexpected bad news (i.e., news suggesting that climate change is likely to be even greater than they previously thought) than in response to unexpected good news (i.e., news suggesting that climate change is likely to be smaller than they previously thought).

2. People who tend to be less certain that man-made climate change is occurring, and less unenthusiastic about an international agreement, show the opposite asymmetry: They change their beliefs far more in response to unexpected good news (i.e., news suggesting that climate change is likely to be (even) smaller than they previously thought) than in response to unexpected bad news (i.e., news suggesting that climate change is likely to be larger than they previously thought). In fact, there is no statistically significant change in their views in response to bad news at all.

3. People with moderate beliefs about climate change show no asymmetry. They update equally, and significantly, in response to both good news and bad news.

These findings have evident connections with other work on the formation and alteration of beliefs. It is well-known that when people are confronted with balanced information on political issues, they often credit the information that supports their antecedent convictions and disregard information that contradicts it (biased assimilation).[4] People decide to believe the information that fits best with

---

[4] *See* Charles G. Lord et al., *Biased Assimilation and Attitude Polarization: The Effects of Prior Theories on Subsequently Considered Evidence*, 37 J. PERSONALITY & SOC. PSYCH. 2098 (1979); Geoffrey D. Munro et al., *Biased Assimilation of Sociopolitical Arguments: Evaluating the 1996 U.S. Presidential Debate*, 24 BASIC & APPLIED SOC.

what they originally thought (confirmation bias). It follows that if people come to a balanced presentation with opposite priors, they are likely to polarize. A more recent finding is that some seemingly credible corrections of erroneous political beliefs *backfire*; they strengthen people's commitment to their original beliefs.[5] Apparently, people decide, at least in some circumstances, to believe the opposite of the correction. We do not know exactly why. People might think: "Why would they deny it, if it were not true?" Alternatively, a correction might trigger strong emotions, which might intensify their commitment to their original beliefs.

Biased assimilation can have multiple sources. People might believe what they want to believe – a form of motivated reasoning. If you receive information that fits with beliefs that you like holding, you might credit it. If you receive information that contradicts beliefs that you like holding, you might dismiss it. Biased assimilation might also be a product of rational updating. I believe that dropped objects fall; if I receive information contradicting that belief, I might well (decide to) dismiss it, given the strength of my conviction. (It's probably an optical illusion.)

These findings bear directly on the operation of practical reason in ordinary life. Outside of the political domain, good news with respect to personal prospects typically has a stronger effect on people's beliefs than bad news, regardless of priors. This is the "good news–bad news effect."[6] Suppose that you are told that you are smarter than you originally thought. Would you believe that? Now suppose that you are told that you are less smart than you originally thought. Would you believe that? Or suppose that you are told that you are better-looking than you originally thought. Would you believe that? Now suppose that you are told that you are less good-looking than you originally thought. How would you react?

The basic answer is that most people find welcome news more credible than unwelcome news. If people are given information

PSYCH. 15 (2002); John W. McHoskey, *Case Closed? On the John F. Kennedy Assassination: Biased Assimilation of Evidence and Attitude Polarization*, 17 BASIC & APPLIED SOC. PSYCH. 395 (1995).

[5] *See* Brendan Nyhan & Jason Reifler, *When Corrections Fail: The Persistence of Political Misperceptions*, 32 POL. BEHAV. 303 (2010).

[6] David Eil & Justin M. Rao, *The Good News-Bad News Effect: Asymmetric Processing of Objective Information about Yourself*, 3 AM. ECON. J.: MICROECON. 114 (2011); *see also* Tali Sharot et al., *How Unrealistic Optimism Is Maintained in the Face of Reality*, 14 NATURE NEUROSCI. 1475 (2011).

suggesting that they are smarter or better-looking than they thought, they update a fair bit. (People tend to think: That's credible!) If they are given information suggesting that they are less smart or worse-looking than they thought, they will update a lot less. (People tend to think: Those mean people cannot be trusted!) The phenomenon is quite widespread. For example, people are more likely to update their beliefs if they receive information suggesting that their likely longevity is greater than they previously estimated than when receiving information suggesting that it is shorter. Not only do they update their beliefs more upon receiving good news, they are also more likely to do so in a fully rational manner than when receiving bad news.[7]

The good news–bad news effect can be seen as a reflection of a form of motivated reasoning known as "desirability bias":[8] People are more likely to shift their beliefs in a direction that pleases them or that makes them feel better. If you hear that you are healthier than you think, you might find that credible, and if you hear that you are less healthy than you think, you might dismiss the messenger. In a sense, the good news–bad news effect is a reflection of the appeal of Pascal's wager. It also suggests that people do, even if unconsciously and rapidly, decide what to believe: Sometimes people decide not to believe bad news, and sometimes they decide to believe good tidings.

In line with these findings is one here: People who do not believe strongly in climate change adjust to unexpected good news about the climate more than they do to unexpected bad news, which has essentially no impact. Good news about the climate is comparable to good news about oneself, and bad news about the climate is comparable to bad news about oneself. With respect to people who do not believe strongly in climate change, the data should be unsurprising. But in apparent contrast, strong believers in climate change adjust to unexpected bad news about the climate to a greater extent than they do to unexpected good news.

This is the surprising finding. Why is bad news more credible than good news? There are two possible explanations. First, people

[7] See Eil & Rao, *supra* note 6; *see also* Tali Sharot & Neil Garrett, The Myth of a Pessimistic View of Optimistic Belief Updating – A Commentary on Shah et al. (September 16, 2016) (manuscript), http://papers.ssrn.com/sol3/papers.cfm?abstract_id=2811752; Bojana Kuzmanovic & Lionel Rigoux, Optimistic Belief Updating Deviates from Bayesian Learning (July 25, 2016) (manuscript), http://ssrn.com/abstract_id=2810063.

[8] Ben M. Tappin et al., *The Heart Trumps the Head: Desirability Bias in Political Belief Revision*, 146 J. Experimental Psych.: Gen. 1143 (2017).

might be showing a form of biased assimilation *in favor of bad news*. In brief, strong believers in climate change may be motivated to believe unexpected bad news, as it confirms their sense of urgency and perhaps even fits with their conception of their identity.[9] By contrast, unexpected good news disconfirms their sense of urgency and may undermine their conception of identity.

The second explanation is that people are simply engaged in rational updating, given their starting points. Strong believers in climate change might be dismissing good new on the grounds that it is simply not credible in light of their original beliefs. At the same time, they might be crediting bad news, on the grounds that it fits with those original beliefs. I will return to these issues later.

Whatever the best explanation, it is clear that this form of asymmetrical updating is likely to be pervasive and quite important. It is strong evidence that we do decide what to believe, and that our motivations, and our prior beliefs, greatly affect how and when we our prepared to change our minds. The possibility that for some, bad news could in a sense be good news, and have special credibility, may help explain why new information can entrench beliefs and increase polarization in many areas of social, political, and legal life.

The Study

Participants

Three hundred and two volunteers (177 males, 125 females) living in the United States were recruited via Amazon Mechanical Turk to participate in an online study. The study took approximately two minutes to complete and participants were paid $0.25 for participation. The characteristics of the participants are shown in Table 4.1.

Tasks

The main goal was to examine whether and by how much people would update their beliefs about the magnitude of climate change after receiving information that was better or worse than previously received.

---

[9] On the relevance of identity and associated concepts, Dan Kahan has done a great deal of informative work. *See, e.g.*, Dan M. Kahan, *The Politically Motivated Reasoning Paradigm, in* EMERGING TRENDS IN SOCIAL & BEHAVIORAL SCIENCES (2015).

Table 4.1 Characteristics of participants

Age	45.7% under 30 41.7% 30–49 11.6% 50–64 1% over 64
Race	73.8% White 11.3% Asian 7.6% Black 5.3% Hispanic 0.3% Native American 1.7% Other
Income	25.8% under $30,000 41.1% $30,000–$59,999 19.2% $60,000–$89,999 7.6% $90,000–$119,999 3.0% $120,000–$150,000 3.3% over $150,000
Party Affiliation	49.7% Democrat 33.4% Independent 16.9% Republican
Highest Level of Education	0.3% did not graduate high school 10.6% high school 38.1% some college 38.4% four-year college degree 1.7% professional degree 9.3% master's degree 1.7% doctoral degree

The hypothesis was that people who strongly believe in climate change would be more reluctant to alter their beliefs after receiving unexpected good news (i.e., the expected temperature rise is in fact lower than previously assumed) than after receiving unexpected bad news (i.e., the expected temperature rise is in fact higher than previously assumed). It was also hypothesized that those who were more skeptical about climate change would show the opposite pattern: They would be more likely to alter their beliefs upon receiving unexpected good news (i.e., the expected temperature rise is in fact lower than previously assumed).

To test these hypotheses, participants' attitudes were initially assessed. Specifically, participants were asked three questions: (1) Do you consider yourself an environmentalist? (2) Do you believe that man-made climate change is occurring? (3) Do you think that the United States was right to sign the recent Paris Agreement to reduce green-house gas emissions? They indicated their answers on a scale of 1 to 5 (where 1 is strongly disagree and 5 is strongly agree).

The responses were correlated (Q1 & Q2: $r = .26$, $p < .001$; Q1 & Q3: $r = .31$, $p < .001$; Q2 & Q3: $r = .72$, $p < .001$) and thus summed up to create an overall "climate change belief" score for every subject (acknowledging that the "environmentalist" question does not directly measure belief in climate change). Participants were then divided into three groups: those with high scores (high climate change belief group, $N = 108$, mean climate change belief $= 13.83 \pm .08$); those with medium scores (medium climate change belief group, $N = 105$, mean climate change belief $= 11.02 \pm .08$); and those with low scores (low climate change belief group, $N = 89$, mean climate change belief $= 7.73 \pm .17$).[10]

Next, participants were given the following information and asked the following question about climate change:

> Many scientists have said that by 2100, the average US temperature will rise *at least 6°F*. How many degrees Fahrenheit do you personally expect the average US temperature to rise by 2100, if further regulatory steps are not taken?

Participants could indicate their answer by selecting a number from 0 to 12.

The average first estimate that participants gave was 5.40°F±0.156 (mean±SE). (This estimate did not differ between participants who subsequently received additional good or bad news, $t(300) = 0.36$, $p = 0.721$, two-tailed t-test.) Across participants, this estimate correlated positively with the climate change belief score ($r = 0.474$, $p < 0.01$). This was true also even after controlling for age, education, and income ($r = 0.408$, $p < 0.01$). For the high climate change score group, the average first estimate was $6.32 \pm .20$. For the

---

[10] Since the questions were on an integer scale, this created clustering of participants, which prevented portioning them into three equal groups. The following formula was therefore used to divide participants into three groups:

$$cutoff_t^* = \underset{cutoff}{argmin}\left|\frac{tN}{3} - \#\{i|i \in S, CCB_i \leq cutoff\}\right|,$$

Where N is the sample size (302 participants), t is the tercile (1,2,3), i is the index for the participant in ascending rank order with respect to climate change belief score, S is the set of all participant indices, and $cutoff^*$ is the cutoff point between the respective terciles.

moderate climate change score group, it was 5.93±.25. For the low climate change score group, it was 3.64±.29. Importantly, the low climate change group did *not* consist of "climate change deniers"; they believed that climate change would occur, but that it would be smaller than the other two groups expected.

After indicating their initial estimate, participants were randomly assigned to one of two conditions. Specifically, they received information that was either better (good news, 152 participants, 72 female) or worse (bad news, 150 participants, 53 female) than originally received. In the good news condition, they were told:

> Assume that in the last few weeks, some prominent scientists have reassessed the science and concluded that the situation is far better than had previously thought. They stated that unless further regulatory steps are taken, by 2100, the average US temperature is projected to increase by about 1°F to 5°F, depending on emissions scenario and climate model.

In the bad news condition, they were told:

> Assume that in the last few weeks, some prominent scientists have reviewed the science and concluded that the situation is far worse than they had previously thought. They stated that unless further regulatory steps are taken, by 2100, the average US temperature is projected to increase by about 7°F to 11°F, depending on emissions scenario and climate model.

They were then asked to provide their updated estimate: "How much do you personally believe that the average US temperature will rise by 2100, if further regulatory steps are not taken?" by selecting a number from 0 to 12 from a dropdown menu.[11] This was followed by a series of demographic questions (age, income, ethnicity, party affiliation).

Each participant's change in beliefs (i.e., update) was calculated as follows: subject's first estimate minus second estimate in the good news condition, and the reverse for the bad news condition. Thus, positive numbers indicated an adjustment downwards in the former and an adjustment upwards in the latter. These updated scores were then entered into a 2 × 3 ANOVA with a between-subject factor of condition

---

[11] This, of course, creates a problem if the subject's true belief is below 0 or above 12. However, this restriction, if anything, would have made it more difficult to observe our results, rather than explain them.

(good news, bad news) and a between-subject factor of group (high/medium/low belief in climate change), with age, education, income, gender, party affiliation, ethnicity, and first estimate controlled for by entering them as covariates.

Results

There was an interaction between condition and group ($F_{(2, 284)}$ = 6.28, p = .002, η^2 = .04), such that subjects in the high climate change belief group updated their beliefs more upon receiving bad news relative to good news ($F_{(1, 95)}$ = 8.35, p = .005, η^2 = .08), whereas those in the low climate change belief group updated their beliefs more upon receiving good news relative to bad news ($F_{(1, 75)}$ = 6.96, p = .01, $\eta2$ = .09). Subjects in the medium climate change belief group did not show any difference in update between conditions ($F_{(1, 93)}$ = 1.94, p = .167, η^2 = .02).

Those in the high climate change belief group updated their beliefs more upon receipt of bad news than did those in the low climate change belief group ($F_{(1, 91)}$ = 20.50, p < .001, η^2 = .18). There was no difference across groups in updating upon receipt of good news ($F_{(1, 79)}$ = 6.89, p = .01, η^2 = .08). All updates were significantly greater than zero, with the important exception of the low belief group in the bad news condition (good news, low belief: $t_{(42)}$ = 3.87, p < .001; bad news, low belief: $t_{(45)}$ = .71, p = .479; good news, medium belief: $t_{(58)}$ = 5.07, p < .001; bad news, medium belief: $t_{(45)}$ = 5.79, p < .001; good news, high belief: $t_{(49)}$ = 4.03, p < .001; bad news, high belief: $t_{(57)}$ = 7.58, p < .001).

There was no main effect of condition ($F_{(1, 284)}$ = .98, p = .324, η^2 = .00) nor significant effect of group ($F_{(2, 284)}$ = 1.45, p = .237, η^2 = .01). None of the covariates were significant except for the first estimate ($F_{(1, 284)}$ = 6.67, p = .01, η^2 = .02). Recall that all the earlier results are given after controlling for subjects' first estimate in the ANOVA.

Figure 4.1 shows the update in climate change belief. The y-axis shows marginal means after controlling for age, education, income, gender, political party, ethnicity, and first estimate. The error bars are standard errors of the mean. * p < .05, ** p < .01, *** p < .001.

With regard to party affiliation, it should be unsurprising that Democrats had a higher climate change belief score than did Republicans ($t_{(199)}$ = 7.68, p < .001, two-tailed t-test) and greater first estimates (Democrats = 6.13±0.18 (mean±SE), Republicans, 3.73±0.40,

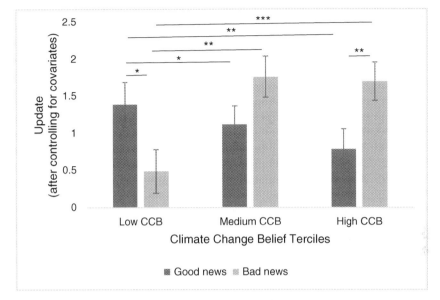

Figure 4.1 Update in climate change belief

t(199) = 6.19, p < .01, two-tailed t-test). Updating behavior across good and bad news did not interact significantly with party affiliation (F(1,191) = 2.72, p = .101, η² = .01), after controlling for all other demographic variables and climate change belief scores.

Uncomfortable Truths

The aim here was to study how people decide to believe, or (if you prefer) how people adjust their beliefs after receiving new information. Those with high climate change belief scores show asymmetrical updating, changing their beliefs more in response to bad news than to good news. Those with low climate change belief scores show the opposite asymmetrical updating, changing their beliefs more in response to good news than bad news (which had essentially no effect at all). Those with moderate climate change belief scores showed no asymmetrical updating. What explains the asymmetrical updating for the former groups? And what are the implications of these findings for the formation of beliefs in general?

As we have seen, the first explanation for the two findings of asymmetrical updating involves motivated reasoning. Recall that with respect to personally relevant information (say, about how good-looking one is, or about how good one's likely health outcomes are), people are more likely to update their beliefs in response to good news than in response to bad news.[12] They are motivated to dismiss the latter or at least to give it less weight. People (decide to) believe what they want to believe. In the context of climate change, those with both low and high belief scores may have an emotional investment in their attitudes toward climate change. For those with low belief scores, good news is good news on all counts; it is pleasing to know that things will not be so bad, and it is also pleasing to learn that one was essentially correct in not being so scared. For these reasons, good news should be expected to have particular weight for low climate change believers. It is somewhat more surprising, and certainly more dramatic, that bad news had essentially no effect. Perhaps low climate change believers were motivated to dismiss the bad news (7-degree to 11-degree warming). After all, it is bad news. Perhaps it could be disregarded as evidence-free alarmism or simply further noise.

The largest puzzle is why those with high beliefs scores were especially likely to credit bad news. One possibility is that, for them, such news is, in a sense, affirming, insofar as it supports their concerns and confirms that they have been right to have them.[13] To that extent, they may well be motivated to accept bad news.

For strong climate change believers, by contrast, good news causes dissonance. It suggests that they have been wrong to focus on climate change, or to be quite alarmed about it, and for that reason it may evoke a negative reaction. With respect to political beliefs (and indeed beliefs of all kinds), good news can evoke such a reaction if and to the extent that it threatens strongly held convictions and people's sense of identity.[14] When society is divided, it follows that, whether good or bad, new information can heighten polarization, because it may trigger a negative emotional reaction for some (and hence be discounted) but a positive emotional reaction for others (and hence not be discounted). It is reasonable to suspect that in daily life, emotional reactions to good news and bad news are a major determinant of whether people decide to find such news to be credible.

---

[12] See Eil & Rao, *supra* note 6; *see also* TALI SHAROT, THE OPTIMISM BIAS (2011).
[13] See Kahan, *supra* note 9, for a series of illuminating observations and findings.
[14] See Nyhan & Reifler, *supra* note 5; Brendan Nyhan et al., *The Hazards of Correcting Myths about Health Care Reform*, 51 MED. CARE 127 (2013).

The second answer does not invoke motivations or emotions; it is purely cognitive and reflects a form of rational updating or Bayesianism.[15] Here is the simplest version of that answer. If you are a weak climate change believer, you tend to think that it will get hot, but not that hot. Suppose that you now hear that scientists think it will get less hot than you originally believed. You might find that information credible and update accordingly. Now suppose you hear that scientists think that if will get hotter than you are originally believed. You might decide not to believe that. Who are those scientists? Are they zealots? Given your starting point, you might find good news from scientists to be credible, and you might dismiss bad news, thinking that those who think that the sky is falling, or that the planet is burning, really cannot be trusted.

Strong climate change believers might be similar. If you are a strong climate change believer, you tend to think that it will get pretty hot. Suppose you hear that scientists think that if will get even hotter than you are originally believed. You might find that information credible and update accordingly. Now suppose you hear that scientists think that if will get less hot than you are originally believed. You might decide not to believe that. Who are those scientists? Are they in the pay of industry?

Here is a more complex version of a Bayesian explanation for the findings. Participants' priors on the likely increase in temperature ate best described as a histogram of probabilities rather than a discrete number (i.e., Joe believes the probability that temperature will rise by 5 degrees is 10%, that the probability that it will rise by 6 degrees is 30%, that the probability that it will rise by 7 degrees is 20%, and so on). When asked to declare the likely increase, Joe will give a number representing the peak of his belief distribution – in this case 6 degrees. Now imagine two scenarios. In one, Joe is told that scientists believe the increase is likely to be 7 degrees (bad news) and in the other that scientists believe it is likely to be 5 degrees (good news). Joe is than asked about his new belief. To form his new belief, Joe will combine his prior with the evidence and report back the peak of that distribution. Because the prior was originally skewed, even if Joe was using Bayesian statistics to form a posterior, the peaks of the posteriors in these two cases will not be equal distance from the peak of the prior.

---

[15] For discussion, *see* Edward Glaeser & Cass R. Sunstein, *Does More Speech Correct False-hoods?*, 43 J. LEGAL STUD. 65 (2014).

It is possible that people who begin with a strong belief that climate change is both serious and real have a negatively skewed prior, and weak believers a positively skewed prior. Although the study controlled for people's peak priors, it did not record the full distribution of their priors.[16] Thus, Bayesianism could be sufficient to account for both forms of asymmetrical updating here.[17]

Asymmetrical Updating Everywhere

These findings have implications for how people will update their beliefs about climate change in particular, and also for beliefs about ordinary life, health, science, and politics more generally. If people receive new information about climate change (as is inevitable), and if it is highly variable (as is predictable), we should expect to see greater polarization. Those most concerned about climate change will be more likely to revise their estimates upwards upon receiving bad news than those who are least concerned. Those who are least concerned about climate change will be more likely to revise their estimates downwards upon receiving good news than those who are most concerned.

This asymmetry undoubtedly contributes to polarization with respect to climate change, as both alarming and less alarming news comes to people's attention. Of course it is true that many factors contribute to polarization about climate change, but asymmetrical updating is an important part of the picture.[18] Recall that those with low climate change belief scores were not skeptics or denialists. They simply believed that the magnitude of change would be lower than the two other groups did. Even so, they were more moved by good

---

[16] Eil & Rao, *supra* note 6, use an elegant technique to capture a subject's full distribution of priors with regards to their IQ and attractiveness. They show that even after accounting for the full distribution of a subject's prior, updating is asymmetric, favoring good news.

[17] There are other potential explanations in addition to the two discussed here. For example, strong climate change believers might be more pessimistic in general, in which case their greater incorporation of bad news would be consistent with their dispositions. We could easily imagine a set of pessimistic people who would be especially likely – for cognitive or affective reasons – to accept information suggesting that the world is likely to end up worse than they originally thought. An early test, however, explored this issue and did not find that strong climate change believers were more pessimistic in general. The question does bear further investigation.

[18] *See, e.g.,* Donald Braman et al., *The Polarizing Impact of Science Literacy and Numeracy on Perceived Climate Change Risks,* 2 NATURE CLIMATE CHANGE 732 (2012).

news than by bad news, as those with moderate climate change belief scores were not.

With respect to beliefs in general, it is likely that in many domains, something similar will occur. We could readily imagine studies of the formation of beliefs about personal health, personal finance, the well-being of one's children, whether an election has been stolen, terrorism (how much terrorism will there be in the next year?), immigration (for how much violence will immigrants be responsible over a specified future period?), and minimum wage legislation (how much of a disemployment effect should be expected from a $15 minimum wage?). For many people, good news – in the form of an apparently credible expert judgment that things will be better than they think – will have far more weight than bad news. It is easy to imagine groups that will be tempted to accept evidence (good news) that immigration is not producing increases in crime or unemployment – and that would be highly reluctant to accept evidence to the opposite effect (bad news).

For some groups, however, apparently good news of exactly these kinds will trigger a sharply negative reaction, in part because of people's desire to be vindicated – to see their actions and concerns affirmed rather than contradicted. Some people have strong investments in their attitudes, even if the implication is that things are getting much worse – that their health is bad, that the economy is failing, that terrorism will increase, that immigration is producing violence, that climate change will be devastating, that the $15 minimum wage produces significant increases in unemployment. For such people, bad news might be entirely welcome, and it might therefore have special weight.

A great deal of belief change, and a great deal of polarization, is created and fueled in this way. Every week, if not every day, it is possible to encounter competing (and apparently plausible) predictions about future states of affairs that suggest that one's own current estimates are too optimistic or too pessimistic. If the evidence involves one's own health, good news will usually have special weight. But if the evidence involves politics and law, what counts as good news may not be nearly so obvious. Some people will receive objectively good news (things will be better than expected) as such and give it particular attention in updating. Other people will find such news to be quite bad, in the sense that it will threaten convictions to which they are deeply committed. Whenever this is true, the circumstances are right for polarization – heightened or produced by asymmetrical updating of diametrically opposite kinds. A great deal remains to be learned on this topic. But this difference helps explain why polarization can increase over time and why agreement can be so hard to obtain, even on highly technical questions.

The implications are broader still. In daily life, we have a choice about what to believe about any number of things – our friends, our employer, our children, our spouse, our car, our clothing, our existing options and opportunities. We might make decisions, often very quickly, about what to believe, based in part on our preexisting beliefs (my car seems terrific, and I am unlikely to credit unfavorable information about it) and in part on our emotions (I adore my children, and I am motivated not to credit unfavorable information about them). So let's broaden the viewscreen.

5 DECIDING TO BELIEVE, 2
In General

Some of our beliefs seem rigid and fixed. Once we form a belief, we tend to keep it, or decide to keep it, and might be reluctant to change it, or to decide to change it. Indeed, most individuals identify with the religious beliefs of their parents,[1] and by the age of seven, many sport fans have established which teams they will support for the rest of their lives.[2] Yet beliefs do change, and people do decide to think something very different from what they once thought. In recent years, many people have changed their beliefs about what constitutes workplace harassment,[3] and about whether smoking in public venues is acceptable.[4] Public health experts changed their minds on whether face masks can help reduce the spread of coronavirus,[5] and on whether electric cigarettes are safe.[6] No one should doubt that new information and experiences can and do lead people to change their beliefs.

[1] See *U.S. Teens Take After Their Parents Religiously, Attend Services Together and Enjoy Family Rituals*, PEW RESEARCH CENTER (September 10, 2020).
[2] See SETH STEPHENS-DAVIDOWITZ, EVERYBODY LIES: BIG DATA, NEW DATA, AND WHAT THE INTERNET CAN TELL US ABOUT WHO WE REALLY ARE (2017).
[3] Sarah Green Carmichael, *Have Our Attitudes about Sexual Harassment Really Changed?* HARV. BUS. REV., April 20, 2017.
[4] See David Burns, *How Far We Have Come in the Last 50 Years in Smoking Attitudes and Actions*, 11 ANNALS AM. THORACIC SOC'Y 224 (2014).
[5] Trisha Greenhalgh et al., *Face Masks for the Public during the Covid-19 Crisis*, 369 BMJ M1435 (2020).
[6] Lauren M. Dutra et al., *Philip Morris Research on Precursors to the Modern E-Cigarette Since 1990*, 26 TOBACCO CONTROL E97 (2016).

John Maynard Keynes, the notable economist, has often been quoted as saying, "When I find new information I change my mind; What do you do?" As Chapter 4 suggests, however, the answer to that question is not straightforward. Sometimes people do not alter their beliefs after receiving new information; they are stubborn, even intransigent. Sometimes people alter their views readily, with apparently little reason to do so.[7] Such inconsistencies have baffled lay people, as well as psychologists, economists, and philosophers.[8]

The central claims of this chapter are that everything turns on *the value of beliefs*, and that the value of beliefs is composed of identifiable elements.[9] Some of these elements are associated with the accuracy of a belief and some are not. By altering what they believe, people can gain or lose "utility," understood to encompass welfare (and hence used here as a synonym). Thus, the process of belief change can be understood as a (conscious or unconscious) process of weighing the value of an old belief against the expected value of a potential new belief. Such a conceptualization can help explain why some beliefs seem intractable; why some beliefs change quickly; and why some strategies for promoting belief change succeed, while others fail dismally.

The process of belief change can be understood as a multidimensional valuation problem, analogous to multidimensional economic decisions. This perspective marries recent findings from decision neuroscience with classic insights from psychology and behavioral economics to describe the process.[10]

---

[7] *See* Tali Sharot & Neil Garrett, Forming Beliefs: Why Valence Matters, 20 TRENDS COGNITIVE SCIS. 25 (2016).

[8] *See, e.g.*, Ziva Kunda, *The Case for Motivated Reasoning*, 108 PSYCH. BULL. 480 (1990); David A. Armor & Shelley E. Taylor, *When Predictions Fail: The Dilemma of Unrealistic Optimism, in* HEURISTIC AND BIASES: THE PSYCHOLOGY OF INTUITIVE JUDGMENT 334 (Thomas Gilovich, Dale Griffin, & Daniel Kahneman, eds., 2002); Don Moore & Deborah Small, *When It Is Rational for the Majority to Believe that They Are Better than Average, in* RATIONALITY AND SOCIAL RESPONSIBILITY: ESSAYS IN HONOR OF ROBYN MASON DAWES 141 (J. I. Krueger, ed., 2008); Andreas Kappes et al., *Confirmation Bias in the Utilization of Others' Opinion Strength*, 23 NATURE NEUROSCIENCE 130 (2019); Joshua Klayman & Young-Won Ha, *Confirmation, Disconfirmation, and Information in Hypothesis Testing*, 94 PSYCH. REV. 211 (1987).

[9] *See* Roland Bénabou & Jean Tirole, *Mindful Economics: The Production, Consumption, and Value of Beliefs*, 30 J. ECON. PERSPS. 141 (2016); Ethan S. Bromberg-Martin & Tali Sharot, *The Value of Beliefs*, 106 NEURON 561 (2020); George Loewenstein & Andras Molnar, *The Renaissance of Belief-Based Utility in Economics*, 2 NATURE HUM. BEHAV. 166 (2018).

[10] *See* Tommy C. Blanchard et al., *Orbitofrontal Cortex Uses Distinct Codes for Different Choice Attributes in Decisions Motivated by Curiosity*, 85 NEURON 602 (2015);

Belief Change as a Multidimensional Valuation Problem

Return to the climate change case discussed in Chapter 4. There, as elsewhere, belief change can be characterized as a *value-based decision*. The suggestion is that every belief carries a utility.[11] People will be more likely to change their beliefs when the expected utility of a new belief is greater than that of an old belief. The utility of a belief is derived by a summation of quantities along multiple dimensions. These dimensions can be roughly categorized into two groups: the external outcomes of holding a belief and the internal outcomes of holding a belief. The outcomes of holding a belief can be accuracy-dependent or accuracy-independent.

External Outcomes

Accuracy-independent

These refer to the external consequences of holding a belief, such as monetary rewards or social acceptance, that are independent of whether the belief is accurate.[12] For example, in certain societies people are more likely to find a job (positive external outcome) if they hold certain religious views. These external outcomes (positive or negative) are independent of whether the belief itself is true or false. (True, people might merely pretend to hold a belief, but let's bracket that point here.)

Accuracy-dependent

These outcomes refer to the external benefits (or rewards) associated with holding an accurate belief and the costs (or punishments) associated with holding an inaccurate belief. For example, if people believe that the stock market will rise and invest in the market, they can gain money if they are right, but they will lose if they are wrong. If they do not have any money to invest in the stock market

Kunda, *supra* note 8; George Loewenstein, *The Pleasures and Pains of Information*, 312 SCIENCE 704 (2006).

[11] See Bénabou & Tirole, *supra* note 9; Bromberg-Martin & Sharot, *supra* note 9; Loewenstein & Molnar, *supra* note 9.

[12] See Jay J. Van Bavel et al., *The Social Function of Rationalization: An Identity Perspective*, 43 BEHAV. BRAIN SCI. E52 (2020).

(and are not advising others), the accuracy-dependent external out-comes are zero. While many beliefs have direct accuracy-dependent consequences for the individual, as they guide actions with positive or negative consequences (e.g., believing whether cigarette smoking is good for you, whether coronavirus vaccines are safe, or whether a colleague is a friend or foe), many others do not (e.g., the positive or negative consequences of believing the earth is flat are not typically a function of the accuracy of the belief, unless perhaps the individual is navigating long distances, but instead involve social benefits of allying with like-minded others). Some beliefs may not have a cor-responding notion of accuracy at all, such as preferences ("chocolate ice cream is better than vanilla" or "dogs are better than cats") or beliefs about what is right and wrong ("people should not sacrifice animals for food"). (This claim raises some contested philosophical questions; let us bracket them here.)

Internal Outcomes

Accuracy-independent

Internal outcomes refer to the positive or negative cognitive and affective outcomes derived *directly* from a belief itself, regardless of whether there are external outcomes associated with such beliefs. These outcomes are often independent of whether the belief is accu-rate or not. For example, holding positive beliefs about the future (e.g., believing one will likely live a very long time or obtain a terrific job) can lead to a positive mental state.[13] This is because people are forward-looking agents who care about their future states.[14] A belief that a future state will be desirable leads to a current positive state known as "positive anticipation."[15] Another example is holding posi-tive beliefs about oneself (such as one's own competence, character, intelligence, or good looks). Yet another example is holding beliefs with high certainty, which gives people a comforting sense that they understand the world around them.

---

[13] *See* Caroline J. Charpentier et al., *Models of Affective Decision Making: How Do Feelings Predict Choice?*, 27 PSYCH. SCI. 763 (2016); Loewenstein, *supra* note 13.

[14] *See* Markus K. Brunnermeier & Jonathan A. Parker, *Optimal Expectations*, 95 AM. ECON. REV. 1092 (2005).

[15] *Id.*

Accuracy-dependent

Internal outcomes can also be accuracy-dependent. For example, holding a belief that one is likely to obtain a good grade can lead to (accuracy-independent) positive feelings in the present moment, but to great disappointment later when a failing grade is revealed.[16] The latter is an internal outcome that is accuracy-dependent yet derived directly from the belief. That is, if one were to expect a failing grade, the magnitude of disappointment would be much smaller and perhaps negligible.

Interactions

Internal and external outcomes can interact. For example, believing that one is likely to perform well on a job interview can in turn improve actual performance in the interview, increasing the likelihood of obtaining the job.[17] However, exaggerated self-confidence can also be self-defeating. If one believes that one will do very well on a test, one might feel better (which means that the belief is pleasant to have) but study much less than one otherwise would.

Combining Expectations

Expectations about all these different outcomes are implicitly combined to derive the overall utility of each belief. Forming a belief can thus be conceptualized as a multi-attribute, value-based decision problem in which the aim is to hold a belief that has the highest value (most likely to lead to desirable outcomes), rather than to form the most accurate belief. People may incorporate these dimensions at an unconscious level (i.e., they do not necessarily have explicit access to these calculations). This is not unusual; the brain engages in many unconscious calculations that drive decisions (e.g., estimating the speed and distance of an upcoming car before crossing the street).[18] Thus,

---

[16] *See* Robb B. Rutledge et al., *A Computational and Neural Model of Momentary Subjective Well-Being*, 111 PROC. NAT'L ACAD. SCI. 12252 (2014).

[17] *See* Albert Bandura, Self-Efficacy: *Toward a Unifying Theory of Behavioral Change*, 84 PSYCH. REV. 191 (1977); Roland Bénabou & Jean Tirole, *Self-Confidence and Personal Motivation*, 117 Q.J. ECON. 871 (2002).

[18] *See* Thomas Goschke, *Implicit Learning and Unconscious Knowledge: Mental Representation, Computational Mechanisms, and Brain Structures*, *in* KNOWLEDGE, CONCEPTS, AND CATEGORIES 247 (Koen Lamberts & David R. Shanks, eds., 1997); Mathias

while the brain may code for the value of the belief and estimate different outcomes, individuals will not necessarily have conscious access to this process and/or to the values of each attribute. This process may lead people to believe that the view with highest utility is the accurate one due to rationalization. Such a belief will feel subjectively justified, due to the automaticity of the belief-formation process.[19]

When new evidence comes to light, the difference in the utilities of a potential new belief and old belief are compared. If the utility of a new belief is greater than that of an old belief, then a change in belief is likely.

This framework can account for cases in which people do not change their beliefs in the face of highly credible new evidence. Recall the findings from chapter 4 and note that, for example, people fail adequately to alter their beliefs in the face of information that points toward unpleasant conclusions, such as that the likelihood of an adverse event (such as an accident or illness) is worse than expected,[20] that others view them as less attractive then they thought,[21] that they are likely to earn less than they expected,[22] or that their preferred presidential candidate is lagging behind in the polls.[23] In all these cases, individuals may hold onto inaccurate beliefs that are associated with non-accuracy-dependent outcomes (e.g., the positive feeling of maintaining a belief that it is pleasant to have) that are greater than the external accuracy-dependent outcomes.

A similar valence-dependent asymmetry has been observed in reinforcement learning tasks, where participants are required to learn which of two cues is associated with the greatest reward. A larger learning

Pessiglione et al., *Subliminal Instrumental Conditioning Demonstrated in the Human Brain*, 59 NEURON 561 (2008).

[19] *See* Leon Festinger, *Cognitive Dissonance*, 207 SCI. AM. 93 (1962); Tali Sharot et al., *Do Decisions Shape Preference? Evidence from Blind Choice*, 21 PSYCH. SCI. 1231 (2010).

[20] *See* Tali Sharot et al., *How Unrealistic Optimism Is Maintained in the Face of Reality*, 14 NATURE NEUROSCI. 1475 (2011); Andreas Kappes & Tali Sharot, *The Automatic Nature of Motivated Belief Updating*, 3 BEHAV. PUB. POL'Y 87 (2019); Christina Moutsiana et al., *Human Frontal-Subcortical Circuit and Asymmetric Belief Updating*, 35 J. NEUROSCI. 14077 (2015).

[21] *See* David Eil & Justin M. Rao, *The Good News-Bad News Effect: Asymmetric Processing of Objective Information about Yourself*, 3 AM. ECON. J.: MICROECON. 114 (2011).

[22] *See* Markus M. Mobius et al., *Managing Self-Confidence: Theory and Experimental Evidence* (Nat'l Bureau of Econ. Rsch., Working Paper No. 17014, 2011).

[23] *See* Ben M. Tappin et al., The Heart Trumps the Head: Desirability Bias in Political Belief Revision, 146 J. EXPERIMENTAL PSYCH.: GEN. 1143 (2017).

rate is observed in response to unexpected positive outcomes than in response to negative outcomes.[24] Interestingly, the bias is observed only when participants select between cues themselves (i.e., when they have control over the outcomes) and not when a computer makes the choices for them.[25] In other words, participants are amplifying the belief that their own choices are correct – a belief that is internally rewarding. It has been suggested that such a learning pattern (also known as "choice-confirmation bias") can lead to greater external rewards in some situations.[26] In such cases, the resulting belief will have high value due to both internal and external outcomes. Note, however, that positivity biases in belief updating have been observed even in situations where people have no control over the outcomes, such as in updating a belief about whether one carries the Huntington gene.[27]

When a person's environment or situation changes, the value of accuracy-dependent outcomes relative to non-accuracy-dependent outcomes can vary. In environments rife with threat, the external accuracy-dependent cost of underweighting negative information could be particularly high. For example, the outcome of holding onto a belief that one is immune to a deadly infectious virus amid a global pandemic may be grave. Indeed, it has been shown that exposing participants to a threatening environment increases the likelihood that they will adequately change their beliefs in response to unpleasant information.[28] (This is very good news.)

Or consider an individual who grows up in an environment where social acceptance is conditional on holding conservative beliefs, but who then moves to a town where both conservatives and progressives are socially accepted. The external non-accuracy-dependent outcomes of holding conservative beliefs are reduced or eliminated, and hence the individual may shift their beliefs based on the other

[24] Germain Lefebvre et al., *Behavioural and Neural Characterization of Optimistic Reinforcement Learning*, 1 NATURE HUM. BEHAV. 67 (2017).
[25] *See* Valérian Chambon et al., *Information about Action Outcomes Differentially Affects Learning from Self-Determined versus Imposed Choices*, 4 NATURE HUM. BEHAV. 1067 (2020).
[26] *See id.*
[27] *See* Emily Oster et al., *Optimal Expectations and Limited Medical Testing: Evidence from Huntington Disease*, 103 AM. ECON. REV. 804 (2013).
[28] *See* Neil Garrett et al., *Updating Beliefs Under Perceived Threat*, 38 J. NEUROSCI. 7901 (2018); Laura K. Globig et al., *Under Threat, Weaker Evidence Is Required to Reach Undesirable Conclusions*, 41 J. NEUROSCI. 6502 (2021).

dimensions. In other words, people may change their beliefs when their environment changes, because those changes bring with them alterations to the value of the different dimensions of a belief. Because people experience different environments and have different personalities and values (e.g., some people may care more/less about social acceptance), the utility of a belief will be different for different people, which can lead to diverse beliefs within a population. Political polarization might well result from this process, as when one environment rewards a certain set of beliefs, and another environment rewards a different set of beliefs; a "belief subsidy" is some places turns into a "belief tax" in others.

Belief change can also occur when one of these attributes is made more salient. For example, if people are nudged to consider accuracy, they may give more weight to accuracy-dependent outcomes than they would otherwise and consequently shift their beliefs. Indeed, a study reported that priming subjects to consider the veracity of social media posts by asking them to rate the accuracy of a single post subsequently resulted in reduced sharing of other false information.[29] Note, however, that whether this manipulation also reduced the likelihood that subjects believe these posts to be true was not tested.

Just as the valuation and comparison of material goods can involve biases and heuristics,[30] so can people's assessment of the value of beliefs, which could lead to mistaken judgments about the benefits and costs of changing beliefs. For example, people might overestimate the short-term adverse emotional impact of a new belief (e.g., about personal vulnerability to some health risk), partially because they underestimate their ability to adapt to negative information.[31] In some cases, people might hold onto their beliefs more tenaciously than they should, given the expected value of changing them, and in other cases, they might change their beliefs too readily, given that same expected value. Present bias and optimistic bias might contribute to unjustified failures to change beliefs, and also to unjustified changes in belief.[32]

---

[29] Gordon Pennycook et al., *Shifting Attention to Accuracy Can Reduce Misinformation Online*, 592 NATURE 590 (2021).

[30] *See* Amos Tversky & Daniel Kahneman, *Judgment Under Uncertainty: Heuristics and Biases*, 185 SCIENCE 1124 (1974).

[31] *See* Tali Sharot & Cass R. Sunstein, *How People Decide What They Want to Know*, 4 NATURE HUM. BEHAV. 14 (2020).

[32] *See id.*

The Role of Confidence and Metacognition in Belief Change

The multidimensional framework described here is analogous to other multidimensional economic decision problems.[33] Determining the subjective value of a banana is a multidimensional estimation problem. An agent needs to estimate how tasty the banana will be, how much sugar and fiber it has, the current level of sugar and fiber in one's body, and so forth.[34] In turn, people may have different levels of uncertainty around their estimate related to each dimension (*dimensional uncertainty*). You may be very certain about how tasty the banana will be but not about the amount of sugar in it. A person may be unsure about whether holding religious beliefs will facilitate or impede job security or how they may feel if they no longer held such beliefs. Uncertainty about a dimension will usually reduce the impact of this dimension on the overall utility calculation, in line with Bayesian rules of information integration, where more precise signals are weighted more heavily.[35] Scientists might have high certainty about the effects of vaccinations on COVID-19 case numbers (external accuracy-dependent dimension) as they are educated in the scientific method, leading to a larger influence of this dimension on their overall belief. In comparison, people who are less familiar with the scientific method might feel less certain about the accuracy-dependent dimension, and thus show less influence of this dimension on their overall belief. Moreover, uncertainty about any of the dimensions will contribute to low certainty in the overall integrated value of a belief (*belief uncertainty*).

Uncertainty about a belief or value is conceptually distinct from confidence in a decision about which belief to hold. This is analogous to the distinction drawn between confidence and certainty in other realms of decision-making.[36] When choosing between material options (such as between a banana and a dragon fruit), you may have higher certainty in the value of a banana than in the value of a dragon fruit, with which you might have less experience. Choosing between

---

[33]   *See* Jerome R. Busemeyer et al., *Cognitive and Neural Bases of Multi-Attribute, Multi-Alternative, Value-Based Decisions*, 23 TRENDS COGNITIVE SCIS. 251 (2019).

[34]   *See generally* Silvia U. Maier et al., *Dissociable Mechanisms Govern When and How Strongly Reward Attributes Affect Decisions*, 4 NATURE HUM. BEHAV. 949 (2020).

[35]   *See* Marc O. Ernst & Martin S. Banks, *Humans Integrate Visual and Haptic Information in a Statistically Optimal Fashion*, 415 NATURE 429 (2002).

[36]   *See* Alexandre Pouget et al., *Confidence and Certainty: Distinct Probabilistic Quantities for Different Goals*, 19 NATURE NEUROSCI. 366 (2016).

the options then gives rise to different degrees of *decision confidence*, a quantity that is thought to be related to the difference in the distributions of the value of one option (e.g., banana) over another option (e.g., dragon fruit).[37] The width of each value distribution is inversely proportional to the certainty about the value, which in turn affects how much the distributions overlap. When the value distributions are overlapping, deciding between the options is typically hard, and decision confidence is typically low. When the distributions are well-separated, the decision is easy and confidence is high.[38] Similarly, when deciding whether to change one's belief, a relative value comparison between opposing beliefs can be made. More distinct value distributions for the opposing beliefs will lead to greater confidence in the adopted belief. For instance, while a person may be unsure about the overall utility of being an atheist (high *belief uncertainty*), they could still hold high *decision confidence* that for them it is preferable to following Pastafarianism, due to a clear relative difference in value.

In standard decision-making tasks, people are more likely to gather additional information when *decision confidence* is low.[39] The process should be similar for beliefs; if people are not confident in an initial belief that vaccines are ineffective and unsafe, they might continue to ask for new information, eventually changing their belief. Information gathering could take various forms: actively seeking new information (e.g., looking up studies on vaccine efficacy),[40] resampling internal evidence (e.g., recalling a past conversation with one's

---

[37] *See* Benedetto De Martino et al., *Confidence in Value-Based Choice* 16 NATURE NEUROSCI. 105 (2013).

[38] *See id.*

[39] *See id.*; *see also* Kobe Desender et al., *Subjective Confidence Predicts Information Seeking in Decision Making*, 29 PSYCH. SCI. 761 (2018); Kobe Desender et al., *A Postdecisional Neural Marker of Confidence Predicts Information-Seeking in Decision-Making*, 39 J. NEUROSCI. 3309 (2019); Florent Meyniel et al., *The Sense of Confidence during Probabilistic Learning: A Normative Account*, 11 PLoS COMPUTATIONAL BIOLOGY E1004305 (2015); Lion Schulz et al., *Dogmatism Manifests in Lowered Information Search Under Uncertainty*, 117 PROC. NAT'L ACAD. SCIS. 31527 (2020); Tomas Folke et al., *Explicit Representation of Confidence Informs Future Value-Based Decisions*, 1 NATURE HUM. BEHAV. 1 (2017); Stephen M. Fleming et al., *Neural Mediators of Changes of Mind about Perceptual Decisions*, 21 NATURE NEUROSCI. 617 (2018).

[40] *See* Desender et al., 2018, *supra* note 41; Desender et al., 2019, *supra* note 41; Schulz et al., *supra* note 41. *See also* Samuel J. Gershman, *Deconstructing the Human Algorithms for Exploration*, 173 COGNITION 34 (2018); Eric Schulz et al., *Structured, Uncertainty-Driven Exploration in Real-World Consumer Choice*, 116 PROC. NAT'L ACAD. SCIS. 13903 (2019); Eric Schulz & Samuel J. Gershman, *The Algorithmic Architecture of Exploration in the Human Brain*, 55 CURRENT OP. NEUROBIOLOGY 7 (2019).

physician about vaccine efficacy),[41] or paying more attention to information accidently encountered in the media environment (i.e., "scanning").[42] If, however, the potential outcomes of a belief (internal or external) are negligible, people are unlikely to invest time and effort in seeking information (e.g., one may be highly uncertain whether vaccines are safe, but will not bother to investigate the matter if one expects never to have access to vaccines).

Low decision confidence has been found to make it more likely that new evidence will induce belief change regardless of whether the new information was actively sought out or not.[43] Confidence levels can thus be adaptive in optimally allocating resources toward acquiring and processing valuable information.[44] In this sense, confidence plays the role of an internal control mechanism indicating the need (or the absence of a need) for further processing and adapting the receptiveness to new information accordingly. As suggested earlier, (high) confidence may itself be a component of an accuracy-independent internal outcome, in that a comforting feeling of confidence in the world may itself be intrinsically valuable. This is in keeping with studies that have shown that value and confidence signals are both represented in a similar region of ventromedial prefrontal cortex,[45] and with the demonstration of interactions between monetary incentives and confidence.[46]

How useful these control signals are will depend on their alignment with the true underlying distribution of the belief utilities.[47] Previous work has shown that confidence can be influenced by factors extraneous to the decision (for instance, fluency and arousal). If

[41] *See* Douglas G. Lee & Jean Daunizeau, *Trading Mental Effort for Confidence in the Metacognitive Control of Value-Based Decision-Making*, 10 ELIFE E63282 (2021).
[42] Robert Hornik & Jeff Niederdeppe, *Information Scanning*, *in* THE INTERNATIONAL ENCYCLOPEDIA OF COMMUNICATION 2257 (Wolfgang Donsbach, ed., 2008).
[43] Florent Meyniel, *Brain Dynamics for Confidence-Weighted Learning*, 16 PLoS COMPUTATIONAL BIOLOGY E1007935 (2020); *see also* Max Rollwage et al., *Confidence Drives a Neural Confirmation Bias*, 11 NATURE COMMC'NS 1 (2020).
[44] *See* Lee & Daunizeau, *supra* note 43; Meyniel, *supra* note 45.
[45] *See* De Martino et al., *supra* note 39; Maël Lebreton et al., *Automatic Integration of Confidence in the Brain Valuation Signal*, 18 NATURE NEUROSCI. 1159 (2015).
[46] *See* Maël Lebreton et al., *Two Sides of the Same Coin: Monetary Incentives Concurrently Improve and Bias Confidence Judgments*, 4 SCI. ADVANCES EAAQ0668 (2018).
[47] *See* Max Rollwage & Stephen M. Fleming, *Confirmation Bias Is Adaptive When Coupled with Efficient Metacognition*, 376 PHIL. TRANSACTIONS ROYAL SOC'Y 20200131 (2020); Lion Schulz et al., *Confidence in Control: Metacognitive Computations for Information Search*, 43 PROC. ANN. MEETING COGNITIVE SCI. SOC'Y 3301 (2021).

confidence is poorly aligned with the true underlying distributions, people might be confident even though they should not be, which would lead them not to invest mental effort in changing beliefs even when there is considerable belief uncertainty. Conversely, people might feel uncertain even though they should not, which could drive them toward a suboptimal belief change.

How well (decision) confidence aligns with true performance is known as metacognitive ability.[48] People with high metacognitive ability will be very confident in their decisions when they are correct and not so confident when they are incorrect. Metacognitive ability is typically measured with respect to judgements that have a ground truth, such as the accuracy of a perceptual decision (e.g., "is an array of dots moving right or left?" "how confident are you?"). But the notion of metacognition can also be extended to belief utility. When metacognitive ability is high, people will tend to have high confidence in high utility beliefs and low confidence in suboptimal beliefs, motivating them to invest mental effort to change their beliefs in the latter case. It is thus possible that increasing people's metacognitive abilities, for example through training,[49] could increase openness to new information, specifically in cases when it could be helpful for ensuring that beliefs and values align.

Policy Applications

The discussion thus far has suggested that the value of a belief can be understood as a weighted summation of four types of belief outcomes; these follow a 2 × 2 categorization (external and internal outcomes that are either dependent or independent of accuracy). Policymakers and practitioners may find it useful to consider *all* four "boxes" when attempting to predict and/or alter people's beliefs.

Many policies requiring disclosure of information are designed to alter beliefs. For example, information regarding health and safety, or labels informing consumers about fuel economy, are meant to bring consumers' beliefs into accordance with reality. Regulators often

---

[48] *See* Stephen M. Fleming & Raymond J. Dolan, *The Neural Basis of Metacognitive Ability*, 367 PHIL. TRANSACTIONS ROYAL SOC'Y 1338 (2012); Stephen M. Fleming & Hakwan C. Lau, *How to Measure Metacognition*, 8 FRONTIERS HUM. NEUROSCI. 443 (2014).

[49] *See* Jason Carpenter et al., *Domain-General Enhancements of Metacognitive Ability through Adaptive Training*, 148 J. EXPERIMENTAL PSYCH.: GEN. 51 (2019).

assume that consumers, workers, investors, and others care only about what is accurate, which means that if they are presented with the truth, they will believe it so long as it is credible. For reasons sketched earlier, that assumption might well be wrong. As we have seen, people also care about accuracy-independent dimensions of holding beliefs, including how beliefs make them feel.

The implication is that when policymakers (as well as advocates and marketers) are seeking to promote belief change (e.g., in the interest of health or safety), they should also pay close attention to people's expectations about the internal outcomes of belief change,[50] as well as perceptions of external outcomes that are not accuracy-dependent. If they do, they might be able to recast or frame information in such a way as to make belief change more appealing.

As an example, consider the campaign to persuade people to believe in the safety and efficacy of COVID-19 vaccines. Most private and public institutions focus only on communicating data indicating the efficacy and safety of the vaccine (external accuracy-dependent outcome). Future studies should examine if highlighting accuracy-independent outcomes will increase belief in vaccine efficacy. Consider, for example, learning that one is immune will greatly reduce anxiety (internal accuracy-independent outcome) or that people who believe in vaccine efficacy are more respected by their relevant peers (external accuracy-independent outcome),

It might be speculated that when fear appeals work,[51] it is because they can generate positive internal and external belief outcomes. Most fear appeals highlight a danger (COVID-19 can lead to death) alongside a controllable solution (get vaccinated). Such fear appeals may be effective because the promoted belief (vaccines work) has both positive accuracy-dependent external outcomes (people who hold such a belief will be more likely to get vaccinated and thus increase disease protection) and accuracy-independent internal outcomes (believing vaccines work reduces fear).

These points also bear on effective responses to misinformation and "fake news." In some cases, factual corrections do not work, in part because people do not want to believe them for reasons unrelated

---

[50] *See* Cass R. Sunstein, *Ruining Popcorn? The Welfare Effects of Information*, 58 J. RISK & UNCERTAINTY 121 (2019).
[51] *See* Melanie B. Tannenbaum et al., *Appealing to Fear: A Meta-Analysis of Fear Appeal Effectiveness and Theories*, 141 PSYCH. BULL. 1178 (2015).

to accuracy;[52] in extreme cases, they can actually backfire, fortifying people's commitment to the belief that were supposed to be debunked.[53] One reason may be people's judgment that if they changed their belief, they would in some sense suffer (perhaps because the new belief would endanger their affiliation with generally like-minded others, perhaps because it would threaten their sense of identity, perhaps because it would make them feel sad or afraid). The implication is that if the correction can be made in a way that does *not* threaten people's affiliations or self-understanding, or the essentials of their view of the world, it is more likely to be effective.[54] "Surprising validators," who are not expected to endorse a new belief (such as a conservative politician who supports gay rights) but who are credible to those who are considering whether to do so, can succeed in promoting belief change in part for this reason.[55] If a new belief about (say) personal safety and health seems more like an opportunity rather than a threat, people may be more likely to be drawn to it.

Finally, the current framework has implications for formal educational settings. The role of confidence and metacognition in guiding students' learning and study time has been long appreciated.[56] In tandem, self-efficacy beliefs (such as believing that I am good at mathematics) have been shown to influence effort and attainment in the classroom – a factor that may contribute to the differential confidence of boys and girls in STEM subjects.[57] In order to bring such beliefs in line with reality (e.g., to ensure that girls realize they are as good at math than boys), it may be fruitful to examine not only factual aspects of belief change (such as test scores) but also accuracy-independent

---

[52] *See* Jay J. Van Bavel et al., *Political Psychology in the Digital (mis)Information Age: A Model of News Belief and Sharing*, 15 Soc. Issues & Pol'y Rev. 84 (2021).

[53] *See* Brendan Nyhan et al., *Effective Messages in Vaccine Promotion: A Randomized Trial*, 133 Pediatrics e835 (2014).

[54] *See* Dan M. Kahan, *Misconceptions, Misinformation, and the Logic of Identity-Protective Cognition* 1 (Cultural Cognition Project, Working Paper No. 164, 2017).

[55] *See* Edward Glaeser & Cass R. Sunstein, *Does More Speech Correct Falsehoods?*, 43 J. Legal Stud. 65 (2014).

[56] *See, e.g.*, Janet Metcalfe, *Metacognitive Judgments and Control of Study*, 18 Current Directions Psych. Sci. 159 (2009).

[57] *See* Bandura, *supra* note 19; *see also* Corina U. Greven et al., *More than Just IQ: School Achievement Is Predicted by Self-Perceived Abilities – But for Genetic Rather than Environmental Reasons*, 20 Psych. Sci. 753 (2009); Programme for International Student Assessment, Results: Ready to Learn: Students' Engagement, Drive and Self-Beliefs (2013).

aspects of self-efficacy beliefs (such as the unwillingness to deviate from the opinions of one's peer group).

Accuracy Is Not All That Matters

The central suggestion here is that a person's goal is to hold beliefs that carry maximum utility. The utility of a belief is equal to the weighted summation of the potential outcomes of holding that belief. Some of these potential outcomes are dependent on the accuracy of the belief, but some are not. For example, the outcomes of holding a religious belief may include reduced stress and social acceptance, neither of which are dependent on the accuracy of that belief. The outcomes of holding a belief about personal vulnerability to health risks may include fear and sadness, which people prefer to avoid.

It follows that the process of belief change is not necessarily an attempt to improve the accuracy of a belief, but rather to adopt a belief with higher utility. Sometimes belief change may not be observed even when highly credible new evidence, inconsistent with the current belief, is introduced; the accuracy-independent costs of changing one's beliefs might be perceived to be too high. Sometimes belief change may occur without any new evidence at all, but simply because the utility of holding it suddenly increases (e.g., due to a new environment, where external rewards are given to those who hold the new belief). Importantly, exposing individuals to new evidence to correct a false belief may not be sufficient for belief change in cases when a potential new belief does not carry higher utility than an old belief. This point underscores the importance of considering all relevant dimensions of a belief when aiming to promote belief change.

6 DECIDING INCONSISTENTLY

Thus far we have explored how people decide (1) how to decide, (2) what information to seek, and (3) what to believe. Let us now shift the viewscreen. Sometimes our decisions are inconsistent. On some occasions, we prefer A to B, but on other occasions, we prefer B to A. This is true whether we are speaking of books, cell phones, cities, jobs, laptops, investments, friends, or romantic partners. My focus in this chapter is on one dimension of that problem, a dimension that might seem a bit technical, but that is, I think, the most fundamental of all. The puzzle that I will be addressing bears directly on decisions about decisions. It suggests the immense importance of thinking about options, and the presentation of options, in a way that avoids the kinds of errors that I will be emphasizing here.

In the last quarter century, one of the most intriguing findings in behavioral science goes under the unlovely name of "preference reversals between joint and separate evaluations of options."[1] The basic idea is that when people evaluate options A and B separately,

---

[1] The initial discovery was in 1992. *See* Max H. Bazerman et al., *Reversals of Preference in Allocation Decisions: Judging an Alternative versus Choosing among Alternatives*, 37 ADMIN. SCI. Q. 220 (1992). For a valuable overview, *see* Christopher K. Hsee et al., *Preference Reversals between Joint and Separate Evaluations of Options: A Review and Theoretical Analysis*, 125 PSYCH. BULL. 576 (1999). For a recent treatment with helpful additional complexity, *see* Yin-Hui Cheng et al., *Preference Reversals between Joint and Separate Evaluations with Multiple Alternatives and Context Effects*, 120 PSYCH. REPS. 1117 (2017).

they prefer A to B; but when they evaluate the two jointly, they prefer B to A. Preference reversals of this kind tell us a great deal about practical reason in daily life. They also raise deep questions about choice, rationality, choice architecture, and the relationship between decisions and welfare.[2]

In many circumstances, people are making decisions in separate evaluation. They are assessing an option: an appliance, a book, a movie, a policy, a political candidate, or a potential romance. They focus intently on the option *in isolation*. In other circumstances, people are making choices in joint evaluation. They are assessing two options, and they compare them along one or another dimension. They focus intently on the two options and the particular dimensions along which they differ.

Of course, they might also assess three options, or four, or 500. The distinction between separate and joint evaluation might be unrealistic in situations in which the alternative to separate is better described as "multiple." I will return to that point, but let us bracket it for now. The central idea is that in assessing an option, people may or may not be comparing them with other options in the same general vicinity.

My principal goal here is to show that both separate and joint evaluation often lead to bad outcomes, though for intriguingly different reasons. To simplify the story, a characteristic problem with separate evaluation is a lack of relevant information. Some features of an option are hard to assess in isolation; their meaning, for life or actual experience, is unclear. For that reason, those characteristics may be ignored. By contrast, a characteristic problem with joint evaluation is the undue salience of a single factor (or a subset of factors). People focus on what distinguishes the two options, whether or not it means much for life or experience.

I devote considerable space to elaborating these problems, which show why individual decisions often go wrong in both markets and politics. Contrary to a widespread view, I argue that there is no justification for preferring separate evaluation to joint evaluation, or

---

[2] There is an extensive literature on other kinds of preference reversals, not discussed here. *See, e.g.*, Amos Tversky & Richard H. Thaler, *Anomalies: Preference Reversals*, 4 J. ECON. PERSPS. 201 (1990); Amos Tversky et al., *The Causes of Preference Reversal*, 80 AM. ECON. REV. 204 (1990). The best explanation of some such reversals – "scale compatibility" – belongs, I think, in the same general family as those explored here, though I cannot establish that proposition in this space.

vice versa. For purposes of producing good decisions and good out-comes, both modes of evaluation run into serious problems. We should try to avoid the problems and pathologies associated with each.

Consumer Goods

For consumers, here is an example of the kind of preference reversal on which I will be focusing here:

Dictionary A
20,000 entries, torn cover but otherwise like new

Dictionary B
10,000 entries, like new

When the two options are assessed separately, people are willing to pay more for B; when they are assessed jointly, they are willing to pay more for A.[3] A prominent explanation for such preference reversals points to "evaluability."[4] In separate evaluation, it is difficult for most people to know how many words a dictionary should have, or whether 10,000 is a lot or a little.[5] For that reason, 10,000 and 20,000 might be taken to be indistinguishable in separate evaluation, and hence produce essentially the same willingness to pay. The numbers do not and indeed cannot matter, to the extent that it is difficult to know what they mean. By contrast, "torn cover" is clearly a negative, and "like new" is clearly a positive, even in separate evaluation. That characteristic looms large. Who wants a dictionary with a torn cover?

---

[3] See Christopher K. Hsee, *The Evaluability Hypothesis: An Explanation for Preference Reversals between Joint and Separate Evaluations of Alternatives*, 67 ORG. BEHAV. & HUM. DECISION PROCESSES 247, 248 (1996).

[4] See id.; see also Christopher K. Hsee, *Attribute Evaluability and Its Implications for Joint-Separate Evaluation Reversals and Beyond*, in CHOICES, VALUES, AND FRAMES 543–65 (Daniel Kahneman & Amos Tversky eds., 2000). Other explanations are explored in Max H. Bazerman et al., *Explaining How Preferences Change across Joint versus Separate Evaluation*, 39 J. ECON. BEHAV. & ORG. 41 (1999); I take them up later.

[5] Compare this to the important finding of "comparison friction" in Jeffrey R. Kling et al., *Comparison Friction: Experimental Evidence from Medicare Drug Plans*, 127 Q.J. ECON. 199 (2012). In brief, Kling and his coauthors describe comparison friction as "the wedge between the availability of comparative information and consumers' use of it." *Id.* at 200. They find that the wedge is significantly larger than people think, in the sense that even when information is readily available, people do not use it. There is a clear relationship between comparison friction and preference reversals of the kind on which I focus here; in real markets, and in politics, it is because of comparison friction that in separate evaluation, people do not obtain the information that they could readily obtain.

The problem of evaluability, used in the psychology literature, is best understood in more conventional economic terms. It points to *a lack of adequate information*, which can be costly to obtain, and which people might not seek out even if obtaining it is not costly. In separate evaluation, insufficient information is a pervasive problem. (We have seen that whether it is a rational to try to obtain it is a separate question, one which depends on the costs and benefits of the effort.) Many characteristics of options – dictionaries, appliances, cell phones, jobs, people, cities – are essentially meaningless in the abstract. Consistent with standard practice, I shall use the term evaluability throughout, understanding it to refer to a lack of adequate information.

Some characteristics that are hard or impossible to evaluate are numbers, whose meaning depends on context and background. For "Geekbench 3 SC 32," a laptop might show a number of 3680, but it might be hard or impossible for consumers to know the consequences of that number for what they care about. With respect to some numbers (such as battery life), many or most consumers might have a good understanding even in separate evaluation. But even for such numbers, separate evaluation might not make it easy for people to make appropriate distinctions between impressive numbers (twenty hours, eighteen hours) or less impressive ones (six hours, five hours). To overcome a problem of evaluability (understood as lack of adequate information), consumers must do some work, and they will often decline to do it.

The problem of evaluability, in this sense, belongs in the same family as "opportunity cost neglect": People might be willing to pay $X for a certain good, but not if they are focused on other things for which they might pay $X.[6] Drawing people's attention to opportunity costs is analytically similar to joint evaluation; it broadens the viewscreen to focus attention on a comparison to which they would otherwise be oblivious.

For consumer goods, and indeed for countless options, evaluability presents a serious challenge, and at the time of choice, characteristics that can be readily evaluated will dominate people's decisions. We can understand the behavioral phenomenon of "present bias" in similar terms.[7] The present is often easy to evaluate; the future is often

---

[6] *See* Shane Frederick et al., *Opportunity Cost Neglect*, 36 J. Consumer Rsch. 553 (2009).
[7] *See* Ted O'Donoghue & Matthew Rabin, *Doing It Now or Later*, 89 Am. Econ. Rev. 103 (1999).

surrounded in some kind of cloud. A challenge of evaluability, with respect to future states of affairs, may well contribute to present bias. For many choices, the evaluability of certain characteristics of options may be especially difficult – a point to which I will return.

In joint evaluation, by contrast, it is easy to see that 10,000 words are less good than 20,000 words. To consumers, those numbers greatly matter, and they become more meaningful in a comparative setting. Because the point of a dictionary is to define words, a dictionary with 20,000 words seems much better than one with 10,000 words. If one dictionary has twice as many words as the other, who cares whether its cover is torn?

Or consider this example (involving an admittedly ancient technology, but work with me here):[8]

CD Changer A
Can hold five CDs; Total Harmonic Distortion = 0.003 percent

CD Changer B
Can hold twenty CDs; Total Harmonic Distortion = 0.01 percent

Subjects were informed that the smaller the Total Harmonic Distortion, the better the sound quality. In separate evaluation, they were willing to pay more for CD Changer B. In joint evaluation, they were willing to pay more for CD Changer A.[9] Here too evaluability is the most plausible explanation. Even if one knows that a lower figure is preferable for Total Harmonic Distortion, 0.01 percent sounds very low in the abstract, and it is not particularly meaningful. In separate evaluation, 0.01 percent and 0.003 percent might seem the same (low). But in joint evaluation, 0.003 percent is obviously much better. Apparently, people think that for a CD changer, what most matters is the sound quality, and hence they would willingly sacrifice a relatively unimportant dimension (the number of CDs held) in return for better sound quality.

Here is one more example, involving data from an actual marketplace:[10]

Baseball Card Package A
10 valuable baseball cards, 3 not-so-valuable baseball cards

---

[8] See Hsee, *supra* note 3, at 253.
[9] *Id.*
[10] See John A. List, *Preferences Reversals of a Different Kind: The "More Is Less" Phenomenon*, 92 AM. ECON. REV. 1636 (2002).

Baseball Card Package B
10 valuable baseball cards

In separate evaluation, inexperienced baseball card traders would pay more for Package B. In joint evaluation, they would pay more for Package A. Intriguingly, experienced traders also show a reversal, though it is less stark. They too would pay more for Package A in joint evaluation. In separate evaluation, they would pay more for Package B (though the difference is not statistically significant). For experienced traders, it is fair to say that in a relatively small population, the preference is for Package A in joint evaluation, but there is no preference in separate evaluation.

The explanation is similar to what we have seen before, and it is straightforward for inexperienced traders. In joint evaluation, it is easy to see that Package A is better. People get something of value that they do not get with Package B. In separate evaluation, it is hard to assess the two packages, or to know which one is better. Some people might use a version of the representativeness heuristic to downgrade Package A; because it contains cards that are not so valuable, the entire package looks worse. As John List explains, this particular reversal, "examining real choices in actual markets," produces a nice test of "the stability of preferences in riskless decisionmaking."[11] The central finding is that preferences are not stable.

Politics

Here is one more example, from a different domain:[12]

Congressional Candidate A
Would create 5,000 jobs; has been convicted of a misdemeanor

Congressional Candidate B
Would create 1,000 jobs; has no criminal convictions

In separate evaluation, people rated Candidate B more favorably, but in joint evaluation, they preferred Candidate A. The best explanation should now be familiar. In the abstract, it is hard to know

---

[11]   *Id.* at 1641.
[12]   *See* GEORGE LOEWENSTEIN, EXOTIC PREFERENCES: BEHAVIORAL ECONOMICS AND HUMAN MOTIVATION 261 (2007).

whether 1,000 or 5,000 jobs is a large number, and a great deal of work would be necessary to make sense of the difference. But a misdemeanor conviction is obviously a strong negative – which explains the relatively greater appeal of Candidate B in separate evaluation. But in joint evaluation, most people think that the benefit of 4,000 additional jobs outweighs the cost of having a member of Congress with a misdemeanor conviction, and hence Candidate A prevails.

Of course, this example is highly stylized, and the outcome depends on predispositions within the relevant population. We could easily imagine a group for which a misdemeanor conviction would be decisive in joint or separate evaluation; we could even imagine a group for which such a conviction would be especially weighty in joint evaluation.[13] Shrewd political consultants should be alert to the possibility that one or another mode of evaluation is in their candidate's interest. I will return to this point, because it raises the specter of manipulation (and poses a challenge for some accounts of rationality). The only point is that in choosing among candidates, as among products, people's preferences, and hence their decisions, may shift as between the two modes.

Global Evaluation and Real Life

It should be emphasized that joint evaluation is not global evaluation, understood as evaluation of all relevant options with all relevant characteristics. In the cases just given, joint evaluation has two distinctive features. First, the two options vary along only two dimensions. Second, there are only two options. In real life, any option has a large assortment of characteristics, some of which will be evaluable in separate evaluation, and some of which will not be. And in real life, there are usually numerous options, not merely two.

For these reasons, experiments involving joint and separate evaluation should be seen as mere approximations of actual decisions, illuminating their characteristics. In well-functioning markets, we might

---

[13] A methodological note: at several points, I will offer some speculations about what imaginable groups would do, without collecting data. My hope is that the speculations will be sufficiently plausible, a logical necessity (given the assumptions), or even self-evident, so that the absence of data is not a problem. But I emphasize that some of the speculations are only that, and that data would be much better.

be inclined to assume that something like global evaluation is involved. But the inclination should be resisted. Recall the baseball card study, involving an actual market, in which experienced traders show a kind of reversal. In real markets, and real decisions, some options are, in fact, evaluated separately, or close to it; people focus on purchasing a product or not doing so. It may take significant effort, and exposure to a kind of friction, to focus as well on alternatives; people may avoid "comparison friction." The point helps explains why global evaluation is usually a mere thought experiment. People cannot easily hold in their minds an entire option set, even if we could agree on how to define it (microwave ovens, books about time travel, hybrid cars). To be sure, many choices involve multiple evaluation rather than joint evaluation, especially when multiple options are squarely faced in front of people (as, e.g., at supermarkets or drug stores).

It is also important to see that in the four cases given, the selection of one other option in joint evaluation is hardly random. It is specifically designed to make one important characteristic more evaluable than it was before, or evaluable when it was not evaluable before. For dictionaries, CD changers, and politicians, we could imagine, in joint evaluation, a wide range of options that would accentuate, and make evaluable, one or another characteristic. As we shall see, there are ample opportunities for manipulation here. We could easily imagine tests not of joint evaluation, but of evaluation of three, four, or forty options.[14] The fact that joint evaluation is not global evaluation, or close to it, has important implications, to which I will return.

Note as well that in actual life, there is a continuum between joint and separate evaluation, rather than a sharp dichotomy.[15] In some cases, people explore an option entirely on its own, but in other cases, another option, or two or more, are in some sense in the background. People might go to a store to purchase a cell phone with a clear understanding that other cell phones are available. In some cases of joint evaluation, two or more options are simultaneously visible, but in others, the chooser has to do some work to make a comparison. The options are not quite side by side.

---

[14] For evidence in this vein, see Cheng et al., supra note 1.

[15] See Christopher K. Hsee et al., Magnitude, Time, and Risk Differ Similarly between Joint and Single Evaluations, 40 J. CONSUMER RSCH. 172 (2013).

Is Less More?

Preference reversals between joint and separate evaluations can be found in multiple domains.[16] It is even possible to predict when they will occur and when they will not. As a first approximation: *If an option has some characteristic X (say, word count for dictionaries) that is*

(1) *difficult to evaluate in separate evaluation,*
(2) *much easier to evaluate in joint evaluation,*
(3) *dominated by characteristic Y (say, torn or intact cover) in separate evaluation (solely because of the problem of evaluability), and*
(4) *deemed to be more important than characteristic Y in joint evaluation, then we will see a preference reversal.*

Sometimes conditions (1) through (4) arise without any conscious efforts by sellers. But sometimes they are deliberately engineered by those whose personal, economic, political, or legal interests are at stake.

There is a relationship here to extremeness aversion, which also produces a kind of preference reversal, and which can also be manipulated.[17] For example: I prefer Option A, the small piece of chocolate cake, to Option B, the medium-sized piece of chocolate cake, in a pairwise comparison. But if I am offered three options – those two sizes and also a large piece – I switch to the medium-sized piece, and thus prefer Option B to Option A. The reason is a kind of heuristic, sometimes understood as a compromise effect: Choose the middle option. Extremeness aversion also makes people susceptible to manipulation. A seller might deliberately add, to Options A and B, some not-so-attractive Option C, so as to shift people from Option A to Option B. They might exploit the compromise effect so as to encourage choosers to select the more expensive option. Politicians might do the same thing.

Restaurants and movie theaters are well aware of this phenomenon. A movie theater might offer Option A, which is regular popcorn, and also Option B, which is large popcorn. Knowing that people will choose Option A, it might introduce Option C, which is jumbo popcorn. Maybe few people will choose Option C, but its existence leads more people to choose Option B.

---

[16] *See* Bazerman et al., *supra* note 4.
[17] *See* Mark Kelman et al., *Context-Dependence in Legal Decision Making*, 25 J. LEGAL STUD. 287 (1996).

When is joint evaluation preferable to separate evaluation, and vice versa? By what criteria? Might both modes of evaluation be subject to characteristic problems?

Resisting Temptation

Let us stipulate that for consumption choices, the question is what will improve consumer welfare. Let us bracket the hardest questions about what, exactly, that means. Even with that bracketing, it is tempting to conclude that joint evaluation is better, simply because it makes one or more relevant considerations easier to evaluate. That is indeed an advantage. Consider the cases given earlier: In all of them, an important variable was discounted or ignored in separate evaluation, simply because people did not know how to evaluate it. Joint evaluation supplied relevant information, and the variable received the attention that people thought that it deserved. The baseball card example is the most straightforward: In joint evaluation, people could see that it is better to have more than less.

But this conclusion is much too simple. First, joint evaluation *might make salient a difference that does not much matter in an actual experience.*[18] For dictionaries, more words are better than fewer (within limits), but how much better? It is possible that for most users, a 10,000-word dictionary is as good as a 20,000-word dictionary. It is also possible that a torn cover is a constant annoyance. Second, life is generally lived in separate evaluation. (I will raise complications about this point in due course.) It might greatly matter whether a CD changer holds five or instead twenty CDs. And in terms of listening experience, the difference between 0.003 percent and 0.01 percent might not matter at all. The bare numbers do not tell us. To be sure, a gain of 4,000 jobs is significant, and in the case of congressional candidates, joint evaluation does seem better. But if a misdemeanor conviction is predictive of corruption or of misconduct that would cause real harm, then joint evaluation might lead to some kind of mistake.

We can even see some choices in joint evaluation as reflecting a disparity between "decision utility" and "experience utility,"[19]

---

[18] *See* Hsee et al., *supra* note 15.

[19] *See* Daniel Kahneman & Richard H. Thaler, *Anomalies: Utility Maximization and Experienced Utility*, 20 J. ECON. PERSPS. 221 (2006); Daniel Kahneman et al., *Back to Bentham? Explorations of Experienced Utility*, 112 Q.J. ECON. 375 (1997).

or (more simply) a hedonic forecasting error,[20] in which people make inaccurate predictions about the effects of their choices on their subjective welfare. There is a specific reason: Joint evaluation often places a bright spotlight on a characteristic that may not much matter.[21] Here is an intuitive example. Jones is deciding between two houses:

House A
Very large, with a long commute to work

House B
Large, with a short commute to work

In separate evaluation, Jones might well be willing to pay more for House B. After all, it is large, and the commute is short. In joint evaluation, Jones might well favor House A. A very large house seems a lot better than a large house, and perhaps the commute will not loom particularly large in his decision. This is a hedonic forecasting error in the sense that Jones is undervaluing the day-to-day inconvenience of a long commute. He is inattentive to that inconvenience because he is focused, in joint evaluation, on something more immediate: the concrete differences in sizes.

Do these points apply outside of the context of consumer choices? Suppose that the goal is to make good personnel decisions. It is reasonable to suppose that joint evaluation is better: If a company is presented with two or more candidates, it might focus on attributes that greatly matter, and so the quality of the decision would be higher in joint evaluation. Consider the following:

Potential Employee A
Strong record, good experience, recommended by a friend, attended the same college as the CEO

Potential Employee B
Exceptional record, exceptional experience, recommended by a stranger, attended a superb college with no alumni at the company

We could easily imagine a preference for Potential Employee A in separate evaluation. But in joint evaluation, Potential Employee B looks better – and might well be chosen. Here too, however, it is important to be

---

[20] Timothy D. Wilson & Daniel T. Gilbert, *Affective Forecasting: Knowing What to Want*, 14 CURRENT DIRECTIONS PSYCH. SCI. 131 (2005).
[21] *See* Hsee et al., *supra* note 15.

careful. On certain assumptions about what matters to employers, separate evaluation could produce better outcomes. Perhaps the chooser cares greatly about a recommendation from a friend, and in joint evaluation, that turns out to be decisive. Or perhaps the chooser cares greatly about cultivating the CEO, and hiring someone who went to the same college would seem to do the trick. If we stipulate that Potential Employee B is better, then joint evaluation might produce mistakes.

In this light, we can raise a question about a prominent account that suggests that in separate evaluation, people make emotional judgments, and that in joint evaluation, their judgments are more deliberative.[22] To be sure, it is possible to devise situations in which that is true, leading to the reasonable suggestion, supported by data, that "emotions play too strong a role in separate decision making."[23] But the opposite may also be true. Consider the following, understood as options for dating:

Person A
Great personality, fun, always kind, attractive

Person B
Good personality, incredibly fun, usually but not always kind, devastatingly attractive

I have not collected data, but we can imagine groups that would prefer Person A in separate evaluation, but Person B in joint evaluation. Is separate evaluation more emotional and less deliberative? Maybe not. The same question raises a concern about the closely related view that in separate evaluation, people focus on what they "want," whereas in joint evaluation, people focus on what they "should" want.[24] The view fits with some of the data. Consider this example:

Option A
Improve air quality in your city

Option B
Get a new cell phone

---

[22] This suggestion can be found in Max H. Bazerman et al., *Negotiating with Yourself and Losing: Making Decisions with Competing Internal Preferences*, 23 ACAD. MGMT. REV. 225, 231 (1998).

[23] Max H. Bazerman et al., *Joint Evaluation as a Real-World Tool for Managing Emotional Assessments of Morality*, 3 EMOTION REV. 290 (2011).

[24] *See* Bazerman et al., *supra* note 4.

It is possible that in separate evaluation, people would be willing to pay more for a new cell phone, but that in joint evaluation, they would be willing to pay more to improve air quality.[25] We could easily devise situations in which separate evaluation triggers a strong desire while joint evaluation produces a response connected with people's normative judgments. But we could devise situations that yield exactly the opposite outcomes. Here is a candidate:

Option A
Contribute to pay down the national debt

Option B
Take your romantic partner out for a romantic dinner

Among some populations, Option A would produce a higher figure in separate evaluation, and Option B would do so in joint evaluation. Everything depends on the antecedent distribution of preferences and on what becomes the focus in joint evaluation – a point to which I now turn.

How to Win Friends and Influence People

In either separate evaluation or joint evaluation, sellers (and others) have identifiable routes by which to influence or to manipulate choosers. The appropriate design should be clear.

Using Separate Evaluation

In separate evaluation, self-interested sellers should show choosers an option with a characteristic that they can easily evaluate (if it is good) and also show them a characteristic that they cannot easily evaluate (if it is not so good). In these circumstances, the option will seem attractive even if it has a serious downside. In fact, sellers should choose separate evaluation, if they can, whenever it is feasible to present an option with these features.

I have emphasized that in real markets, options do not simply have two characteristics; they have an assortment of them. Recall that much of the experimental evidence is a radical simplification. But the

---

[25] I borrow here from *id.* at 46, which uses a video recorder instead of a cell phone.

essential point remains – in fact, it is fortified. Sellers (and others) can present options with a range of easily evaluable characteristics (appealing ones) and also a range of other characteristics that are difficult or impossible to assess (not so appealing ones). It is well known that some product attributes are "shrouded," in the sense that they are hidden from view, either because of selective attention on the part of choosers or because of deliberative action on the part of sellers.[26] A problem of evaluability belongs in the same category; it is a close cousin. Nothing is literally shrouded, but choosers cannot make much sense of the information they are given. In some real markets, they might be able to find out. In fact, that might be easy. But because of comparison friction – defined as people's unwillingness to obtain comparative information, even when it is available – a problem of evaluability in separate evaluation might persist.

Using Joint Evaluation

In joint evaluation, by contrast, self-interested sellers should allow an easy comparison along a dimension that is self-evidently important to choosers, whether or not the difference along that dimension matters little or not at all to experience or to what actually matters. The trick is to highlight a characteristic on which the product in question looks good, or better, or great. It is best, of course, if that characteristic does matter a great deal in reality. But even if it does not, use of joint evaluation, putting a spotlight on the characteristic whose appeal is heightened by way of comparison, is a good strategy. The point holds for consumer products and political candidates, but it should work for options of all kinds.

An imaginable example: A new computer is introduced with a reduction in size and weight; it is easier to transport and it has a better screen than that of existing models. When the existing models are compared with the new one, the difference in weight and between the screens is easy to see. They stand out. Assume, however, that consumers have no problem with existing weight and screens; they find them inferior only in joint evaluation. Assume finally that the new computer has to sacrifice along an important dimension in order to have the

---

[26] *See* Xavier Gabaix & David Laibson, *Shrouded Attributes, Consumer Myopia, and Information Suppression in Competitive Markets*, 121 Q.J. ECON. 505 (2006).

spectacular screen – say, its battery time is much reduced, or its keyboard is much less comfortable to use. It is easy to imagine that in joint evaluation, people will choose (and purchase) the new computer, but that in separate evaluation, they will have a much better experience with the old one.[27] A more general way to put the point is to suggest that in joint evaluation, people might overweight attributes that have become simple to evaluate or that trigger a strong response, including a visceral one.[28]

Net Welfare Gains

These points should be sufficient to show that there is no abstract answer to the question whether joint evaluation or separate evaluation produces better decisions on the part of consumers and choosers of all kinds. Neither is ideal, and both might lead to mistakes. In fact, both modes of evaluation have characteristic problems and pathologies. With separate evaluation, the most important of these is incomplete information, producing a failure of evaluability. With joint evaluation, the most important of these is a focus on one characteristic, producing excessive salience.

In the baseball card case, joint evaluation is obviously better; more is better than less. But in the dictionary and CD cases, we need more information to know whether joint evaluation is better. The same is probably true for the case of the congressional candidates. In the context of consumption choices, the question is whether in joint evaluation, the ability to evaluate a characteristic of an option, and the salience of that characteristic, produces decisions with net welfare gains for choosers. If the factor that is evaluable in joint evaluation does not matter much, and if the factor that is downplayed or ignored in joint evaluation is actually important, then separate evaluation is likely to be better.

There is a psychological wrinkle here. It is tempting to think that life is lived in separate evaluation, which helps explain why and when joint evaluation leads to mistakes. But is life really lived in separate evaluation? The answer depends on the context and on

---

[27] True, this is based on personal mistake. I love the old 11" MacBook Air, but I bought the new MacBook, with its terrific screen and its awful keyboard. (I am writing this on the former. The latter is in some drawer somewhere.)

[28] See Bazerman et al., *supra* note 4.

the person. Suppose that a consumer buys a dictionary with 10,000 words or a computer with a terrific keyboard but a less-than-ideal screen. If that consumer does not think about dictionaries with more words or computers with ideal screens, her purchasing decision will be shown to be correct. If her attention is not spent on issues of comparison, she will live in separate evaluation. But suppose that she does think about those products, at least some of the time, and focuses on her dictionary with limited words or her computer with a screen that, while excellent, pales by comparison with a screen that she rejected. If so, she is living, to a greater or lesser extent, in joint evaluation.

People of course vary in their propensity to engage in product comparisons. The point helps underline that the universe of comparison products defines the frame of reference by which people define their experiences – and helps explain why product improvements may impose serious welfare losses on people who had been enjoying their goods a great deal.

Law and Policy

I have emphasized that preference reversals between joint and separate evaluation have been found in law and politics as well. The domain for analysis here is very large, and research remains in an early state. One of my goals here is to vindicate the suggestion with which I began: The choice between joint and separate evaluation depends on the relevant task and the underlying goals of the enterprise. For that reason, we might well end up rejecting both modes of evaluation. We might simply block some grounds for action (such as racial prejudice). We might seek to rely on global evaluation. We might want to use some kind of algorithm. If, for example, optimal deterrence is the goal, neither joint nor separate evaluation is likely to do a great deal of good.

Consider three examples.

Discrimination

Let us stipulate that in many domains, some people discriminate on legally impermissible grounds: race, sex, religion, disability, age. Discrimination might be a product of conscious bias, in the form of a desire to benefit or burden members of specific social groups. Alternatively, it might be a product of unconscious bias, in the form of automatic devaluation of which people are not aware, and which they might deplore, or be embarrassed by, if they were made aware of it. Whether conscious or unconscious, discrimination raises puzzles for preference reversals. Does joint or separate evaluation matter? If so, is one better? As we shall see, no simple answer makes sense. But there is a fortunate qualification, which is that if the goal is to stop discrimination, we can specify the circumstances in which joint or separate evaluation will be more likely to achieve that goal.

Iris Bohnet and her coauthors have found that in joint evaluation, people decide on the merits, but that in separate evaluation, gender matters, so that men have an advantage over women.[29] To simplify the story: Suppose that an employer is evaluating two candidates, Jack and Jill. In separate evaluation, Jack has an advantage, because he is male; the employer automatically values men more highly than women, and in separate evaluation, that automatic assessment matters. But in joint evaluation, the advantage dissipates. The employer compares the two candidates, and if Jill's qualifications are better, she will be hired. Merit becomes decisive. That is the central finding by Bohnet et al.: discrimination occurs in separate evaluation; merit dominates in joint evaluation.[30]

The mechanism here seems straightforward. It does not involve evaluability. In the relevant population, there is a bias in favor of men, which means that in separate evaluation, they will do better. But people know, in some sense, that they should not discriminate, and in joint evaluation, the fact that they are discriminating will stare them in the face. If they see that they are discriminating, they will be embarrassed – and stop. It follows that when women have stronger qualifications than men, women will be chosen. We could easily imagine similar findings in the context of discrimination on the basis of race, religion, age, or disability.

From this finding, however, it would be a mistake to conclude that joint evaluation is *generally* a safeguard against discrimination. It works in that way only under specified conditions, and under different

---

[29] Iris Bohnet et al., *When Performance Trumps Gender Bias: Joint vs. Separate Evaluation,* 62 Mgmt. Sci. 1225 (2016).

[30] *Id.*

conditions, it might actually aggravate discrimination. Suppose, for example, that people have a self-conscious bias of some kind and that they are not at all ashamed of it. In joint evaluation, those who have such a bias might discriminate more, not less, than in separate evaluation. In separate evaluation, sex or race might not loom so large; discriminators might focus mainly on qualifications. But if people are biased against women or racial minorities, they might discriminate more in joint evaluation, simply because sex or race might crowd out other considerations; it might operate like Total Harmonic Distortion in the case of the CD changers.

Imagine, for example, these cases:

Potential Employee A
Very strong record, excellent experience

Potential Employee B
Strong record, good experience, from a prominent family, not Jewish

In separate evaluation, Potential Employee A might well be preferred. (Let us suppose that Potential Employee A is not from a prominent family, and is Jewish, but that neither of those characteristics is salient in separate evaluation.) But if social attitudes take a particular form, Potential Employee B might well be preferred in joint evaluation. With respect to discrimination, everything depends on the relevant constellation of attitudes.

Punitive Damages

In the US legal system (and some others), juries are allowed to award punitive damages in order to punish wrongdoing. There is a pervasive question, to which the Supreme Court has occasionally been attentive, whether such awards are arbitrary or excessive.[31] In deciding whether to give punitive damages, and choosing what amount to award, juries are not permitted to consider comparison cases. They are making decisions in separate evaluation. Does that matter? If so, how?

---

[31] *See* State Farm Mut. Auto. Ins. Co. v. Campbell, 538 U.S. 408 (2003); TXO Prod. Corp. v. Alliance Res. Corp., 509 U.S. 443 (1993).

Normalization

For a glimpse, consider these pairs of cases:

Case A
Childproof safety cap fails, and child needs hospital stay

Case B
Repainted cars sold as new to a leasing agency

When people see two cases of this kind in isolation, they tend to receive similar punishment ratings (on a bounded scale of 1 to 8) and similar monetary awards.[32] But when they see them jointly, Case A receives much higher punishment ratings and much higher punitive awards.[33] There is a clear reversal. But the mechanism is different from what we have seen previously. There is no problem of evaluability, at least not in the same sense. Nor is there anything like a characteristic that people might find relevant only or mostly in separate evaluation. When people see a case of physical harm in separate evaluation, *they spontaneously "normalize" it by comparing it to other cases of physical harm.*[34] A failed childproof safety cap is, in the category of physical harms, not good – but it is not all that bad. When people see a case of financial harm in separate evaluation, they engage in a similar act of normalization. Repainted cars are, in that category, not good – but not all that bad. Hence the two receive similar ratings and similar awards.

At the same time, people agree that a case of physical harm is generally worse than one of financial harm. It follows that in joint evaluation, the failed safety caps look significantly worse, in the sense that they deserve more severe punishment. The effect of joint evaluation is to dislodge people from their spontaneous use of category-bound judgments. They will think more broadly. In experiments of this kind, joint evaluation has a significant effect because it enlarges the universe of cases about which participants will think. The mechanism is related to that in the context of sex discrimination, where joint evaluation forces a different and better form of deliberation.

There is a broad point about outrage here. Outrage is category-bound, in the sense that the level of felt outrage will be a function of

---

[32] *See* Cass R. Sunstein et al., *Predictably Incoherent Judgments*, 54 STAN. L. REV. 1153 (2002).

[33] *See id.*

[34] *See id.*

category in which the offending behavior falls. If someone cuts in line at an airport security line or makes a rude comment on social media, people might feel high levels of outrage. But if they compare such behavior to (say) child abuse or assault, they might be a bit embarrassed (and feel far less outrage). Punitive damage judgments are a product of outrage.[35] Because outrage is category-bound, preference reversals are essentially inevitable.

Manipulation again

Here again, joint evaluation affords ample opportunity for manipulation in selection of the comparison cases. Suppose that people are thinking about cases involving financial harm. If they are exposed to cases involving rape, financial harm might seem trivial and receive significantly lower ratings. But if they are exposed to cases involving minor acts of trespass on private property, financial harm might seem serious and receive significantly higher ratings. To see the point, compare these cases:

Case A
Jones, an editor at a national news magazine, sexually harassed a female employee; he tried, on several occasions, to kiss her against her will, and he made her extremely uncomfortable at work

Case B
Smith, who has had several tickets for reckless driving, recently hit a pedestrian at night; the pedestrian suffered five broken bones (including a severe concussion)

It is easily imaginable that in separate evaluation, Jones and Smith would receive equally severe punishment, or even that Jones' punishment would be more severe – but that in joint evaluation, Smith's punishment would be more severe. Now imagine a different Case B:

Case B
Smith, a high school student in a rock band, has repeatedly played very loud music late at night, keeping awake his neighbor, Wilson

---

[35] *See* Daniel Kahneman et al., *Shared Outrage and Erratic Awards: The Psychology of Punitive Damages*, 16 J. RISK & UNCERTAINTY 49 (1998).

It is easily imaginable that with joint evaluation, this Case B would produce a higher punishment for Jones than Jones would receive in separate evaluation.

Normative considerations

Notwithstanding these points, it is true that for problems of this kind, joint evaluation has an important advantage over separate evaluation: The latter will produce a pattern of results that people will themselves reject, on reflection.[36] In other words, separate evaluation will yield what separate evaluators will consider to be an incoherent set of results. As noted, punitive damage awards are generally assessed in isolation. The U.S. legal system now forbids juries from considering comparison cases.

That does seem to be a mistake. If we want coherent patterns, joint evaluation is better. But there are two problems with joint evaluation. The first is that it is not global evaluation. If the goal is to produce reasoned outcomes and to prevent what decisionmakers would themselves consider unfairness, they should look at a universe of cases, not two, and not a handful. The second problem is that in these kinds of cases, we might not want to celebrate what comes from either mode of evaluation. In the context of punitive damage awards, we cannot offer a normative judgment without some kind of theory of what punitive damages are *for*. (This point bears on choices and decisions in general.)

Suppose that we adopt an economic perspective, focused on optimal deterrence, and see punitive damage awards as justified to make up for the fact that the probability of detection and compensation is less than 100 percent. If so, the question is whether separate or joint evaluation focuses people on how to achieve optimal deterrence. Unfortunately, neither does so. People are intuitive retributivists.[37] They do not naturally think in terms of optimal deterrence, and they will be reluctant to do so even if they are asked.[38] From the standpoint

---

[36] *See* Daniel Kahneman & Cass R. Sunstein, *Cognitive Psychology of Moral Intuitions, in* NEUROBIOLOGY OF HUMAN VALUES: RESEARCH AND PERSPECTIVES IN NEURO-SCIENCES 91 (Jean-Pierre Changeux, Antonio R. Damasio, Wolf Singer & Yves Christen eds., (2005).

[37] *See* Kahneman et al., *supra* note 35.

[38] *See* Cass R. Sunstein et al., *Do People Want Optimal Deterrence?*, 29 J. LEGAL STUD. 237 (2000).

of optimal deterrence, the conclusion about joint and separate evaluation is simple: a pox on both your houses.

If we embrace a retributive theory of punishment, joint evaluation seems better. On one view, the question is how best to capture the moral outrage of the community, and in separate evaluation, category-bound thinking ensures that the question will not be answered properly (by the community's own lights). But one more time: The major problem with joint evaluation is that it is not global evaluation. That point argues in favor of some effort to broaden the jury's viewscreen to consider cases in light of a range of other cases; to allow reviewing judges to do the same; or to create a damage schedule of some kind.

These conclusions bear on some philosophical questions on which preference reversals have been observed.[39] To summarize a complex story,[40] most people say that they would not push a person off a bridge and in front of a train, even if that is the only way to divert the train and thus to save five people who are in the train's path. But most people say that they would be willing to flip a switch that would divert the train away from the five people and kill a bystander. Typically, the two problems (usually called the footbridge and the trolley problems) are tested separately, and moral intuitions in the two cases diverge.

But what if people assess the problems jointly? The simple answer is that they endeavor to give the same answer to the two questions – either to say that they would save the five or that they would refuse to kill the one. (Perhaps surprisingly, there appears to be no strong movement in the direction of the utilitarian direction, which counsels in favor of saving the five.) But it is not clear how to evaluate this shift. Nor is it even clear that in joint evaluation, people are showing moral consistency. Whether they are doing so depends on *whether, on normative grounds, the footbridge and trolley problems are the same.* The answer depends on whether we accept a utilitarian or nonutilitarian account, and whether we should be utilitarians cannot be dictated by how people respond in joint or separate evaluation.

---

[39] *See* Netta Barak-Corren et al., *If You're Going to Do Wrong, At Least Do It Right: Considering Two Moral Dilemmas at the Same Time Promotes Moral Consistency,* 64 MGMT. SCI. 1528 (2017).

[40] *See* Cass R. Sunstein, *How Do We Know What's Moral?*, N.Y. REV., April 24, 2014.

Contingent Valuation

When regulators engage in cost-benefit analysis, they sometimes have to value goods that are not traded on markets, or for which market evidence is unavailable or unreliable. In such circumstances, they engage in surveys, sometimes described as involving "stated preference" or "contingent valuation."[41] Let us bracket the serious controversies over the usefulness and reliability of these methods and ask a simple question:[42] Do people's valuations differ, depending on whether they see cases separately or jointly?

Consider these cases, in which people were asked about their satisfaction from providing help, on a bounded scale, and also their willingness to pay:

Cause A
Program to improve detection of skin cancer in farm workers

Cause B
Fund to clean up and protect dolphin-breeding locations

When people see the two in isolation, they show a higher satisfaction rating from giving to Cause B, and they are willing to pay about the same.[43] But when they evaluate them jointly, they show a much higher satisfaction rating from A, and they want to pay far more for it.[44] Here, as well, the best explanation involves category-bound thinking.[45] Detection of skin cancer among farm workers is important, but in terms of human health, it may not be the most pressing priority. Protection of dolphins plucks at the heart strings. But most people would want to pay more for the former than the latter, if they are choosing between them.

For contingent valuation, is joint evaluation better than separate evaluation, or vice versa? Is either approach reliable? For those who embrace contingent valuation methods, the goal is to discern how

[41] See J. A. HAUSMAN, CONTINGENT VALUATION: A CRITICAL ASSESSMENT (1993); see also HANDBOOK ON CONTINGENT VALUATION (Anna Alberini & James R. Kahn eds., 2006).

[42] See, e.g., Peter A. Diamond & Jerry A. Hausman, Contingent Valuation: Is Some Number Better than No Number?, 8 J. ECON. PERSPS. 45 (1994).

[43] Daniel Kahneman et al., Economic Preferences or Attitude Expressions?: An Analysis of Dollar Responses to Public Issues, 19 J. RISK & UNCERTAINTY 203, 220 (1999).

[44] Id.

[45] See id.

much informed people value various goods, replicating the idealized use of the willingness-to-pay criterion in well-functioning markets. If that is the goal, separate evaluation faces a serious problem, which is that people make judgments with a narrow viewscreen. On that count, joint evaluation seems better to the extent that it broadens the viewscreen – which means that joint evaluation cannot involve cases from the same category. But even with that proviso, from what category do we find Case B? There is a risk of manipulation here, driving judgments about Case A up or down.

Yet again, global evaluation, or something like it, seems better than joint evaluation, but it is challenging to design anything like it in practice. If the theory of contingent valuation is generally plausible – a big if – then preference reversals give us new reason to emphasize the importance of broad viewscreens for participants.

Evaluating Policies

Do people approve of policies? Which ones? In recent years, that question has produced a growing literature in the context of "nudges" – interventions that respect freedom of choice, but that nonetheless move people in predictable directions.[46] A central finding is that in the domains of safety, health, and the environment, people generally approve of freedom-preserving interventions of the kind that have been adopted or seriously considered in various democracies in recent years.[47] At the same time, majorities generally seem to favor educative nudges, such as mandatory information disclosure, over noneducative nudges, such as default rules.[48]

But do they really? Shai Davidai and Eldar Shafir have shown that in joint evaluation, they do – but that in separate evaluation, they do not.[49] Consider this stylized example:

Policy A
Promote savings by automatically enrolling employees into pension plans, subject to opt out

---

[46] See Janice Y. Jung & Barbara A. Mellers, *American Attitudes toward Nudges*, 11 JUDGMENT & DECISION MAKING 62 (2016) (finding general support for nudges).

[47] See id.; see also CASS R. SUNSTEIN, THE ETHICS OF INFLUENCE (2016).

[48] See Jung & Mellers, *supra* note 46.

[49] Shai Davidai & Eldar Shafir, *Are 'Nudges' Getting a Fair Shot? Joint versus Separate Evaluation*, 4 BEHAV. PUB. POL'Y 1 (2018).

Policy B

Promote savings by giving employees clear, simple information about the benefits of enrolling into pension plans

In joint evaluation, we might find that most people will prefer an educative nudge and also rank it higher on a bounded scale. But in separate evaluation, the rankings might be identical or at least similar.[50] The best explanation, which should now be familiar, involves salience. In separate evaluation, people do not specifically focus on whether a nudge is or is not educative. In joint evaluation, the distinction along that dimension (educative or not?) becomes highly salient, and it drives people's judgments.

Is joint or separate evaluation better? Note that in this context, the question is whether we have reason to trust one or another evaluative judgment. At first glance, the answer seems straightforward. Joint evaluation would be better if, on normative grounds, it is appropriate to make a sharp distinction between the two kinds of nudges. If it is indeed appropriate, joint evaluation is best because it places a bright spotlight on that distinction. But if, on normative grounds, that distinction is entitled to little or no weight, its salience in joint evaluation leads people in the wrong direction. One more time: The problem with joint evaluation is that it draws people's attention very directly to a factor that might deserve little normative weight.

With respect to evaluation of policies, there is a much broader point here, connected with what we have seen in the context of consumer goods. Policy A might look good or bad in the abstract; it might be difficult to evaluate it unless its features are placed in some kind of context. The opportunity to see Policy B can provide helpful information, but it might focus people on what distinguishes Policy A from Policy B, and give it undue prominence. Here again, experimenters, or politicians, can engage in manipulation on this count. Global evaluation would be better, but as before, it is challenging to implement. In cases like those presented by Davidai and Shafir, there is no escaping a normative question: Does the distinction made salient in joint evaluation matter, or not? The normative question must be engaged on its merits, not by asking what people

---

[50] *Id.*

prefer, and how the answer differs depending on joint or separate evaluation. It is tempting, and not wrong, to emphasize that in separate evaluation, people will not pay attention to a factor that might turn out to be critical in joint evaluation. But that is not an answer to the normative question.

What if we are trying to discover what people actually think, or what they think on reflection? In this context, it is reasonable to wonder whether there is an answer to that question, at least for purposes of choosing between joint and separate evaluation. Since people's answers are a product of which kind of evaluation is being asked of them, all that can be said is that to that extent, their preferences are shifting and labile.

How to Decide

For consumer goods, the central question (putting externalities to one side) is which choice will improve the welfare of choosers. In cases subject to preference reversals, the problem is that in separate evaluation, some characteristic of an option is difficult or impossible to evaluate – which means that it will not receive the attention that it may deserve. The risk, then, is that a characteristic that is important to welfare, or actual experience, will be ignored. In joint evaluation, the problem is that the characteristic that is evaluable may receive undue attention. The risk, then, is that a characteristic that is unimportant to welfare, or to actual experience, will be ignored.

Sellers can manipulate choosers in either separate evaluation or joint evaluation, and the design of the manipulation should now be clear. In separate evaluation, the challenge is to show choosers an option with a characteristic that they can evaluate, if it is good (intact dictionary cover), and with a characteristic that they cannot evaluate, if it is not so good (.01 percent Total Harmonic Distortion). In joint evaluation, the challenge is to allow an easy comparison along a dimension that is self-evidently important, even if the difference along that dimension matters little or not at all to experience or to what matters.

If external observers had perfect information, they could of course decide what the chooser should do. The problem is that external observers usually have imperfect information. Among other things, they tend to lack a full sense of the chooser's preferences and values. Nonetheless, we can find easy cases in which separate evaluation is best, and easy cases in which joint evaluation is best, and we are now in a position to understand why some cases are hard. The larger lesson is that separate evaluation and joint evaluation have serious and characteristic defects. Decisions about decisions should be made in a way that structures situations of choice in such a way as to avoid those defects.

7 DECIDING TO CONSUME, 1
In General

To this point, I have not focused directly on actions – on what people *do*. I focus in this chapter on an important subset of those decisions, involving consumption. Here is the central puzzle. Many critics of market relationships have emphasized what they see as their apparently atomistic and alienating nature, and the asocial, highly individualistic attitudes that markets seem to express and to inculcate.[1] Undoubtedly, this account contains a degree of truth; but there is another side. Daily consumption patterns reflect a range of social, even communal impulses. In their consumption choices, consumers relate not only to products but to other customers as well. In consuming mass-produced goods, people often decide to seek, and find, a sense of solidarity and belonging. The impulse toward shared experiences and toward multiple forms of solidarity – sometimes toward simultaneous inclusion and exclusion – persistently reasserts itself.

In these respects, the decisions of ordinary consumers are enmeshed in efforts to build networks of common experiences and identifications. Advertisers of goods are well aware of this point and sometimes attempt to exploit it for economic gain. But even when they do not, an emphatically social impulse plays a large role in consumption choices and in the practices that emerge from them.

---

[1] For an illuminating discussion of the themes of commodity fetishism and alienation, *see* Jon Elster, Making Sense of Marx 100–07 (1985).

Consumers' enjoyment in finding solidarity thus offers another perspective on mass consumption, one very different from that offered by those who emphasize the risks of alienation and fragmentation. That enjoyment also helps explain an assortment of decisions, and decisions about decisions.

Goods and Persons

There are many possible relationships between individual choices and the perceived choices of others. Some goods have the value they do independently of whether other people are enjoying or consuming them. Call these *solitary goods*. The value of a cup of coffee in the morning, or of exercising on a treadmill, may be unaffected by whether others are drinking coffee or exercising. The value of other goods depends, at least in part, on whether or not other people are enjoying or consuming them too. Call these *social goods*. Social goods divide into *solidarity goods* and *exclusivity goods*. Solidarity goods have more value to the extent that other people are enjoying them.[2] The value of a magazine or television program focusing on a current topic may increase significantly if many other people watch or read them. Exclusivity goods, in contrast, diminish in value to the extent that other people are enjoying them. The value of owning an art lithograph, or of vacationing at a holiday resort, may go down, perhaps dramatically, if many others have the same lithograph or access to the same resort. Both producers and consumers attempt to generate a wide range of solidarity goods and exclusivity goods.

It is worthwhile to note here the possibility of complex and varying value functions. Consider Harley-Davidson motorcycles. They sell well for many reasons, but one of them is simple: People want to identify with the set of Harley-Davidson users. It is reasonable to think that the value of identification would be reduced if the number of users increased dramatically, or if the Harley-Davidson became known as the vehicle of choice among, say, investment bankers. A number of goods and activities have characteristics of this kind.

[2] To some people, the term "solidarity" might be taken to suggest more intentional agency than is being suggested here, as in the view that solidarity connotes a conscious decision to associate with or stand by certain people or goals, notwithstanding the risks or costs involved. In most of the cases, a somewhat weaker kind of solidarity is involved. Indeed, solidarity is a possible unintended by-product of solidarity goods.

Solidarity Goods: In General

In many cases, goods become more valuable because and to the extent that they are being widely enjoyed. Consider a popular movie, a presidential debate, a national monument, a drink before dinner, a visit to a historic site, or a millennium celebration. These are goods that are worth less, and are possibly worthless, if many others are not enjoying or "purchasing" them too. Part of what people are willing to pay for, when they enjoy or buy the good, stems from the range of benefits coming from the fact that other people are also enjoying or buying it. Some goods would not be worth consuming, or even having for free, if others did not consume them too. Sometimes the good, taken as a solitary good, has negative value. Producers of goods and services are well aware of this fact; they know that the number of viewers and users will increase, sometimes exponentially, once popularity is known to exceed a certain threshold. When solidarity goods are involved, the fact that many other people are enjoying them creates *positive solidarity externalities*.

The value associated with a solidarity good may be intrinsic, instrumental, or both. People may find it intrinsically pleasurable to enjoy something that others are enjoying too, like a best-selling novel or a song on the car radio. Or they may think that if many people enjoy the good, this will lead to valuable social interactions, even to friendships, business associations, or shared policy initiatives.[3]

---

[3] Solidarity goods have an interesting relationship to network effects, which have received extensive investigation. The standard definition of network externalities refers to increases in the value of some goods that come from the mere fact that many people are using those goods. For example, use of a social media platform may be worth a great deal more by virtue of the fact that other users constitute a network. Who wants to be the only person on a social media platform? Network effects can be understood to turn some goods into solidarity goods of a specific kind. But solidarity goods and network effects are not the same, and the category of solidarity externalities is different from the category of network externalities, above all because of the phenomenon of solidarity in consumption. One might feel solidarity in consumption from being part of a group of people who like Star Wars or Star Trek; one might enjoy the network effect of being on Facebook or Twitter without feeling any kind of solidarity in consumption, from being part of that network. The increase in value from watching a particular television show, stemming from the wide viewing audience for that show and the sense that one is part of a set of people who enjoy that show, is not what is meant by a network externality. Relatedly, many solidarity goods are not restricted to the causal connection that leads to the standard consequence of network effects, which is increasing returns to scale. *See* Michael L. Katz & Carl Shapiro, *Network Externalities, Competition, and Compatibility*, 75 Am. Econ. Rev. 424 (1985); Philip H. Dybvig & Chester S. Spatt, *Adoption Externalities as Public Goods*, 20 J. Pub.

To qualify as solidarity goods, it is not necessary that the relevant goods be enjoyed by people who are literally in each other's company. Some goods are *public* solidarity goods, whereas others are *private* solidarity goods. Public solidarity goods are those that people like to enjoy in the company of others (consider civic celebrations, as for national holidays). Private solidarity goods are those that people like to enjoy by themselves, but with the knowledge that others are enjoying them too. Movies in the theater have, for many, the quality of public solidarity goods; movies viewed online have, for many, the quality of private solidarity goods.

Solitary Goods and Exclusivity Goods

Many goods are solitary goods. Their value is quite independent of whether other people enjoy them. For such goods, it does not matter whether many, few, or none are involved. Some people have this attitude toward sporting events and television programs; drinking a glass of orange juice in the morning, driving a Toyota Camry, or exercising on your treadmill are typical examples for many people.

Exclusivity goods are valued to the extent that they can be enjoyed in small groups or alone. The fact that others are enjoying them makes them worth less, perhaps much less. This is true for certain status-related goods, sometimes described as positional goods,[4] and it is also true for goods that allow or create solitude – a beach house, for example, in a remote area. Often exclusive or near-exclusive enjoyment is a large part of value. In the extreme case, an exclusivity good has the value it has because only one person is able to enjoy it. Of course, producers exploit this property of some goods, by emphasizing their rare or unique character; scarcity may be intentionally manufactured for this purpose, as in the case of the "rare commemorative coin" struck in a limited edition.

ECON. 231 (1983); Mark A. Lemley & David McGowan, *Legal Implications of Network Economic Effects*, 86 CAL. L. REV. 479 (1998). On the distinction between network effects and network externalities – terms often used interchangeably – *see* S. J. Liebowitz & Stephen E. Margolis, *Network Externality: An Uncommon Tragedy*, 8 J. ECON. PERSPS. 133, 135 (1994) (suggesting that "network effects" apply to markets with increasing returns to scale and that "network externalities" should be restricted to markets in which increasing returns create suboptimal conditions).

[4] The term was coined in FRED HIRSCH, SOCIAL LIMITS TO GROWTH (1976). For general discussion, *see* ROBERT H. FRANK, LUXURY FEVER (1999).

Demi-Solidarity Goods and Club Goods

As the Harley-Davidson example suggests, there is an interesting class of goods that do not quite fit any of the three categories; call these *demi-solidarity goods*. For such goods, it is undesirable to see *either* increases in use above a certain point *or* decreases below a certain point. You may want to go to a restaurant, but you will not go either if it is very crowded or if you will be almost alone there. You might choose to attend a political rally only if it is neither very large nor very small. Something similar is often true for decisions about clothing. Many people do not want simply to follow the crowd, but they also do not want to stand out too much. The goods should be popular, but not too popular. For demi-solidarity goods, the number of users matters and may be crucial to choice. But value neither increases nor decreases continuously as a function of that number.

In a related process, people may want to create organizations that represent an ideal combination of solidarity and exclusivity. Many clubs thus provide a special set of demi-solidarity goods. Such clubs are valued partly because they allow a certain group, defined in specified terms, to enjoy goods and activities in common, while at the same time excluding others, also defined in specified terms. Within economics, considerable attention has been given to "club goods," created when a group of people bands together and benefits from sharing a public good, from which they exclude others.[5] Examples include athletic associations, exercise facilities, health maintenance organizations, and political groups with common activities. Club goods typically suffer from crowding, which leads to a reduction in the quality or experience of the relevant services. It is partly for this reason that clubs erect certain barriers to participation through, for example, membership and initiation fees, ceremonies of various sorts, and selection procedures.[6]

For many clubs, moreover, members enjoy not only the provision of some shared service, but also certain common characteristics with other members; this enjoyment has an exclusionary aspect. The preferred characteristics may include gender, geography, education,

---

[5] *See* RICHARD CORNES & TODD SANDLER, THE THEORY OF EXTERNALITIES, PUBLIC GOODS, AND CLUB GOODS 347 (1986).

[6] *See* Laurence R. Iannaccone, *Sacrifice and Stigma: Reducing Free-Riding in Cults, Communes, and Other Collectives*, 100 J. POL. ECON. 271, 276–89 (1992), for a discussion, in this vein, of religious organizations as clubs.

wealth, religion, or race. Here the sharing of club goods may well produce increasing benefits as the number of desired members increases (subject to the risk of crowding), but the benefits decline, for many or for all, if undesired members join. What members like is not only a set of common experiences, but the fact that other people, not defined in the same way, cannot enjoy those experiences. In fact, group identity often depends on the right mix of solidarity and exclusivity.

Who, Not How Many: Partnership and Fraternity Goods

Sometimes people care not only about the sheer number of consumers but also (and perhaps more importantly) about their *identity*, understood in some specific way. Six, or sixty, relevant people may be the critical ones for you; the fact that those people, in particular, are enjoying the relevant good (or not enjoying it) is what makes you especially like it. When the relevant group is relatively small, the choice may help establish or signal a partnership, and people may be said to be enjoying *partnership goods*. In the limiting case, consider a love affair, a close friendship, or a marriage, where the fact of joint consumption may be crucial to the underlying choice (of books, restaurants, movies, or vacation resorts). If more than the two people are also enjoying it, consumption by others may be irrelevant and value may stay constant.

An important feature of some goods is that value increases when a certain number of relevant people enjoy them, but consumption by others reduces value. We have seen that this is true for some clubs; it can also be true in friendships and fraternities, and also in neighborhoods, teams, clubs, ethnic groups, and nations. People may like a good more when it is enjoyed by a large number of people thought to be relevantly like them; advertisers often try to exploit this fact and consumers may react accordingly whether or not they do. But once people in another category start enjoying the good, value decreases, sometimes dramatically.

In the case of "pure" solidarity goods, people care about the sheer number of consumers, and in the case of partnership goods, people care about who the consumers are. But the preceding points suggest an additional class of goods, call them *fraternity goods*, where people care about fellow consumers falling under a certain description or belonging to a particular category (e.g., students, Catholics, athletes). Fraternity goods have a discriminatory element: Not only do you enjoy the party more to the extent that more Catholics come, but your enjoyment decreases if non-Catholics participate too. This is a generalization of the idea of discriminatory clubs – groups self-consciously formed to create club goods that include the local public good of exclusion (subject perhaps to legal controls, themselves subject in turn to constitutional constraints). Ordinary consumer products can have the same feature, with more informal rules of inclusion and exclusion, as, for example, when people of a certain type wear certain clothing, perhaps displaying signals (consider the Harley-Davidson motorcyclists) that outsiders fear, reject, or do not entirely understand.

The Relational Character of Goods

Thus far the discussion has proceeded as if goods qualify or fail to qualify as one of the various types because of what they "are." But this is an oversimplification. The nature of a good, for any particular person, depends not only on its innate qualities but also on how particular people relate to it. Here people differ from one another, often dramatically. It is not possible to "read" the nature of the good off the good itself; it is necessary to know how people react to it, and people, groups, and even cultures typically vary along relevant dimensions.

A workplace lounge may be a solidarity good for some people, who like it best when it is crowded. But it may be a solitary good for others, who go for the coffee, and who do not care how many people are there. And it may be an exclusivity good for others, who like it best or perhaps only when it is empty. A Jane Austen novel may be a solitary good for some, but for the members of a Jane Austen Society, it may be a solidarity (or a demi-solidarity) good instead. Strictly speaking, then, the notion of a solidarity good is a relational one: A given good may be a solidarity good to me, or to you, but not a solidarity good as such. It is therefore more precise to say not that goods "are" solidarity, solitary, or exclusivity goods, but that the value of a good is a function of its solidarity value, solitary value, and exclusivity value. These values can be combined in different ways, both for different people and in the social aggregate. For some people and some goods, exclusivity value is crucial and makes consumption likely, while for others the exclusivity value of the good may be positive but of trivial importance. It is easy to imagine a continuum of values and many possible variations.

Varying Value Functions

We have seen that there can be complex value functions with respect to both solidarity goods and exclusivity goods. These functions include both discontinuities and sudden shifts in direction. There are goods for which value steadily increases with the number of people who consume or enjoy them. There are goods for which value increases up to a certain number of consumers, but does not increase after that point. Perhaps those who watch a presidential debate need to know that millions of people are watching, but the number of millions is not important. We can imagine an exclusivity good for which value decreases with the increase in the number of consumers, but from a certain point it stays constant. Perhaps a beach is an example: Once it is crowded, it does not much matter, to the privacy lover, how much more crowded it gets.

Decreases and Increases in Value

Why do some goods decrease or increase in value when others are enjoying them? The case of decreases is the simplest. Some goods, to some people, are status goods or, somewhat more broadly, positional goods. Their value comes from the fact that they are not widely accessible, and people like them because ownership provides a signal about the owner's status. Sometimes the most important point is the person's self-conception. Ownership of a rare good may enable the owner to think of herself as original or as a person of refined taste; mass consumption of the good will make it seem vulgar. In addition, sometimes people value solitude and often people dislike crowds. Some exclusivity goods help to ensure solitude or relative solitude, and to prevent congestion or intrusion. People might enjoy going to a nature preserve, a museum, or a beach most when few others are there; and they might be willing to pay a premium to be able to do so.

There are several reasons why value might increase with the number of users:

1. People may be able to participate in valuable social interactions, and other activities, because of their consumption of certain goods. Part of what they get from those goods is the relevant social interactions. For example, those who watch a sports event or a popular television show may be able to have a range of conversations by the water cooler at work. Those who visit national parks may be able

to talk about the visit with their friends (whether this creates or reduces value for the friends is another question). People who follow a presidential campaign may be able to understand and enjoy a range of newspaper articles and television programs that would otherwise be unintelligible.

2. The fact that a good is widely enjoyed may relieve people's anxiety about whether it is reasonable or legitimate to enjoy that good. People may not know whether it is appropriate or proper to enjoy a football game or a romantic comedy or a cigar; the fact that other people enjoy it removes a potential sense of embarrassment or shame. Or people may feel proud that they are enjoying something on which others have placed a kind of stamp of approval.

3. People care about their reputations, and if other people are doing something, it is often reasonable to infer that other people will think well of those who do the same thing, and possibly less well of those who do something different. The value of a certain activity or purchase may increase as its popularity increases, not because of the information provided by popularity, but because of the desirable reputational effects of joining the crowd (or the undesirable reputational effects of not joining the crowd). We can imagine cases in which reputational effects are the most important consideration in consumption choices. The phenomena of cascade effects and tipping points can sometimes be understood in the light of perceived reputational factors; when a critical mass is reached, a very large number of people may end up doing the same thing. A related point is that people may engage in a certain activity in order to signal their "type," and if large numbers of people will be listening, or if the signal is a distinctive one, the signal might be amplified, or amplified in the right way.[7]

The Role of Markets and States

Solidarity goods are often generated spontaneously and without any governmental effort to steer people in their direction. But in some cases, people will have difficulty in coordinating their actions, often because of transaction costs, including a lack of information. In addition, some solidarity goods cause harm to those who use or enjoy them. When

---

[7] On signaling, see ERIC POSNER, LAW AND SOCIAL NORMS (2000).

people choose certain goods because of an *inaccurate* belief that other people are choosing them, it is entirely legitimate for the state to correct their misperceptions. In the most interesting cases, people choose a good because of an *accurate* belief about what other people are choosing, but they wish that other people were choosing otherwise. There is an important sense in which the autonomy of these people is being violated.

Under reasonable assumptions, the relevant choices cannot be changed without public intervention. The government might therefore seek to alter an undesirable equilibrium in which people fail to converge on a solidarity good, when such convergence would be in their interest as they perceive it. Or the government might intervene when people succeed in converging on a bad solidarity good, when non-convergence, or convergence on another good, would be in their interest as they perceive it. People might fail to converge on a good or service, or end up with a shared, bad course of action, even though non-excludability is not a problem in the least. Hence government action will be justified even if no public good is involved. This is the sense in which an understanding of solidarity goods provides a distinctive rationale for state intervention.

Social Glue and External Benefits

In thinking about the role of the law, it is important to begin with a general point: A society that contains few solidarity goods is likely to have a wide range of problems. The claim is not that shared experiences and memories are always pleasant (they may in fact be traumatic), but that they are important to the sense that diverse people are engaged in a shared endeavor, to social stability, and to many important social values. To the extent that solidarity goods help unify diverse people around common symbols and experiences, they can be an ingredient in social cohesion and peace (consider national celebrations, discussed later). When such goods are salient and numerous, people may be more likely to exhibit solidarity: They can come to see one another more distinctly and more directly as fellow citizens with common interests and experiences. A great deal of attention has been given to the idea of "social capital," a term that refers largely to relationships that promote reciprocity.[8] But it is also helpful to see that societies require a large degree of "solidarity capital," that is, shared endeavors and experiences

---

[8] *See* ROBERT D. PUTNAM, BOWLING ALONE (2000).

that will help spur relations of trust. Other things being equal, a large amount of solidarity capital will help spur altruistic behavior and help promote social norms that solve collective action problems.

Solidarity goods may also produce external benefits that are not adequately captured by individual choices. Assume, for example, that the benefits of educational programming, or public affairs television, are not captured by individual viewers; much of the benefit is obtained by others, who learn from those who watch. This is a conventional third-party benefit, and such benefits can come from solidarity goods, as from all other kinds. But there are also distinctive externalities associated with solidarity goods – above all, the externalities that follow from various forms of social glue. If people are able to interact in productive and congenial ways in part because of the existence of solidarity goods, they themselves will certainly benefit, and third parties will benefit as well. The inculcation of group identity, or patriotism and a general interest in public affairs, are cases in point. (This is not to deny the potential bad effects of patriotism and citizen engagement.) The problem here is generating a sufficient number and density of solidarity goods of the socially desirable kind.

Thus far the emphasis has been on subjective values. But if the evaluation of social well-being does not depend solely on aggregated pains and pleasures, we might think that there is objective solidarity value to (for example) programs on civic topics, or to visits to pristine areas and cultural institutions, and that this objective value outruns their subjective solidarity value. If the good effects of these experiences cannot be measured solely by reference to private preferences, the objective solidarity value may be higher than the aggregate of subjective solidarity values. There are of course questions here about the extent to which the government's role is merely to satisfy existing preferences, or whether it is legitimate for it to subject some such preferences to critical evaluation. For many people, some solidarity goods deserve public protection not merely to solve coordination problems but because of the desirable effects of some of those goods on the development of preferences and beliefs; consider cultural subsidies and environmental protection.

A Solidarity Game

As we have seen, people can and will generate solidarity goods spontaneously. Acting as a result of producer efforts or entirely on

Table 7.1 A solidarity game

	Debate watch	Sleep
Debate watch	(5,5)	(3,4)
Sleep	(4,3)	(4,4)

their own, groups of consumers turn certain products into solidarity goods. But in some circumstances, people will not be able to succeed independently. More particularly, the generation of solidarity goods can create a collective action problem involving coordination.[9] Here the government has a possible role.

To see the basic point, imagine a simple two-person society. On plausible assumptions, such a society will fail to produce a solidarity good – for illustration, a shared viewing of a late-night presidential debate – unless the collective action problem can be overcome. Assume that the benefit of individual viewing of the debate is 3; that the benefit of sleep, at the relevant time, is 4; and that the benefit of joint viewing of the debate is 5. The pay-off structure will be as in Table 7.1.

Note that the best cell overall is obviously the upper left. It also provides a stable equilibrium, in the sense that once both parties are there, there is no incentive to deviate; this is not a prisoner's dilemma. It may, however, be a problem for the participants to get to the right place in the first instance. Row-chooser, not knowing what column-chooser will choose, will think this: If I choose to watch the debate, the worst I can get is 3 (when I'm a lone debate-watcher, while column-chooser sleeps). If I choose sleep, I get 4 no matter what column-chooser does. If row-chooser has no idea what column-chooser will do, and if he seeks to be on the safe side and to maximize his worst-case scenario, he will choose to sleep. Since the situation is symmetrical, column-chooser thinks the same way. The result may well be that the two will end up at (4,4), which is also a stable equilibrium. What they need is a method that will bring them to (5,5) instead.[10]

The situation captured by this matrix may bring to mind the coordination case known as the battle of the sexes: While she may

---

[9] See, e.g., EDNA ULLMANN-MARGALIT, THE EMERGENCE OF NORMS 77–133 (1977); DOUGLAS G. BAIRD ET AL., GAME THEORY AND THE LAW 191–95 (1994).

[10] This is a version of the so-called assurance game. See AMARTYA SEN, CHOICE, WELFARE AND MEASUREMENT 78–79 (1982).

prefer going to the cinema and he to the football game, both still prefer to go together rather than going their own separate ways. This is a situation in which the participants want above all else to do the same thing, and the problem is how to coordinate on the one thing that each will choose. The battle-of-the-sexes case may therefore be seen as involving two or more solidarity goods, and it is in this sense a special case of the collective action problem we are here discussing. In the general case of solidarity goods there is no assumption that the participants' overall preference is to coordinate. They simply have, among their options, one whose value for them increases to the extent that others choose it too.

Two people, or small groups, can usually solve this kind of problem on their own. A brief discussion, providing mutual assurances, should be sufficient.[11] ("Let us read this book together.") The difficulty is far more acute in larger groups, where rational and boundedly rational people may settle on inferior options simply because communication and mutual assurance can be costly and difficult. Suppose, for example, that many people seek a method to celebrate the memory of Martin Luther King, Jr. or of Yitzhak Rabin. It is possible to make some progress simply through private efforts and educational campaigns, dedicating a certain period to their memory. Some successful efforts might eventually generate significant solidarity benefits. But it is easy to imagine circumstances in which this will not happen. Perhaps people have difficulty communicating with one another, or perhaps they lack the relevant information (involving, for example, the solidarity benefits that would follow from simultaneity).

Under certain assumptions, the best approach would be a government advertising campaign or even the declaration of a national memorial event or holiday. Note that the main function of the advertising campaign or of the declaration is not coercive, but rather coordinating. The goal is to signal a solution that is preferred by all or most. Similarly, consider a situation in which a certain television program would have a great deal of value, both individual and collective, but if and only if large numbers of people watched it. In a period of numerous entertainment options, it might be difficult to coordinate on the best outcome, in which most or all watch.

---

[11] For evidence, *see* ROBERT C. ELLICKSON, ORDER WITHOUT LAW: HOW NEIGHBORS SETTLE DISPUTES (1994).

Once the government provides the focal point, the desirable outcome is self-enforcing and does not require further monitoring and enforcement (as opposed to, say, paying taxes or maintaining clean air). As a real-world analogue, consider the widespread phenomenon of "compliance without enforcement" – private compliance with laws that are enforced rarely or not at all, where compliance often reflects a solution to a problem of coordination,[12] and sometimes involves the production of solidarity goods.

It follows that when a solidarity good is involved, the government might want to consider going beyond the provision of information and mandate consumption, on the theory that such a mandate will not, by hypothesis, have high costs or produce significant complaints. If people really want to embark on a shared course of action, a government mandate will ensure that they are able to do what they want to do. Of course, information might well be sufficient, and because it is less intrusive, it should be presumed preferable to mandates.

Where the Law Can Help

If an unregulated market underproduces solidarity goods, the government and the law might help. Of course, a detailed investigation would be necessary to establish whether and how coordination problems might be solved in the relevant domains. Consider a few possibilities.

Media Policy

Much news and entertainment programming has the quality of a solidarity good. For many people, the value of such programming dramatically increases when many people are watching. There is a no mystery why this should be so. Part of the reason is the social benefits that come after the show has been watched; various interactions are made possible through this route. Sometimes such programming provides desirable third-party effects. Sometimes it generates a range of external social benefits.

Consider in this regard Elihu Katz's discussion of Israel's one-channel television policy, ensuring, when it was first introduced to the

---

[12] See Robert A. Kagan & Jerome H. Skolnick, *Banning Smoking: Compliance without Enforcement, in* SMOKING POLICY: LAW, POLITICS AND CULTURE (Stephen D. Sugarman & Robert L. Rabin eds., 1993).

country in the late 1960s, that television "controlled by the Broadcasting Authority was the only show in town."[13] From the standpoint of democracy, any such policy is obviously troublesome. But from that same standpoint, it is not only troublesome: Within two years of the inauguration television,

> almost all households owned television sets, and almost everybody watched almost everything on the one monopolistic channel. ... [H]awks and doves watched it—and largely believed it; Jews and Arabs watched it—and largely believed it; even Arabs across the borders paid attention. ... Moreover, the shared experience of viewing often made for conversation across ideological divides. ... [T]he shared central space of television news and public affairs constituted a virtual town meeting. ... The lesson of the first twenty years of Israeli television is that participatory democracy may be enhanced, rather than impeded, by gathering its citizens in a single public space set aside for receiving and discussing reliable reports on the issues of the day.[14]

Katz draws attention to the dark side of the increasing segmentation of the television market and hence the decreased provision of solidarity goods on the media, in the form of dangers for "altruism, patriotism, collectivity orientation, ideological politics, or the civic need for a shared public space."[15] It is not necessary to think that a one-channel policy is best or even tolerable in order to recognize that shared viewing, providing common experiences for most or all, can be extremely valuable from the democratic point of view. In a period in which online experiences, with countless options, have helped to create social fragmentation, and a high degree of enmity and outrage. Katz' argument should have particular resonance. And if Katz is right, it makes sense for the government to consider policies (for example, through public subsidies) that would promote widely viewed, high-quality programming; consider public television. It also makes sense for the government to consider other routes by which to promote goods that will have a large solidarity value. Many cities, for example, subsidize sports teams through taxpayer funds, a subsidy that might easier to justify

---

[13] Elihu Katz, *And Deliver Us from Segmentation*, 546 ANNALS AM. ACAD. POL. SOC. SCI. 22, 28 (1996).

[14] *Id.* at 28–29.

[15] *Id.* at 33.

with reference to the solidarity value, for many people in a heteroge-neous city, of shared entertainment of this kind.

In the United States, compare the Federal Communication Commission's "fairness doctrine," now largely abandoned but once requiring radio and television broadcasters to devote time to public issues and to allow an opportunity for opposing views to speak. The latter prong of the doctrine was designed to ensure that listeners would not be exposed to a single view without being exposed to others – if one view was covered, the opposing position would have to be allowed a right of access. When the Federal Communications Commission aban-doned the fairness doctrine, it did so on the ground that this second prong led broadcasters, much of the time, to avoid controversial issues entirely, and to present views in a way that suggested blandness and uniformity.[16] The elimination of the fairness doctrine did indeed pro-duce a flowering of controversial substantive programming, frequently expressing extreme views of one kind or another.[17]

Typically, this is regarded as a story of wonderfully success-ful deregulation, because the effects of eliminating the fairness doc-trine were precisely what was sought and intended. But if solidarity goods are important, the picture is far more complicated. The growth of issues-oriented programming – expressing strong, often extreme views – has resulted in further balkanization of the speech market and greatly diminished the range of common experiences. To say the least, it is reasonable to think that this is a problem for a democracy with diverse people.[18]

Public Celebrations and Holidays

Public celebrations become widely shared events, enjoyed by large numbers of people at the same time. For many people, a national holiday is emphatically a solidarity good, helping members of a hetero-geneous nation create, and benefit from, a shared identity and shared experiences. When the government devotes a day to celebrate national independence, or to honor the memory of a person of significance, it

---

[16] See Syracuse Peace Council v. FCC, 867 F.2d 654, 665 (D.C. Cir. 1989).

[17] See Thomas W. Hazlett & David W. Sosa, Was the Fairness Doctrine a "Chilling Effect"? Evidence from the Postderegulation Radio Market, 26 J. LEGAL STUD. 279 (1997) (offering an affirmative answer to the question in the title).

[18] See CASS R. SUNSTEIN, REPUBLIC.COM (2001), for a more detailed discussion.

is, on plausible assumptions, ensuring a form of coordination that private persons cannot easily provide on their own. National holidays, so deemed by the law and accompanied by taxpayer funds, can be justified on this ground.

A particular point here has to do with the *expressive* function of official (as opposed to purely private) action.[19] If the celebration does not have the imprimatur of the public as a whole, it is less likely to carry with it the signal that would produce the desired broad response. True, the public imprimatur may backfire when people do not trust the government, and it is also possible that some people will feel that the government has unjustifiably intruded on their freedom of action. But these adverse reactions are less likely to occur when the event in question is perceived to be a solidarity good.

Culture and the Environment

Environmental and cultural amenities often have the value they do because they have been enjoyed by many people over time, and will be enjoyed by many people in the future. When the law protects a historic site and immunizes it from development, part of the justification is to ensure the solidarity value that comes from its continued existence. The same is true for protection of museums and pristine areas, enjoyed by many people as such. Wildlife refuges, operating as focal points that are also solidarity goods, have a similar function. This is not at all to claim that initiatives of this kind are defensible only or mostly as a means of providing solidarity goods. The basic justification must be made on other grounds.[20] But insofar as public expenditures support areas and activities that can be enjoyed by many or all, the gains associated with solidarity value count in their favor.

Dissipating Pluralistic Ignorance

Notwithstanding their status as such, many solidarity goods can cause serious problems, stemming from the existence of harm to others or to self. Consider in this regard the following possible solidarity goods:

---

[19] *See* Cass R. Sunstein, *On the Expressive Function of Law*, 144 U. Pa. L. Rev. 2021 (1996).

[20] *See, e.g.*, Ronald Dworkin, *Can a Liberal State Support Art?*, *in* A Matter of Principle 221 (1985).

criminal conduct, including conspiracy; use of illegal drugs or guns; dangerous driving; smoking; discriminating on the basis of race and sex. Many people are far more likely to engage in the relevant conduct if other people are doing so, partly because of informational and reputational effects, but also if and when the relevant experiences are genuine solidarity goods, providing increased enjoyment and reduced risk. The individual interest in engaging in activity that is harmful, to self and to others, may well increase if other people are doing the same thing.

If many important social bads are also solidarity goods, it is possible to imagine some distinctive strategies for the state, strategies that are both legitimate and promising. An initial goal should be to correct mistaken signals of large social involvement, to the point where the numbers begin to "tip" in the opposite direction. Suppose that the government wishes (by hypothesis, legitimately) to deter people from engaging in certain activity. Suppose too that most people who are choosing that activity do so with a mistaken belief about the number of other people who are choosing it too. For example, people might be purchasing unlawful drugs, or violating the tax laws, or engaging in "binge drinking" because they believe that this is what most people are doing. There should be no objection to government efforts to clarify the situation, by making clear what the facts actually are.

Of various efforts to increase the level of voluntary compliance with the tax laws, one of the more promising is simply to publicize the currently high level of voluntary compliance.[21] Once informed that most people comply fully, and voluntarily, many of those who would otherwise violate the law end up complying too. With respect to binge drinking, the evidence is also striking.[22] Here, universities have had great difficulty in producing successful strategies. But the level of binge drinking on most campuses, while high, tends to be far lower than most students think. Once the actual level is publicized, binge drinking is reduced still further. Part of the reason is that drinking is a solidarity good, and once the number of binge drinkers is shown to be surprisingly low, its solidarity value decreases accordingly. The example is easily generalizable.

[21] See, e.g., STEPHEN COLEMAN, THE MINNESOTA INCOME TAX COMPLIANCE EXPERIMENT: STATE TAX RESULTS (Minn. Dep't Revenue, 1996).

[22] See H. Wesley Perkins, *College Student Misperceptions of Alcohol and Other Drug Norms among Peers, in* DESIGNING ALCOHOL AND OTHER DRUG PREVENTION PROGRAMS IN HIGHER EDUCATION 177–206 (US Dep't Educ. 1997).

In such cases, the government is attempting to counteract pluralistic ignorance – people's lack of information about what other people are thinking and doing. When the choice of goods or actions is a product of the perceived behavior of others, and when the perception is false, the most successful way of controlling behavior may well be to tell people the truth. It follows that if the government wants to increase the level of an activity, and when solidarity value is motivating the behavior of many people, an appropriate strategy is to inform people that most other people are doing the same thing. So long as the government's end is legitimate, there should be no objection to efforts of this sort.

A more difficult problem will arise if the government decides that it is hard to dissipate pluralistic ignorance, or expensive to do so, and seeks to reduce or ban the relevant behavior on the grounds that if well informed, people would not engage in it. Ordinarily, the proper response to insufficiently informed choices is to provide information. But if this is not feasible, it seems reasonable to say that the government should steer people (through incentives if not through bans) in the direction of the choices that they would make if they knew the facts. Where the lack of information involves the relevant actions of others, however, the best way to respect autonomy is to have a strong presumption in favor of more information, and against more aggressive intervention.

Yet another problem, and possibly a less tractable one, will arise when the criminal conduct in question is not strictly a solidarity good but rather falls under the category of partnership goods. Suppose that certain people are more likely to engage in the relevant conduct not because many or most others do, but because particular others do. When it is a specific reference group that matters, rather than sheer numbers, providing more information about sheer numbers will not solve the problem. Other strategies will have to be devised.

Bad Solidarity Goods: Solidarity and Norms

In many cases, people are far from ignorant about the number of others who are choosing the relevant goods. They know the facts and they are responding to what they know. On a standard view, the analysis is then straightforward: Does the government have a legitimate reason to interfere with private choices because, for example, a public good is involved? The standard view overlooks a collective action problem of a distinctive kind. This problem occurs when the typical chooser is choosing as he does because of the actual (not merely perceived) choices of others, and when the typical chooser wishes that those actual choices were otherwise. Of course, it is possible, under certain conditions, for people to solve this problem on their own, simply by communicating their wishes. But especially when large numbers are involved, people may have a hard time finding their way to their preferred solution.

The situation here is likely to be a coordination game of the type outlined earlier, with an important difference. The choice of the solidarity good for both (say, joint use of drugs) produces less value, for both players, than does either the choice of a solitary good for each (say, an early night at home for one, a night at the library for the other), or a solidarity good of a different kind for both. For risk-taking or discriminatory activity of various sorts, this will often be the situation. Sometimes people will engage in activity together even though they would be better off if they could agree not to do so, or perhaps to converge on some other joint project. People are stuck in a bad equilibrium, and it is difficult for them to find their way to a new one. Here the analysis would be similar in structure to that offered with debate–sleep, but with the government helping people to shift away from, rather than toward, the solidarity good.

In many of these cases, people receive little solitary value from the good or activity in question. Possible examples, for many people, include committing crimes, using drugs, carrying a gun, and driving dangerously. In cases of this kind, the solidarity value is all or part of what drives behavior. The problem is that the relevant choosers wish to stop their practice.[23] They wish to be discouraged from doing what they do, through a general change in the practices of other people. Often their desire is to alter a prevailing social norm, which helps make the solidarity good attractive. Notice in this connection that many employers, hotels, and restaurants that were forbidden from discriminating by the Civil Rights Act of 1964 actually supported the prohibition, as a way of breaking a self-defeating equilibrium.[24] Or people might want, for example, to produce a population-wide norm against engaging in such risk-producing activity as reckless driving or smoking (solidarity

---

[23] *See* the treatment of second-order desires in Harry G. Frankfurt, *Freedom of the Will and the Concept of a Person*, 68 J. PHIL. 5 (1971).

[24] *See* Lawrence Lessig, *The Regulation of Social Meaning*, 62 U. CHI. L. REV. 943 (1995).

goods for many), in part so that the social meaning of either action is not "bravery" or "rejecting oppressive convention" but "stupidity" or "irredeemable recklessness."

Sometimes solidarity entrepreneurs succeed in this endeavor. But even assertive people can have difficulty in changing the prevailing norm, and the resulting social meaning, on their own.[25] Here the government and the law might help, and there should be no objection, in terms of legitimacy, to remedial efforts, even if no public goods are involved. If the problem is only one of coordination, information might be sufficient. If people nonetheless are unable to coordinate, a more coercive approach might be justified. Here the government might attempt to produce a new situation, perhaps one in which solidarity value comes from shared activity of the different kind. Of course, an approach of this sort might be ineffectual. The point is not that the government will succeed, but that there is no objection, in principle, to an effort, by the state as well as private actors, to establish a new equilibrium. An understanding of the solidarity value associated with certain activities thus suggests the legitimacy of policy initiatives designed to move people away from (harmful) existing choices and toward an equilibrium that they genuinely prefer.

[25] See id.

8 DECIDING TO CONSUME, 2
The Case of Social Media

In this chapter, I am going to cover a lot of territory, and it will be useful to put the main point on the table at the outset. As we shall see, there is evidence that use of Facebook makes people, on average, a bit less happy – more likely to be depressed, more likely to be anxious, less satisfied with their lives. The effect should not be overstated. It isn't large. But it is real. At the same time, people who have ceased using Facebook, and experienced evident increases in well-being, *very much want to continue to use Facebook*. In fact, they would demand a lot of money to give it up. Why is that? We do not know for sure, but a plausible explanation is that the experience of using Facebook, including the information its use provides, is valuable even if it does not make people happier. Ignorance isn't bliss. People know that. They want the relevant information *because they like or even cherish a sense of connection with relevant others*. Consistent with the discussion in Chapter 7, they want to use Facebook because other people are using Facebook.

It is important to emphasize that social media do not simply provide information, at least not in the sense that I have been emphasizing here. You might decide to use Facebook to connect with family or friends. You may or may not think that you will learn something that matters to your economic situation or to your health. But social media are, in one or another respect, about the transmission of information, even if the category is understood more broadly than I have been doing thus far. A central question is this: How valuable are they, really?

On social media, much of the relevant information is free, at least in the sense that you can get it without turning over money. You might be paying by providing your attention or your data. Companies such as Facebook and Twitter obtain revenue from advertising. But in light of continuing controversies, there have been serious discussions about changing the business model to one in which users are asked to pay for use of the relevant platforms and the services that they provide.[1] These discussions have been accompanied by more theoretical discussions about the appropriate economic valuation of their platforms. What if people were required to pay to use Facebook? How much would they be willing to spend?

The answers would tell us something important about decisions to use social media and to seek information in general. Answering those questions might also help answer more fundamental questions about economic valuation; about the potentially expressive quality of some consumption decisions; and about the disparity between traditional economic measures and actual human welfare. An answer would bear on policy and regulation as well.

A general issue, of special interest in behavioral economics, is the potential disparity between willingness to pay (WTP) and willingness to accept (WTA). If we are interested in welfare, is the best question how much people would be willing to pay to use (say) Facebook, or instead how much they would demand to stop using it? A great deal of work has explored the *endowment effect*,[2] which suggests that people demand far more to give up certain goods than they would pay to obtain those goods in the first instance. The endowment effect is controversial, at least in the sense that there is a debate about its domain, its sources, and its magnitude.[3] We might wonder whether WTA to use social media is greater than WTP not to use social media and, if so, whether the standard explanations account for any such disparity.

---

[1] There are also controversies, of course, centered on whether people's privacy is being invaded and whether they know how their information is being used. For relevant discussion, overlapping with the analysis here, *see* Angela G. Winegar & Cass R. Sunstein, *How Much Is Data Privacy Worth? A Preliminary Investigation*, 42 J. CONSUMER POL'Y 425 (2019).

[2] *See, e.g.,* RICHARD H. THALER, MISBEHAVING: THE MAKING OF BEHAVIORAL ECONOMICS (2015).

[3] *See* Charles R. Plott & Kathryn Zeiler, *The Willingness to Pay-Willingness to Accept Gap, the "Endowment Effect," Subject Misconceptions, and Experimental Procedures for Eliciting Valuations*, 95 AM. ECON. REV. 530 (2005).

An equally general and even more basic question involves the relationship between WTP (or WTA) measures and human welfare. We have seen that within economics, it is common to say that people's WTP for goods is the best available measure of the welfare effects of having those goods. Of course, WTP is the standard measure in actual markets. Note, however, that to produce a WTP figure, people have to solve a prediction problem – that is, they have to predict the effects of the good on their welfare. Solving that problem may seem easy, especially for familiar commodities with which people have experience (shoes, shirts, soap). But for some goods, finding a solution may be especially difficult, especially for unfamiliar commodities for which people lack experience. How is it possible for people to generate a monetary measure to capture the likely welfare effects of a good that they have never had?

For many people, Facebook, Twitter, Instagram, and other social media platforms are anything but unfamiliar; people have a great deal of experience with them. But it is not easy for users of social media to value such platforms in monetary terms. An understanding of WTP in the context of social media tells us something general about the uncertain link between WTP and welfare in the context of information-seeking (see chapter 3) – and should motivate a more direct inquiry into welfare effects. WTP is a mere proxy for those effects, and in some cases, is not a good one. The task is to figure out exactly why and to design substitutes. My goal here is to make some progress on that task.

A Superendowment Effect

In April 2018, I conducted a pilot experiment to obtain some preliminary answers to valuation questions. Using Amazon Mechanical Turk, I asked 439 Facebook users to say how much their use of the platform is worth. More specifically, I asked 215 Facebook users a simple question: "Suppose that you had to pay for the use of Facebook. How much would you be willing to pay, at most, per month?" At the same time, I asked 234 other Facebook users a different question: "Suppose that you are being offered money to stop using Facebook. How much would you have to be paid per month, at a minimum, to make it worth your while to stop using Facebook?"

The first question asks about WTP, whereas the second focuses on WTA. According to standard economic theory, the two questions should produce identical answers. But behavioral economists have shown that in important contexts, they do not.[4] In many experiments, WTA is about twice as much as WTP. This is evidence of the endowment effect, which means that people value what they have far more than they value what they do not have, even if the two commodities are identical.[5] For example, people would pay less to buy a coffee mug or lottery ticket than they would demand to give up a coffee mug or a lottery ticket that they already own.[6] One question I sought to answer is whether an endowment effect would be observed for use of social media; another question is its magnitude.

For WTP, the median answer was just $1 per month. The average was $7.38. Most strikingly, nearly half of participants (46 percent) said that they would pay $0 for a month of Facebook use. In the context of WTP, valuation of Facebook was extremely low. Many users appear to think that it is worthless!

For WTA, by contrast, the median answer was $59 per month. The average was $74.99.[7] In the context of WTA, Facebook has genuine value, and it is not small. It should be clear that the disparity between WTP and WTA is unusually large. We might describe it as a *superendowment effect*. This is in contrast to the 1:2 ratio often observed in previous studies (and also in contrast, of course, to the finding of no

---

[4] *See* Daniel Kahneman et al., *Experimental Tests of the Endowment Effect and the Coase Theorem*, 98 J. POL. ECON. 1325 (1990).

[5] *See id.; see also* Keith M. Marzilli Ericson & Andreas Fuster, *The Endowment Effect*, 6 ANN. REV. ECON. 555 (2014); Carey K. Morewedge & Colleen E. Giblin, *Explanations of the Endowment Effect: An Integrative Review*, 19 TRENDS COGNITIVE SCI. 339 (2015).

[6] *See, e.g.*, Christoph Kogler et al., *Real and Hypothetical Endowment Effects when Exchanging Lottery Tickets: Is Regret a Better Explanation than Loss Aversion?*, 37 J. ECON. PSYCH. 42 (2013). The endowment effect is often attributed to loss aversion, but that explanation does not appear to be complete. *See id.; see also* Morewedge & Giblin, *supra* note 5.

[7] None of the demographic differences (sex, race, education, income, region) was significant, but in light of the small sample, it would be a mistake to make much of this. I might note, however, that for both men and women, the median response to the first question was $1 and that the male average was $7.98 and the female $6.92; that the Republican median was $2, with an average of $11; that the Democratic median was $1, with an average of $8.74; and that the Independent median was zero, with an average of $3.36. For the second question, the male median was $57, and the average was $75.44; the female median was $59, and the average was $74.63. The Republican median was $59, with an average of $78.25; the Democratic median was $53, with an average of $71.34; the Independent median was $60, with an average of $77.14.

Table 8.1 Results from nationally representative survey

	WTP		WTA	
	Median	Mean	Median	Mean
Instagram	$5	$21.67	$100	$102.60
LinkedIn	$8	$25.71	$99	$97.80
Pinterest	$5	$20.97	$100	$102.92
Reddit	$10	$27.73	$99	$97.73
Snapchat	$5	$24.92	$100	$106.20
Twitter	$5	$19.94	$100	$104.18
WhatsApp	$10	$34.90	$100	$101.16
YouTube	$5	$17.27	$88	$90.78

endowment effect for money tokens, for goods held for resale, and sometimes for goods with well-established economic values).[8]

I followed my first survey with a larger one, involving a nationally representative sample. The survey also divided people into two groups, asking the same two questions. But it focused on a wide assortment of social media platforms, and it included people who did not use those platforms. The results were broadly in line with those in the pilot survey, but with some interesting differences across platforms.

For the entire population, the median WTP for the use of Facebook was $5, with a mean of $16.99. The WTA numbers were much higher: $87.50 and $89.17. The figures were close for Facebook users: a median of $5 and a mean of $17.40 for WTP, and $64.00 and $75.16 for WTA. For people who do not use Facebook, the median WTP number was $4, with a mean of $16.70. The WTA answers were surprisingly high: a median of $98.50 and a mean of $98.90. (The relatively high mean for people who do not use Facebook is a bit of a mystery.)

The patterns were broadly similar for other social media platforms, as shown in Table 8.1. For simplicity, I will restrict the figures to actual users:

---

[8] Some questions about the underpinnings and domain of the endowment effect are raised in Plott & Zeiler, *supra* note 3. Clarifying discussions can be found in Ericson & Fuster, *supra* note 5, and Andrea Isoni et al., *The Willingness to Pay-Willingness to Accept Gap, the "Endowment Effect," Subject Misconceptions, and Experimental Procedures for Eliciting Valuations: Comment*, 101 AM. ECON. REV. 991 (2011).

For all of the tested social media outlets, the patterns are strikingly similar. Most intriguingly, WTP is far lower than WTA, sometimes with a ratio (for the medians) of 1:20. I am unaware of any area in which the disparity between WTP and WTA is so high.

The magnitude of the difference raises a puzzle, to which I will turn shortly. By way of comparison, it is useful to consider the environmental setting, in which large disparities have also been observed between WTP and WTA in surveys.[9] One study found that people would demand about five times as much to allow the destruction of trees in a park as they would pay to prevent the destruction of those same trees.[10] When hunters were questioned about the potential destruction of a duck habitat, they said that they would be willing to pay an average of $247 to prevent the loss – but would demand no less than $1,044 to allow it.[11] In another study, participants required payments to accept the degradation of visibility from air pollution ranging from five to more than sixteen times higher than their valuations based on how much they were willing to pay to prevent the same degradation.[12] These disparities are not as high as those observed in the context of social media, but they are also unusually large.

Wasting Time Goods

We will return shortly to the environmental domain. In the social media surveys, the most obvious mystery is the very low median for WTP (with many people saying that they would be willing to pay nothing at all). It is plausible to think that for many digital goods, a similarly low WTP would be observed, at least in surveys. This is a puzzle. From actual behavior, social media seem to have real value for users. Their use, sometimes extending to many hours per week, would seem to be demonstrative of a positive valuation. Is it even plausible to think that for a substantial percentage of them, the value is zero, or close to it?

---

[9] *See, e.g.,* Cass R. Sunstein, *Endogenous Preferences, Environmental Law*, 22 J. Legal Stud. 217 (1993); Simon Dietz & Frank Venmans, *The Endowment Effect, Discounting and the Environment*, 97 J. Env't Econ. & Mgmt. 67 (2019).

[10] David S. Brookshire & Don L. Coursey, *Measuring the Value of a Public Good: An Empirical Comparison of Elicitation Procedures*, 77 Am. Econ. Rev. 554 (1987).

[11] Judd Hammack & Gardner Mallard Brown Jr., Waterfowl and Wetlands: Toward Bioeconomic Analysis (1974).

[12] Robert D. Rowe et al., *An Experiment on the Economic Value of Visibility*, 7 J. Env't Econ. & Mgmt. 1 (1980).

One possibility is that for such people, social media represent a good that they use, but that they also consider, on reflection, to be useless or valueless. Facebook might be a way of spending time, through habit or perhaps even a kind of addiction – but people might nonetheless think that they would be better off, or as well off, doing something else instead. On this account, there are some goods – call them *wasting time goods* – for which there is an interesting but explicable disparity between choices and valuation. People choose to use or consume wasting time goods, but they would not be willing to pay much, if anything, for the right to continue to do so. Or they might decide to use such goods, but they would decide to decide not to do so, if only they were put in a good position to make a second-order decision.

In my view, wasting time goods are real, important, and understudied. Social media may well count as such for some users. But I speculate that the low WTP numbers are not adequately or fully explicable in those terms. The reason for the low WTP figures may well be *expressive*. For some people, they are in the nature of protest answers, and to that extent, they are not at all a reliable measure of the welfare benefits of using Facebook, Twitter, or YouTube. In short: Having had to pay nothing to use such platforms, people much dislike the idea of suddenly having to pay a monthly fee. When people say that they are willing to pay zero or only slightly more, they are effectively announcing: "If you are going to start charging me, well, then, forget about it!" The reference point has been zero, and a sudden charge (even if it is small) is taken to be unfair, not least because it is a loss from the status quo.[13]

Something similar might be said about those who said that they would pay only a small monthly amount (say, $5). They might well have been registering their displeasure at the idea of suddenly having to buy something that has long been provided gratis. Here, then, is a reason to think that the low median WTP does not offer adequate information about the welfare effects of using social media platforms.

Return to the environmental studies in this light. It would be easy to imagine studies of clean air or clean water that would also generate puzzlingly low WTP figures, and for the same reasons: A good once enjoyed for free is now being subject to some kind of charge. Loss

[13] *See* Daniel Kahneman et al., *Fairness and the Assumptions of Economics*, 59 J. Bus. S285 (1986).

aversion undoubtedly plays some kind of role here as well. If people are asked to pay more than the reference point (in this case, zero), they will rebel. They might well think that the change is unfair, and hence gice the protest answer. If so, there is a fair question whether the response to survey questions would be predictive of actual behavior in real markets. People might say that they would pay nothing or give a very low number in a survey, but once a price actually emerged, they might be willing to pay it. After a short period, or after the norm changes, they might get over their initial feelings of outrage. Whether and to what extent this is so is of course an empirical question.

But in the environmental studies listed earlier, the real puzzles come from the high WTA numbers. In general, such numbers can be a questionable proxy for welfare effects. One reason is that in the environmental context, a high figure for WTA might reflect a kind of *moral outrage* (no less than a zero answer for WTP). For an environmental good (clean air, safe drinking water, an endangered species), the WTA question undoubtedly triggers moral concerns, producing protest answers of their own. Some people might even think that it is morally abhorrent to allow members of endangered species to be lost or the air to be made dirtier in return for a specified amount of money. Trading money for some such loss might be seen as a taboo trade-off. The same moral outrage might lead to a high WTA figure.

Protest answers can also be found when moral concerns are not present and when people are asked how much they would accept to give up some entitlement that they enjoy, such as a right to vacation time. Some people might well think: "There is no amount of money that can get me to give up my vacation time!"[14] In some settings, people might resent the very idea that "someone" is trying to pay them to stop doing what they are planning to do. Their resentment might well manifest itself in a high WTA figure (including for use of social media).

Here as well, there remains a question whether and to what extent answers in survey questions would map onto actual behavior. It is easy to decline money in a hypothetical survey setting, and much harder to do so when real money is on the line. Nonetheless, it might well be the case that moral concerns, or a sense of entitlement, will be expressed in market settings.[15]

[14] *See id.*
[15] *See* TRUMAN F. BEWLEY, WHY WAGES DON'T FALL DURING A RECESSION (1999).

There is a separate point, and it involves opportunity costs. The WTP question puts opportunity costs on the cognitive table, at least for many people much of the time: When people are asked how much they are willing to pay for some good X, they are often going to think about what else they could do with that money. The WTA question is different. When people say that they would demand a very high amount of money to give up some good that they own (coffee mugs, lottery tickets), they might not be focused on the potential uses of that money.[16] For that reason, there is reason to doubt whether a high median, in response to the WTA question, is sufficiently informative about the welfare effects of using a social media platform.

Welfare

These points suggest severe limitations to both WTP and WTA surveys as measures of the welfare effects of digital goods that have formerly been provided for free. Expressive answers might well be found for WTP questions, and resentment might infect answers to WTA questions.

In real markets, of course, different results might be expected. Some media outlets, such as the *New York Times* and the *Washington Post*, have shifted to require paid subscriptions, rather than providing free content (as they previously did). In surveys, elicited WTP might have been far lower than actual WTP as observed through behavior. For subscribers to formerly free services, initial resentment, resulting in some kind of expressive reaction, might recede in favor of a welfare calculation, in which people decide how much the good is worth to them. As I have noted, it remains to be determined when and by how much WTP or WTA figures, elicited in surveys, would differ from those that are observed in behavior.

In a much more elaborate study, Brynjolfsson et al. tried to value use of Facebook by asking consumers if they would prefer (a)

---

[16] *See* Shane Frederick et al., *Opportunity Cost Neglect*, 36 J. CONSUMER RSCH. 553 (2009). In the environmental context, another factor is at work: conscience. If people are being asked how much they would demand to allow destruction of (say) polar bears, they might say that no amount is high enough, or they might give an amount that signals not the welfare effects (for them) of destruction of polar bears, but their feeling of responsibility for a terrible loss. On some of the issues here, *see* Eric Posner & Cass R. Sunstein, *Moral Commitments in Cost-Benefit Analysis*, 103 VA. L. REV. 1809 (2017).

to maintain access to the platform or (b) to give it up for one month in response to a specified payment.[17] With their method – a *discrete choice experiment* – they asked people to choose between two identified options and to specify the one they valued more. It is important to see that a discrete choice experiment ought to avoid some of the distortions of both WTP and WTA.[18] At the same time, it cannot avoid an endowment effect: The relevant questions will be asked to people who either are, or are not, current "owners" of the good at issue.

Brynjolfsson et al. also used a large, nationally representative sample, limited to Facebook users. The median answer was in the general vicinity of $50 to give up Facebook for a month (significantly higher than my WTP answers, and significantly lower than my WTA answers). Aware of various technical limitations in their study, Brynjolfsson et al. do not insist on those particular numbers. But they do urge that digital goods, including social media, are producing large, monetizable benefits that are not included in conventional measures of well-being, such as gross domestic product. That conclusion is both important and plausible. Nonetheless, it is important to add two qualifications.

The first, signaled by my own surveys, is that whatever numbers are generated will be an artifact of the particular method that is used. If different methods produce different numbers, then it might be challenging to decide which one is the best measure of economic value. For goods that have been provided free, WTP numbers might not be reliable because they might well reflect resentment about being asked to pay for such goods. WTA numbers might be better, but they have the problems outlined earlier. If the goal is to capture welfare effects, discrete choice experiments are probably best, but insofar as the relevant questions are posed to current users, they will embody a kind of endowment effect.

The second and more fundamental, point is that we need better measures of the effects of such goods on people's experienced well-being.[19] Brynjolfsson et al. title their impressive paper "Using Massive Online Choice Experiments to Measure Changes in Well-Being," but

[17] Erik Brynjolfsson et al., *Using Massive Online Choice Experiments to Measure Changes in Well-Being*, 116 PROC. NAT'L ACAD. SCI. 7250 (2019). I am focusing only on a portion of their study here; it has a number of illuminating findings.

[18] *See* Edward J. McCaffery et al., *Framing the Jury: Cognitive Perspectives on Pain and Suffering Awards*, 81 VA. L. REV. 1341 (1995).

[19] For relevant discussion, *see* PAUL DOLAN, HAPPINESS BY DESIGN (2014).

well-being is emphatically not what they are measuring. At best, they are measuring *predictions* of well-being.[20]

People might be willing to pay $5 each month for the right to use Facebook, or demand $100 to give up that right. In discrete choice experiments, the median value might turn out to be $50. But what are the effects of Facebook on actual experience? Are people enjoying life more or less or the same? Those are the important questions. WTP and WTA numbers and the outcomes of discrete choice experiments are best understood as reflecting people's predictions about effects on well-being, translated into monetary terms. Once more: The actual effects are what matter.[21]

Paying to Be Sadder

Another group of economists, led by Hunt Allcott of New York University, tried to explore those actual effects. They found that getting off Facebook appears to increase people's well-being (and significantly decreases political polarization).[22] As we shall see, there is a real puzzle here.

Allcott and his coauthors began by asking 2,884 Facebook users, in November 2018, how much money they would demand to deactivate their accounts for a period of four weeks, ending just after the midterm election. To make their experiment manageable, the researchers focused on about 60 percent of users, who said that they would be willing to deactivate their accounts for under $102. The researchers divided those users into two groups. The treatment group was paid to deactivate. The control group was not. Members of both groups were asked a battery of questions, exploring how getting off Facebook affected their lives.

---

[20] I am bracketing here the possibility that the answers may reflect reactions, cognitive or emotional, to being asked the questions, as in the case of protest answers.

[21] *See* John Bronsteen et al., *Well-Being Analysis vs. Cost-Benefit Analysis*, 62 Duke L.J. 1603 (2013); Cass R. Sunstein, The Cost-Benefit Revolution (2018). On two of the different components of well-being – pleasure and purpose – *see* Dolan, *supra* note 19. It is possible that for many users of social media, pleasure is increased, but not purpose. It is possible that for many users, neither pleasure nor purpose is increased, and use is in the nature of an addiction, reducing rather than increasing welfare. It is also true that an analysis of welfare effects will ultimately lead to serious philosophical issues. *See* Matthew D. Adler, Well-Being and Fair Distribution (2011).

[22] Hunt Allcott et al., *The Welfare Effects of Social Media*, 110 Am. Econ. Rev. 629 (2020).

The most striking finding is that even in that short period, those who deactivated their accounts seemed to enjoy their lives more as a result. In response to survey questions, they showed significant decreases in depression and anxiety. They also showed significant improvements in both happiness and life satisfaction. Why is that? One reason may be that deactivating Facebook gave people a nice gift: about sixty minutes per day on average. Those who got off the platform spent that time with friends and family, and also watching television alone. Interestingly, they did not spend more time online (which means that contrary to what you might expect, they did not replace Facebook with other social media platforms, such as Instagram).

Getting off Facebook also led people to pay less attention to politics. Those in the treatment group were less likely to give the right answers to questions about recent news events. They were also less likely to say that they followed political news. Perhaps as a result, deactivating Facebook led to a major decrease in political polarization. On political questions, Democrats and Republicans in the treatment group disagreed less sharply than did those in the control group. (This is not because the groups were different; members of both groups, selected randomly, were equally willing to give up use of Facebook for the right amount of money.) It is reasonable to speculate that while people learn about politics on their Facebook page, what they see is skewed in the direction they prefer – which leads to greater polarization.

At this point, it is reasonable to think that getting off Facebook really does improve well-being, properly understood. But there is a serious complication. After one month without Facebook, the median amount that users would demand to deactivate their account for another month was still pretty high: $87. The United States has 240 million Facebook users. If we assume that the median user demands $87 to give up use of the platform for a month, a little multiplication suggests that the platform is providing Americans with massive benefits: if each user gets the equivalent of $87 in benefits per month, the total amount is in the hundreds of billions annually.

With that finding in mind, Allcott and his coauthors offer a strong conclusion: Facebook produces "enormous flows of consumer surplus," in the form of those hundreds of billions of dollars in benefits, for which users pay nothing at all (at least not in monetary terms). But that might not be right. Recall that those who deactivated their accounts reported that they were better off along multiple dimensions – happier, more satisfied with their lives, less anxious, less depressed. So here is a real paradox: Facebook users are willing to pay a significant sum of money, each month, to make themselves more miserable!

The Paradox

To resolve the paradox, consider two possibilities. The first is that what matters is people's actual experience. When people say that they would demand $87 to give up use of Facebook for a month, they are making a big mistake. The monetary figure might reflect a simple habit (maybe people are just used to having Facebook in their lives), or a prevailing social norm, or even a kind of addiction. The second possibility is that when people say that they would demand $87, they are *not making a mistake at all*. They are telling us something important about what they value.

Mistaken Forecasts

Begin with the first possibility. People who decide to use social media platforms might not know that they are being made sad or anxious. They might simply lack that information. They might go online because that is the norm in their social group, or because doing that has become habitual. As with other addictions, the problem might be that the pain of not going online is intense; it is not as if going online is pleasurable. When they break the habit or addiction, they are better off.

If that is so, the mystery is why they demand $87 to stop using Facebook for another month even after they have had a pretty good month without it. Recall that when people decide to buy goods or services, they are usually making forecasts about welfare effects. We have seen that if the good is familiar and if the chooser has experience with it, the prediction problem might not be so serious. But we have also seen that even in such cases, that problem has other dimensions, if it is to be solved properly. *The chooser has to figure out the welfare effects of alternative uses of the money.* That is a complex endeavor.

In a sense, the chooser is in the position of a social(ist) planner, as discussed by F. A. Hayek: He faces a serious epistemic problem. Suppose that the planner is trying to decide on prices or quantities of goods – shoes, socks, pens, cell phones, cars. As Hayek showed, the problem is that the market, reflecting the judgments and tastes of numerous people, will incorporate an extraordinary amount of dispersed knowledge, inaccessible to the planner who seeks to set prices or to decide quantity.[23] Along one dimension, the case of the individual chooser is analogous. The problem is that at time 1, the chooser may know far too little about his likely experience at times 2, 3, 4, 5, 6, and so forth. The chooser may lack important facts about those items for which he is now deciding how much to pay. The chooser may also lack facts about his future self – about exactly what he will be like and will like. The problem is especially acute if people are likely to change in relevant ways.

As I have emphasized, the epistemic problem is harder for some options than for others. As between ice cream and cake, people know what they like best, and in that sense what will promote their welfare. They also have a rough-and-ready sense of alternative uses of the money; even if they do not, the stakes are not so high. But for many options, people lack experience. What is it like to vacation in Bermuda? To see the Mona Lisa? To go to the best restaurant in Los Angeles? To live with ringing in the ears or chronic bronchitis? To have heart disease? To lose a child? The prediction problem is formidable. And yet the WTP measure requires people to try to solve it, certainly when they are deciding how much to pay to eliminate risks.

For social media platforms, some of these problems dissipate. Users have relevant experience; the platforms are part of their lives. For that reason, we might trust WTP or WTA measures, if expressive values could be purged, and we might think that discrete choice experiments tell us something important. Even so, welfare is the master value, and monetary amounts, however elicited, are unlikely to tell us everything that we need to know about welfare.

What People Value

The underlying data raise another point, and it may be equally fundamental. Survey answers about personal well-being – including anxiety and depression – fail to capture everything that people really care about. For example, Allcott and his coauthors show that Facebook users know more about politics. Those who follow politics might become more anxious and depressed – but a lot of people still follow

[23] F. A. Hayek, *The Use of Knowledge in Society*, 35 AM. ECON. REV. 519 (1945).

politics. They don't follow politics to be happy. They follow politics because they are curious and because they think that's what good citizens do. Similarly, Facebook users might want to know what their friends are doing and thinking because that's good to know, whether or not that knowledge makes them happier (recall the discussion of solidarity goods in chapter 7).

Answers to hard questions about the welfare effects of social media platforms are starting to emerge.[24] Aside from the Allcott et al. study just described, the results are complicated and mixed. In terms of depression and anxiety, those effects can be very bad. Use of Facebook and other social media platforms seems to have different effects on people with different personality traits and on members of different demographic groups.[25] It certainly has different effects on qualitatively different *components* of well-being.[26] Moreover, Facebook does not provide a uniform or unitary experience. Different uses of Facebook, and different ways of spending time on the platform, undoubtedly have different effects on users' well-being.

There is a large point here. As we have seen, people often want information for reasons that have nothing to do with the hedonic effects. In Chapter 3, I emphasized the instrumental value of information – as, for example, when people want health-related information even if it makes them sad, because they might be able to use that information to become healthier. Undoubtedly many people who use social media like doing so for instrumental reasons. But the motivation is surely broader than that. Many of them think that it is good to know things about family and friends or about the world, even if that information cannot be used in any way. They are undoubtedly thinking about what it means to have a good or full life. Having that kind of information is valuable even if it has no instrumental value and even if its hedonic value is negative.

---

[24] *See* Xiaomeng Hu et al., *The Facebook Paradox: Effects of Facebooking on Individuals' Social Relationships and Psychological Well-Being*, 8 FRONTIERS PSYCH. 87 (2017); Sebastián Valenzuela et al., *Is There Social Capital in a Social Network Site?: Facebook Use and College Students' Life Satisfaction, Trust, and Participation*, 14 J. COMPUT.-MEDIATED COMMC'N 875 (2009); Edson C. Tandoc, Jr. et al., *Facebook Use, Envy, and Depression among College Students: Is Facebook Depressing?*, 43 COMPUTS. HUM. BEHAV. 139 (2015); Ethan Kross et al., *Facebook Use Predicts Declines in Subjective Well-Being in Young Adults*, 14 PLoS ONE E69841 (2013).

[25] *See* Kross et al., *supra* note 24.

[26] *See* Valenzuela et al., *supra* note 24.

9 DECIDING BY ALGORITHM

Deciding by algorithm is an increasingly pervasive second-order strategy. It is often chosen under a framework very much like that in Chapter 1. Suppose, for example, that a doctor is deciding how to treat a patient who has chest pains; that an employer is deciding whom to hire; that a chess player is deciding what move to make in a high-stakes competition; that a homeowner is deciding whether to purchase flood insurance; that officials at the Internal Revenue Service are deciding whom to audit; that a customer is deciding what car to buy; that a recently divorced woman is deciding whom to date. In cases of this kind, would an algorithm be helpful? How helpful? Should people be making decisions by algorithms? Are algorithms biased? If so, in what respect?

I offer a simple claim here, one that is meant to offer two-and-a-half cheers for deciding by algorithm. The claim is that *algorithms can overcome the harmful effects of cognitive biases, which often have a strong hold on people whose job it is to avoid them, and whose training and experience might be expected to allow them to do so.* The background fact, and the motivation for that claim, is that many questions present *prediction problems*, in which people must make some prediction about a future state of the world. In many contexts, algorithms will make better predictions than people will, and to that extent, it might well make sense to decide by algorithm.

There are important qualifications. As we have seen, accuracy may not be the only goal. People may or may not like to decide. If they like to decide, and if they prefer to exercise their own agency, they might not want to rely on an algorithm, even if the algorithm is really accurate. But if people do *not* like to decide, and if they do not want to exercise their own agency, deciding by algorithm might be especially appealing, even if the algorithm is not terribly accurate. We need to know, in short, whether deciding is a cost, a benefit, or neither. What is clear is that in many domains, consultation of an algorithm, or even a decision by algorithm, might greatly increase accuracy.

In a way, this should be an unsurprising claim. Some of the oldest and most influential work in behavioral science shows that statistical prediction often outperforms clinical prediction; one reason involves cognitive biases on the part of clinicians.[1] Algorithms can be seen as a modern form of statistical prediction, and if they avoid biases, no one should be amazed. What I hope to add here is a concrete demonstration of this point in some important contexts, with some general remarks designed to address the concern that algorithms are "biased."

Before we begin, we need to define "algorithm." Consider a procedure for deciding when to drink alcohol: one drink every week, on Saturday night. Is that an algorithm? Consider a procedure for deciding whether to exercise: once a day, late in the afternoon. Is that an algorithm? Consider a procedure for deciding whether to exceed the speed limit: never. We can think of a rule, or a set of rules, as an algorithm, and a rule, or a set of rules, might greatly simplify decisions (see Chapter 1). In ordinary language, however, the term is usually reserved for computers, machine learning, and artificial intelligence. I will be adopting that ordinary usage here.

Jail, Bail, and Heart Attacks

Let us begin with some research from Jon Kleinberg, Himabindu Lakkaraju, Jure Leskovec, Jens Ludwig, and Sendhil Mullainathan, who explore judges' decisions about whether to release criminal defendants pending trial.[2] Their goal is to compare the performance of an algorithm with that of actual human judges, with particular emphasis on the solution to prediction problems. It should be obvious that

[1] *See* Paul E. Meehl, Clinical Versus Statistical Prediction (2013 ed. 1953).
[2] Jon Kleinberg et al., *Human Decisions and Machine Predictions*, 133 Q.J. Econ. 237 (2017).

the decision whether to release defendants has large consequences. If defendants are incarcerated, the long-term consequences can be very severe. Their lives can be ruined. But if defendants are released, they might flee the jurisdiction or commit crimes. People might be assaulted, raped, or killed. And while the decision whether to release criminal defendants pending trial is highly unusual in many ways, my goal here is to draw some general lessons, applicable to ordinary life, about the choice between decision by human beings and decision by algorithms, and about the decision to decide by one or the other.

In some jurisdictions in the United States, the decision whether to allow pretrial release turns on a single question: flight risk. It follows that judges have to solve a prediction problem: *What is the likelihood that a defendant will flee the jurisdiction?* In other jurisdictions, the likelihood of crime also matters, and it too presents a prediction problem: *What is the likelihood that a defendant will commit a crime?* (As it turns out, flight risk and crime are closely correlated, so that if one accurately predicts the first, one will accurately predict the second as well.) Kleinberg and his colleagues built an algorithm that uses, as inputs, the same data available to judges at the time of the bail hearing, such as prior criminal history and the offense with which the defendant has been charged. Their central finding is that *along every dimension that matters, the algorithm does much better than real-world judges.* Among other things:

1. Use of the algorithm could maintain the same detention rate now produced by human judges and reduce crime by up to 24.7 percent. Alternatively, use of the algorithm could maintain the current level of crime reduction and reduce jail rates by as much as 41.9 percent. That means that if the algorithm were used instead of judges, thousands of crimes could be prevented without jailing even one additional person! Alternatively, thousands of people could be released, pending trial, without adding to the crime rate. It should be clear that use of the algorithm would allow any number of political choices about how to balance decreases in the crime rate against decreases in the detention rate.
2. A major mistake made by human judges is that they release many people identified by the algorithm as especially high risk (meaning likely to flee or to commit crimes). More specifically, judges release 48.5 percent of the defendants judged by the algorithm to fall in the riskiest

1 percent. Those defendants fail to reappear in court 56.3 percent of the time. They are rearrested at a rate of 62.7 percent. Judges show leniency to a population that is more likely to commit crimes.

3. Some judges are especially strict, in the sense that they are especially reluctant to allow bail – but their strictness is not limited to the riskiest defendants. If it were, the strictest judges could jail as many people as they now do, but with a 75.8 percent increase in reduction of crime. Alternatively, they could keep the current crime reduction, and jail only 48.2 percent as many people as they now do.

A full account of why the algorithm outperforms judges would require an elaborate treatment. But for my purposes here, a central part of the explanation is particularly revealing. As point (3) suggests, judges do poorly with the highest-risk cases. (This point holds for the whole population of judges, not merely for those who are most strict.) The reason is an identifiable bias; call it *Current Offense Bias.*[3] We are talking about judges, of course, but the point holds for decisions of all kinds, including those that we make every day. If we are subject to similar biases – and we are – we might be interested in consulting an algorithm, and possibly even in letting it decide for us.

In focusing on Current Offense Bias, Kleinberg and his colleagues restrict their analysis to two brief sentences, but those sentences have immense importance.[4] As it turns out, judges make two fundamental mistakes. First, they treat high-risk defendants as if they were low-risk *when their current charge is relatively minor* (e.g., the charge may be a misdemeanor). Second, they treat low-risk people as if they were high-risk *when their current charge is especially serious.* The algorithm makes neither mistake. It gives the current charge its appropriate weight. It takes that charge in the context of other relevant features of the defendant's background, neither overweighting nor underweighting it. The fact that judges release a number of the high-risk defendants is attributable, in large part, to overweighting the current charge (when it is not especially serious).

Intriguing work by Ludwig and Mullainathan has suggested another reason that algorithms do better than human judges.[5] Even

[3] *Id.* at 284.

[4] *Id.*

[5] Jens Ludwig & Sendhil Mullainathan, *Algorithmic Behavioral Science: Machine Learning as a Tool for Scientific Discovery* (Chicago Booth, Working Paper No. 22–15, 2022).

after controlling for race, skin color, and demographics, judges give more weight than do algorithms to the defendant's mugshot! As Ludwig and Mullainathan put it, "the mugshot predicts judge behavior: how the defendant looks correlates strongly with whether the judge chooses to jail them or not."[6] Perhaps unsurprisingly, judges are responsive to whether the mugshot shows that defendant as "well-groomed": Judges are more likely to release defendants whose faces are clean and tidy as opposed to unkempt, disheveled, and messy. Perhaps surprisingly, judges are more likely to release defendants whose mugshots show them as "heavy-faced" (with a wider or puffier face). Call it *Mugshot Bias*.

The bail study has a sibling, one that involves doctors.[7] The central question here involves diagnosis of heart attacks. Whom do doctors test, and when do they test them? Would an algorithm do better? Here as well, doctors must solve a prediction problem: What is the probability that a patient is suffering from a certain condition, such that a test is worthwhile? In the domain of heart attacks, it turns out that doctors test a lot of people who should not be tested, and fail to test a lot of people who should be tested. More specifically, doctors order a number of tests that are unlikely to find anything of interest – and thus waste a lot of money. It also turns out that doctors do not test many patients that the algorithm rightly predicts will be "high-yield," in the sense that they indeed have acute coronary syndromes. The central results are precisely parallel to those in the bail study. Use of the algorithm could save a great deal of money (by reducing unnecessary and unhelpful tests), could prevent a number of deaths, or both.

Why do doctors err, compared to algorithms? As in the bail study, much of the answer lies in cognitive biases. Doctors give excessive weight to highly salient symptoms, such as chest pain, especially when those symptoms fit the stereotype of a heart attack. It is true, of course, that chest pains can be associated with heart attacks. The problem is that doctors give them more weight than they should. By contrast, the algorithm gives such symptoms something closer to the appropriate weight. Call it *Current Symptoms Bias*. Doctors also give undue weight to demographics; call it *Demographic Bias*. For example, doctors over-test older patients relative to their actual risks. If doctors

---

[6] *Id.* at 2 (emphasis omitted).

[7] Sendhil Mullainathan & Ziad Obermeyer, *Diagnosing Physician Error: A Machine Learning Approach to Low-Value Health Care*, 137 Q.J. ECON. 679 (2022).

had relied on algorithms in deciding whom to test, they could have avoided those biases, again saving money, lives, or both.

Biases Everywhere

When human beings suffer from a cognitive bias, a well-designed algorithm, attempting to solve a prediction problem, can do much better. Here is a simple illustration. When a baby is born, the nurse or doctor might well give them an Apgar score, developed in 1952 by Virginia Apgar, an obstetric anesthesiologist. The evaluator measures the baby's color, heart rate, reflexes, muscle tone, and respiratory effort, sometimes described as a "backronym" for Apgar's name. The Apgar score refers to *appearance* (skin color), *pulse* (heart rate), *grimace* (reflexes), *activity* (muscle tone), and *respiration* (breathing rate and effort). In the Apgar test, each of these five measures is given a score of 0, 1, or 2. The highest possible total score is 10, which is rare. A score of 7 or above is considered indicative of good health. You can think of an Apgar score as a simple algorithm, even though it does not involve a computer or artificial intelligence. And the Apgar test works; a central reason is that it greatly reduces the potential effects of biases in human judgment.

It is worth emphasizing that in both law and medicine, we are dealing not with novices, but with human beings who are both trained and experienced. They are experts. Nonetheless, they suffer from cognitive biases that produce severe and systematic errors. Current Offense Bias is best understood as a close cousin of *availability bias*: When we make judgments about probability, we often ask whether relevant examples are easily brought to mind.[8] In general, doctors are subject to availability bias;[9] for example, their decisions about whether to test patients for pulmonary embolism are affected by whether they have recently had a patient diagnosed with pulmonary embolism.[10]

---

[8] *See* Amos Tversky & Daniel Kahneman, *Judgment Under Uncertainty: Heuristics and Biases, in* JUDGMENT UNDER UNCERTAINTY: HEURISTICS AND BIASES 3 (Daniel Kahneman et al. eds., 1982).

[9] *See* Ping Li et al., *Availability Bias Causes Misdiagnoses by Physicians: Direct Evidence from a Randomized Control Trial*, 59 INTERNAL MED. 3141 (2020).

[10] *See* Dan P. Ly, *The Influence of the Availability Heuristic on Physicians in the Emergency Department*, 78 ANALYSIS EMERGENCY MED. 650 (2021); *see also* Carmen Fernández-Aguilar et al., *Use of Heuristics during the Clinical Decision Process from Family Care Physicians in Real Conditions*, 28 J. EVALUATION CLINICAL PRAC. 135 (2022).

Mugshot Bias, Current Symptom Bias, and Demographic Bias are best understood as forms of *representativeness bias*: Individual judgments about probability are frequently based on whether the known feature of a person or situation is representative of, or similar to, some unknown fact or condition.

All these biases involve *attribute substitution.*[11] Availability bias is product of the availability heuristic, which people use to solve prediction problems. We substitute a relatively easy question ("Does an example come to mind?") for a difficult one ("What is the statistical risk?"). Current Offense Bias reflects what we might call the Current Offense Heuristic, which also involves a relatively easy question ("How bad was the current offense?"), substituted for a harder one ("What is the flight risk?"). Representativeness bias is a product of the representativeness heuristic, which people also use to solve prediction problems. They substitute a relatively easy question ("Is the feature of the case representative of or similar to some fact?") for a difficult one ("What is the statistical fact?"). Apparently judges fall prey to the Mugshot Heuristic (an example of the representativeness heuristic, and doctors use the Current Symptom Heuristic (an example of the availability heuristic) and the Demography Heuristic (the representativeness heuristic once more).

Because of the availability heuristic, people are likely to think that more words, on a random page, end with the letters "ing" than have "n" as their next to last letter – even though a moment's reflection will show that this could not possibly be the case.[12] Furthermore, "a class whose instances are easily retrieved will appear more numerous than a class of equal frequency whose instances are less retrievable."[13] Consider a simple study showing people a list of well-known people of both sexes, and asking them whether the list contains more names of women or more names of men. In lists in which the men were especially famous, people thought that there were more names of men, whereas in lists in which the women were the more famous, people thought that there were more names of women.[14]

---

[11] *See* Daniel Kahneman & Shane Frederick, *Representativeness Revisited: Attribute Substitution in Intuitive Judgment, in* HEURISTICS AND BIASES: THE PSYCHOLOGY OF INTUITIVE JUDGMENT 49, 49–81 (Thomas Gilovich et al. eds., 2002); DANIEL KAHNEMAN, THINKING, FAST AND SLOW (2011).

[12] *See* Tversky & Kahneman, *supra* note 8.

[13] *Id.* at 11.

[14] *Id.*

This is a point about how *familiarity* can affect the availability of instances, and thus produce mistaken solutions to prediction problems. A risk that is familiar, like that associated with smoking, will be seen as more serious than a risk that is less familiar, like that associated with sunbathing. But *salience* is important as well. For example, "the impact of seeing a house burning on the subjective probability of such accidents is probably greater than the impact of reading about a fire in the local paper."[15] Current Symptom Bias reflects the power of salience. *Recency* matters as well. Because recent events tend to be more easily recalled, they will have a disproportionate effect on probability judgments. Availability bias thus helps account for "recency bias."[16] Current Offense Bias can be understood as a sibling to recency bias.

In many domains, people have to solve prediction problems in order to make decisions, and availability bias and representativeness bias can lead to damaging and costly mistakes. Whether people buy insurance for natural disasters is greatly affected by recent experiences.[17] If floods have not occurred in the immediate past, people who live on flood plains are far less likely to purchase insurance. In the aftermath of an earthquake, purchases of insurance for earthquakes rise sharply – but they decline steadily from that point, as vivid memories recede. Note that the use of the availability heuristic, in these contexts, is hardly irrational. Both insurance and precautionary measures can be expensive, and what has happened before seems, much of the time, to be the best available guide to what will happen again. The problem is that the availability heuristic can lead to serious errors, in terms of both excessive fear and neglect.

If the goal is to make accurate predictions, use of algorithms can be a great boon. For individuals, and for both private and public institutions (including governments all over the world), it can reduce or eliminate the effects of cognitive biases. Suppose that the question is whether to open an office in a new city; whether a project will be completed within six months; whether a particular intervention will help a patient who suffers from diabetes and cancer. In all of these cases, some kind of cognitive bias may well distort human decisions. There is a good chance that availability bias, representative bias, or one of their

---

[15] *Id.*
[16] *See* Robert H. Ashton & Jane Kennedy, *Eliminating Recency with Self-Review: The Case of Auditors' 'Going Concern' Judgments*, 15 J. BEHAV. DECISION MAKING 221 (2002).
[17] *See* PAUL SLOVIC, THE PERCEPTION OF RISK 40 (2000).

cousins will play a large role. Algorithms have extraordinary promise. They can save both money and lives.

There is an important qualification. We might easily imagine that in some contexts, algorithms generally perform better than human beings do – but also that in those very contexts, algorithms do not perform better than *all* human beings do. In other words, the best doctors might do better than algorithms, and the best human judges might do better than algorithms. What about the top 5 percent of human beings? Do they do better than algorithms do? Some important work suggests that while algorithms outperform 90 percent of human judges in the context of bail decisions, the best 10 percent of people outperform algorithms.[18] The reason appears to be that the best judges have and use private information to make better decisions. For example, they might learn something about the particular defendant, perhaps from the courtroom discussion, that the algorithm does not know.

There is a large lesson here: Algorithms may lack information that human beings have, and for that reason, some human beings might be able to outperform algorithms. By contrast, the low-performing judges do not use such information for the better; on the contrary, they become more likely to keep low-risk defendants in prison if they have recently heard about a case, unrelated to the current one, in which another defendant committed a violent offense during release. This overreaction appears to reflect a behavioral bias, closely akin to or perhaps a form of the availability bias.

Noise

There is an independent problem. People are not merely biased; they are also noisy.[19] To see the difference between bias and noise, imagine two bathroom scales. The first scale is cruel: Every day, it shows you as ten pounds heavier than you actually are. The second scale is capricious: On some days, it shows you as ten pounds heavier than you actually are; on other days, it shows you as ten pounds lighter than you actually are. The cruel scale is biased, in the sense that it is systematically wrong, and in a predictable direction. The capricious scale is noisy, in the sense that it shows unwanted variability. Note that the

---

[18] *See* Victoria Angelova et al., Algorithmic Recommendations and Human Discretion (October 25, 2022; unpublished manuscript).

[19] *See* DANIEL KAHNEMAN ET AL., NOISE: A FLAW IN HUMAN JUDGMENT (2021).

capricious scale is terrible even if it is right on average. On some days, it will give you unwelcome news, and on other days, it might delight you, but on all days, it is not telling you the truth.

Human judgment can be biased, noisy, or both. An obvious advantage of a good algorithm is that it can avoid bias. If you rely on it, you will not make a systematic error. A less obvious advantage of a good algorithm is that it can avoid noise. It will yield the same answer every time. It will not show unwanted variability. To be sure, a biased but noise-free algorithm is nothing to celebrate; it will go systematically wrong in every case. But the elimination of noise is a great gain in itself.[20]

To see why noise can be a problem, return to the medical context. Suppose that doctors order a large number of tests in the morning, but that in the afternoon, they ask patients to go home and take aspirin. Or suppose that when doctors are in a good mood, they make very different decisions from those they make when they are grumpy. If so, doctors might not show a systemic bias of any kind. But they will be noisy, and the noise will be produce plenty of mistaken decisions. They will be like the capricious scale. For all of us, algorithms can eliminate the caprice. And indeed, judges are noisy when they are making bail decisions, and doctors are noisy when they are deciding whom to test for heart attacks. The noiselessness of the relevant algorithms, and not just their freedom from cognitive biases, helps account for their superiority over human beings.

The focus here is on individual decisions, where both bias and noise can be problems. But across institutions or systems, the problem can be even worse. A group might amplify the bias of individual members, ensuring that it is even more biased than its median member.[21] Systems are often noisy. In a hospital, patients might find themselves in a lottery: Which doctor do they draw? One doctor might recommend a very different treatment from another. A large advantage of algorithms is that they eliminate the lottery.[22]

Algorithm Aversion, Sometimes

To say the least, many people do not love the idea of making decisions by algorithm. One reason, briefly noted earlier, appears to be

---

[20] For more details, *see id.*

[21] *See* CASS R. SUNSTEIN & REID HASTIE, WISER: GETTING BEYOND GROUPTHINK TO MAKE GROUPS SMARTER (2014).

[22] *See* KAHNEMAN ET AL., *supra* note 19.

a *general preference for personal agency*. Sometimes people decide to decide, because they like being the ones who decide.[23] Indeed, many people want to retain agency even if they know that if they delegated the decision to another (including an algorithm), they would end up with better outcomes. A general lesson is that agency has intrinsic value, which means that many people in many contexts would demand a significant premium to give it up.[24] At the same time, it is reasonable to think that if people find it difficult or unpleasant to exercise agency, they will not want to do so, and they might even be willing to pay something to have access to a delegate, including an algorithm.[25] When might that be? Suppose that the decision involves highly technical issues. Or suppose that people are facing a high level of stress in their lives, or multiple tasks and burdens. If so, algorithm aversion might be converted into algorithm attraction.

Some evidence identifies a particular source of algorithm aversion: People are far more willing to forgive mistakes by human beings than they are willing to forgive mistakes by algorithms.[26] If your investment adviser makes a terrible mistake, and if you lose money as a result, you might well think something like, "nobody's perfect," or "to err is human." If, by contrast, an algorithm makes a mistake, and if you lose money as a result, you might lose faith in it. Hence a key empirical finding: *People are especially averse to algorithmic forecasters after seeing them err, even if they do better than human forecasters.*[27] In short, people are less forgiving of algorithms than they are of human beings. This evidence strongly supports a speculation, which is that when making their own decisions, people will not want to rely on algorithmic forecasters that make mistakes, and will prefer to decide themselves, even if they know that algorithmic forecasters are better than they are.

Is that rational? If people want to make the correct decision, it is not. If their goal is to make money or to improve their health, they should rely on the better decider. But one more time: If people *enjoy* making

---

[23] *See* Roy Shoval et al., *Choosing to Choose or Not*, 17 JUDGMENT & DECISION MAKING 768 (2022); Sebastian Bobadilla-Suarez et al., *The Intrinsic Value of Choice: The Propensity to Under-Delegate in the Face of Potential Gains and Losses*, 54 J. RISK & UNCERTAINTY 187 (2017).

[24] *See* Bobadilla-Suarez et al., *supra* note 23.

[25] *See* Shoval et al., *supra* note 23.

[26] *See* Berkeley J. Dietvorst et al., *Algorithm Aversion: People Erroneously Avoid Algorithms After Seeing Them Err*, 144 J. EXPERIMENTAL PSYCH. 114 (2015).

[27] *Id.*

decisions, a preference for making one's own decisions might be perfectly rational. Perhaps people find the relevant decisions fun to make. Perhaps they like learning. Perhaps decision-making is a kind of game. Perhaps they like the feeling of responsibility. Perhaps they like the actuality of responsibility. If so, algorithm aversion is no mistake at all.

There is another factor. People have been found not to trust algorithms, and not to want to use them, in part because they do not know how they work.[28] Suppose that you learn that an algorithm can predict what jokes your best friend will find funny, and indeed that an algorithm can make better predictions, on that count, than you will. Will you consult the algorithm in deciding what jokes to tell your friend? For many reasons, you might not. You might want to tell her *your* jokes, not those recommended by an algorithm, even if it is more accurate. But research finds that people are more likely to trust algorithms, and to be willing to rely on them, if they are given a simple account of why they work.[29]

In the context of jokes, for example, algorithms can make good predictions about what jokes Erika or Paul will find funny if they obtain some data about what jokes Erika or Paul have found funny in the past. The reason is that algorithms have a great deal of data about what jokes people find funny, and they can "match" the answers of Erika and Paul to the answers of numerous other people. Having done that, they predict that if Erika and Paul find certain jokes funny, they will find other jokes funny, because people who like the jokes that Erika and Paul find funny find those other jokes funny as well. Once people learn that algorithms work for that reason, they tend to trust algorithms much more.[30] We can imagine analogies in many contexts. You might be willing to make decisions by algorithms once you are given more clarity about why their predictions are accurate.

Indeed, findings of algorithm aversion are complemented by findings of algorithm appreciation.[31] In many contexts, people seem to prefer decision by algorithms to decision by human beings. In estimating the weight of people in a photograph, for example, people were

[28] *See* Michael Yeomans et al., *Making Sense of Recommendations*, 32 J. BEHAV. DECISION MAKING 403 (2019).

[29] *Id.*

[30] *See id.*

[31] *See* Jennifer Logg et al., Algorithm Appreciation: People Prefer Algorithmic to Human Judgment, 51 Organizational Behavior and Human Decision Processes 90 (2019).

more likely to update their judgments in response to the assessment of an algorithm than in response to an assessment from a human being. People showed a similar preference for an algorithm in predicting the rank of a song on Billboard's "Hot 100" and in predicting whether someone would enjoy a date with a particular person. (There is an irony here, and we will get to it shortly.) People were also more likely to update in response to the advice of an algorithm in response to these questions:

- "What is the probability that Tesla Motors will deliver more than 80,000 battery-powered electric vehicles (BEVs) to customers in the calendar year 2016?"
- "What is the probability that a North American country, the EU, or an EU member state will impose sanctions on another country in response to a cyber attack or cyber espionage before the end of 2016?"
- "What is the probability that the United Kingdom will invoke Article 50 of the Lisbon Treaty before July 1, 2017?"

Interestingly, national security experts discounted the advice of the algorithm; in fact they discounted advice from all sources. This finding fits well with work attempting to reconcile algorithm aversion and algorithm appreciation, and finding that people are highly attentive to whether there is good reason to trust the algorithm or the human alternative.[32] If, for example, the human being is described as a "human expert" or a "physician," we might find algorithm aversion; if the human being is described as "another participant" or "a randomly chosen participant from a pool of 314 participants who took a past study," we might find algorithm appreciation. People seem to make rational, intuitive judgments about comparative expertise.

What Algorithms Cannot Do

There are, of course, continuing debates about what algorithms are likely to do well. For example: Can they predict whether you will fall in love with a stranger? Can they help people to find romantic partners? Thus far, the results on such counts are not promising. Samantha Joel

---

[32] *See* Yoyo Hou and Malte Yung, Who Is the Expert? Reconciling Algorithm Aversion and Algorithm Appreciation in AI-Supported Decision Making, 5 Proceedings of the ACM on Human-Computer Interaction 1 (2021).

and colleagues find that algorithms struggle to predict "the compatibility elements of human mating ... before two people meet," even if one has a very large number of "self-report measures about traits and preferences that past researchers have identified as being relevant to mate selection." Joel and her colleagues suggest that romantic attraction may well be less like a chemical reaction with predictable elements than "like an earthquake, such that the dynamic and chaos-like processes that cause its occurrence require considerable additional scientific inquiry before prediction is realistic."[33]

It is worth pondering exactly what this means. Most modestly, it might mean that algorithms need far more data in order to make accurate predictions – far more, at least, than is provided by self-report measures about traits and preferences. Such measures might tell us far too little about whether one person will be attracted to another. Perhaps we need more data, and perhaps we should focus on something other than such measures. It is possible than if we learn not that Jane is an extrovert and that she likes baseball and Chinese food, but that Jane fell for John, who had certain characteristics, and also for Tom and Frank, who had certain characteristics, she is mostly unlikely to fall for Fred, who has none of those characteristics, but is quite likely to fall for Eric, who shares important characteristics with John, Tom, and Frank. On this view, the right way to predict romantic attraction is to say, "If you like X and Y and Z, you will also like A and B, but not C and D." Or perhaps we should ask whether people who are like Jane, in the relevant respects, are also drawn to Eric – an approach that is not unrelated to that described earlier in connection with humor. (Of course, it would be necessary to identify the relevant respects in which people are like Jane, and that might be challenging.)

More radically, we might read the findings by Joel and her colleagues to suggest that romantic attraction is not predictable by algorithms *in principle* – that it depends on so many diverse factors, and so many features of the particular context and the particular moment, that algorithms will not be able to do much better than chance in specifying the probability that Jane will fall for Eric. Recall the reference to "dynamic and chaos-like processes," which might be a shorthand way of capturing mood, weather, location, time of day, and an assortment

[33] *See* Samantha Joel et al., Is Romantic Desire Predicable? Machine Learning Applied to Initial Romantic Attraction, 28 Psych. Science 1478 (2017).

of other factors that help produce – or fail to produce – a sense of romantic connection.

We do have to be careful here. We might be able to say that there is essentially no chance that Jane will like Carl (because there are things about Carl that we know, in advance, to be deal-breakers for Jane); that there is some chance that Jane will like Bruce; and that Eric is within the category of "it might well happen" for Jane, because Eric is in some sense "her type." The real question is whether and to what extent algorithms will eventually be able to do much better than that. We might speculate that the importance of particular factors – the concrete circumstances – is such that there are real limits on their predictive power (even if they might be able to outperform human beings, whose own predictive power is sharply limited in this context).

The topic of romantic attraction is intriguing in itself, and it can be seen as overlapping with an assortment of other prediction problems: whether you will enjoy living in Paris; whether you will become friends with a coworker; whether you will like a new job; whether a pandemic will occur in the next five years; whether a recession will occur in the next six months; whether a new movie will make a specified amount of money; whether a new book will hit the bestseller list; whether there will be a revolution in a specific nation by a certain date. It is generally agreed that in stable environments with fixed rules, algorithms, armed with a great deal of data, are able to make accurate predictions. But if the future is unlikely to be like the past, or if we are facing a high level of uncertainty, there is continuing debate about whether, where, and when algorithms will do well or even outperform human beings.[34]

Consider the predictability of revolutions. In work that predated the rise of algorithms, the economist Timur Kuran urged that they were unpredictable by their nature.[35] Kuran urged that an underlying problem lies in "preference falsification": People do not disclose their preferences, which means that we cannot know whether they will, in fact, be receptive to a revolutionary movement. If we do not know what people's preferences are, we will not know whether they might be willing to participate in a rebellion once the circumstances become propitious. Kuran added that we cannot observe people's thresholds for

34 See GERD GIGERENZER, HOW TO STAY SMART IN A SMART WORLD (2022).
35 See TIMUR KURAN, PRIVATE TRUTHS, PUBLIC LIES (1995).

joining such a movement. How many people would be willing to join when a movement is in its early stages? Who will require something like strong minority support before joining it? Kuran also noted that social interactions are critical, and that they too cannot be observed in advance. For a revolution to occur, people must see other people saying and doing certain things at certain times. How can we know, before the fact, who will see whom, and when, and doing what? The answer might well be that we cannot possibly do that. Kuran was not writing about algorithms, but they might not be able to do it, either. Algorithms might find it challenging it know what people's preferences are, and they might not be able to specify thresholds. Even if they could do both, they would not have an easy time predicting social interactions, and they might not even be able to identify their probability. In some ways, the challenge of predicting a revolution is not so different from the challenge of predicting a romantic spark.

Kuran did not deny that we might be able to make some progress in seeing when a revolution is improbable in the extreme, and also in seeing when a revolution is at least possible. For one thing, we might be able to make some progress in identifying private preferences – for example, by helping people feel safe to say that they dislike the status quo, perhaps by showing sympathy with that view, or perhaps by guaranteeing anonymity. Kuran wrote before the emergence of the internet, which gives us unprecedented opportunities to observe hitherto unobservable preferences (for example, via Google searches, which might show us widespread dissatisfaction with the current government). Perhaps algorithms can say something about probabilities, based on data of this kind. But if Kuran is right, they will not be able to say a lot, because their knowledge of preferences and thresholds will be limited, and because they will not be able to foresee social interactions. (Is that conclusion premature? Who knows?)

The general analysis need not be limited to revolutions. Preference falsification, diverse thresholds, and social interactions – one or more of these are in play in many domains. Consider the question whether books, movies, or musical albums are likely to succeed. Of course, we might know that a new album by Taylor Swift is likely to do well, and that a new album by a singer who is both terrible and unknown is likely to fail. But across a wide range, a great deal depends on serendipity, and on who says or does what exactly when. Early popularity might be crucial, and early popularity can turn on luck. Because of the sheer number of variables that can produce success or failure, algorithms might well struggle to make successful predictions at early stages (though they can do better if they are given data on an ongoing basis). And in the case of financial markets, there is a special problem: Once it is made, a prediction by a terrific algorithm will automatically be priced into the market, which will immediately make that prediction less reliable, and possibly not reliable at all.

There is far more to learn on these questions, but we should keep the various points in mind in deciding whether to make decisions by algorithms. Let us not lose sight of the central point: Across a wide range of settings, environments are stable enough, and deciding by algorithm is likely to improve accuracy, because algorithms will reduce both bias and noise. As we have seen, the stakes may be very high.

Discrimination

In the current period, there is a great deal of concern that algorithms might discriminate on illegitimate grounds, such as race or sex.[36] The concern appears to be growing. The possibility that algorithms will promote discrimination raises an assortment of difficult questions. But the bail research casts new light on them. Above all, it suggests a powerful and simple point: Use of algorithms will reveal, with great clarity, the need to make tradeoffs between the value of racial (or other) equality and other important values, such as public safety.

A (Very) Little Law

For background: Discrimination law has long been focused on two different problems. The first is *disparate treatment*, understood as treating people differently because of some forbidden characteristic (such as race); the second is *disparate impact,* understood as adopting a practice that disproportionately harms members of certain groups, even though that disproportionate harm is not intended.[37] The US Constitution and all civil rights laws forbid disparate treatment. The U.S. Constitution does not concern itself with disparate impact, though some civil rights statutes do. Different nations make different choices on these topics.

[36] *See*, for a brilliant discussion, Duncan Watts, EVERYTHING IS OBVIOUS (2011).
[37] For an overview, *see* Solon Barocas & Andrew D. Selbst, *Big Data's Disparate Impact*, 104 CAL. L REV. 671 (2016).

Disparate treatment

The prohibition on disparate treatment reflects a commitment to a kind of neutrality. Public officials are not permitted to favor members of one group over another unless there is a sufficiently neutral reason for doing so. In many nations, the law forbids disparate treatment along a variety of specified grounds, such as race, sex, religion, and age. In extreme cases, the existence of disparate treatment is obvious, because a discriminatory practice or rule can be shown to be in place ("no women may apply"). In other cases, no such practice or rule can be identified, and for that reason, violations are more difficult to police. A plaintiff might claim that a seemingly neutral practice or requirement (such as a written test for employment) was actually adopted in order to favor one group (White people) or to disfavor another (Black people). To police discrimination, the legal system is required to use what tools it has to discern the motivation of decisionmakers.

Violations might arise because of explicit prejudice, sometimes described as "animus." Alternatively, they might arise because of unconscious prejudice, operating outside of the awareness of the decisionmaker; unconscious prejudice is sometimes described as an "implicit bias." An official might discriminate against women not because he intends to do so, but because of an automatic preference for men, which he might not acknowledge and might even (consciously) deplore.

Disparate impact

The prohibition on disparate impact means, in brief, that if some requirement or practice has a disproportionate adverse effect on members of specified groups (Black people, women), those who adopt that requirement or practice must show that it is adequately justified. Suppose, for example, that an employer requires members of its sales force to take some kind of written examination, or that the head of a police department institutes a rule requiring new employees to be able to run at a specified speed. If these practices have disproportionate adverse effects on Black people, women, or other protected classes, they will be invalidated unless they can show a strong connection to the actual requirements of the job. They might be required to show that the practices are justified by "business necessity."

The theory behind disparate impact remains disputed. On one view, the goal is to ferret out disparate treatment. If, for example, an employer has adopted a practice with disproportionate adverse effects on Black people, we might suspect that it is intending to produce those adverse effects. The required justification is a way of seeing whether the suspicion is justified. Alternatively, disparate impact might be thought to be disturbing in itself, in the sense that a practice that produces such an impact helps entrench something like a caste system. If so, it is necessary for those who adopt such practices to demonstrate that they have a good and sufficiently neutral reason for doing so.

Algorithms, Judges, and Bail

Human Judges

In the context of bail decisions, we would have disparate treatment if it could be shown that judges discriminate against Black defendants, either through a formal practice (counting race as a "minus") or through a demonstrable discriminatory motive (established perhaps with some kind of extrinsic evidence). We would have disparate impact if it could be shown that some factor or rule of decision (taking account, for example, of employment history) had a disproportionate adverse effect on Black defendants; the question would be whether that effect could be adequately justified in neutral terms.

For present purposes, let us simply assume that the decisions of human judges, with respect to bail decisions, show neither disparate treatment nor disparate impact. In New York City in a relevant period, it is nonetheless true that for Black and Hispanic defendants, the detention rate is 28.5 percent.[38] More specifically, Black defendants are detained at a rate of 31 percent, and Hispanic defendants are detained at a rate of 25 percent. (The detention rate for White defendants is between those two figures.)

The Algorithm

Importantly, the algorithm is made blind to race. Whether a defendant is Black or Hispanic is not one of the factors that it considers in assessing flight risk. But with respect to outcomes, how does the algorithm compare to human judges?

[38] *Id.*

The answer, of course, depends on what the algorithm is asked to do. If the algorithm is directed to match the judges' overall detention rate, its numbers, with respect to race, look quite close to the corresponding numbers for those judges. Its overall detention rate for Black and Hispanic defendants is 29 percent, with a 32 percent rate for Black defendants and a 24 percent rate for Hispanic defendants. At the same time, the crime rate drops, relative to judges, by a whopping 25 percent. It would be fair to say that on any view, the algorithm is not a discriminator, at least not when compared with human judges. There is no disparate treatment. It would be difficult to find disparate impact. And in terms of outcomes, it is not worse than human beings along the dimension of racial fairness. (Whether the numbers are nonetheless objectionable is a separate question.)

Kleinberg and his coauthors show that it is also possible to constrain the algorithm to see what happens if we aim to reduce that 29 percent detention rate for Black and Hispanic defendants. Suppose that the algorithm is constrained so that the detention rate for Black and Hispanic defendants has to stay at 28.5 percent. It turns out that the crime reduction is about the same as would be obtained with the 29 percent rate. Moreover, it would be possible to instruct the algorithm in multiple different ways, so as to produce different tradeoffs among social goals. Kleinberg and his coauthors give some illustrations: *Maintain the same detention rate, but equalize the release rate for all races.* The result is that the algorithm reduces the crime rate by 23 percent – significantly but not massively lower than the 25 percent rate achieved without the instruction to equalize the release rate. A particularly revealing finding: If the algorithm is instructed to produce the same crime rate that judges currently achieve, it will jail 40.8 percent fewer Black defendants and 44.6 percent fewer Hispanic defendants. It does this because it detains many fewer people, focused as it is on the riskiest defendants; many Black and Hispanic defendants benefit from its more accurate judgments.

The most important point here does not involve the particular numbers, but instead the clarity of the tradeoffs. The algorithm would permit any number of choices with respect to the racial composition of the population of defendants denied bail. It would also make explicit the consequences of those choices for the crime rate.

Broader Considerations

When it is said that algorithms can correct for biases, what is often meant is cognitive biases (such as availability bias or representativeness bias). The case of discrimination is more challenging. To be sure, disparate treatment can be prevented; algorithms do not have motivations, and they can be designed so as not to draw lines on the basis of race or sex, or to take race or sex into account. The case of disparate impact is trickier. If the goal is accurate predictions, an algorithm might use a factor that is genuinely predictive of what matters (flight risk, educational attainment, job performance) – but that factor might have a disparate impact on Black people or women. If disparate impact is best understood as an effort to ferret out disparate treatment, that might not be a problem (at least so long as no human being, armed with a discriminatory motive, is behind its use). But if disparate impact is an effort to prevent something like a caste system, it might deserve scrutiny.

Difficult problems are also presented if an algorithm uses a factor that is in some sense an outgrowth of discrimination. For example, a poor credit rating, or a troubling arrest record, might be an artifact of discrimination, by human beings, before the algorithm was asked to do its predictive work. There is a risk here that algorithms might perpetuate discrimination, and extend its reach, by using factors that are genuinely predictive, but that are products of unequal treatment.[39] It might make discrimination into a kind of self-fulfilling prophecy.

One of the signal virtues of algorithms is that they present the relevant tradeoffs in an unprecedently clear light. We might learn that if we pursue racial balance, we will sacrifice other goals, and we might be able to see, with real precision, the magnitude of the gains and the losses. The tradeoffs might well be painful, but in general, it is best to know what they are.

Beyond Intuitions

Let us return to the largest points. In the private and public sectors, people are often asked to make predictions under conditions of uncertainty, and because of cognitive biases, their intuitions can lead

---

[39] *See* Kleinberg et al., *supra* note 3.

them astray.[40] It takes a great deal of work to provide corrections.[41] It is often believed that experts can develop reliable intuitions, or rely instead on statistical thinking. That is frequently true, at least when they receive prompt feedback. But as Current Offense Bias and Mugshot Bias make clear, experienced judges (in the literal sense) can do significantly worse than algorithms. The same is true of Current Symptom Bias and Demographic Bias.

To the extent that algorithms do not display biases of this kind, both experts and ordinary people would do well to consult them, and even to follow their advice. Deciding by algorithm may not bring a bright smile to the face, but in important domains, it is the best decision about decisions.

[40] For a different perspective, *see* RALPH HERTWIG ET AL., TAMING UNCERTAINTY (2019).

[41] For an engaging and still-relevant treatment, *see* RUTH BEYTH-MAROM & SHLOMITH DEKEL, AN ELEMENTARY APPROACH TO THINKING UNDER UNCERTAINTY (Sarah Lichtenstein et al. trans., 1985).

10 DECIDING FOR ONESELF

When we make decisions, or decisions about decisions, we usually dislike being manipulated. If you learn that someone tricked you into making a decision, you might well feel outraged. Coercion is visible; manipulation is hidden. Being manipulated can feel insidious. In ordinary life, we expect to be treated with respect, and manipulators do not treat us with respect. If we are fooled by someone in a superior position, or by an algorithm (as we will increasingly be), we feel demeaned. To understand these points and their possible implications, let us back up a bit.

Regulators all over the world direct their efforts against "fraud" and "deceptive trade practices." Neither of those terms is self-defining, and understandings vary. In ordinary language as well as in law, fraud typically includes lies and misrepresentations intended to produce some kind of gain: "If you purchase this product, you will never get cancer!" Deception typically includes words or conduct intended to convince people to believe something that is untrue: "Vaccines against COVID-19 do not work!" In ordinary language, manipulation is different and in important respects broader. If a box is prechecked ("automatically renew my subscription every year, with a price that triples annually"), we may not be speaking of fraud, and no one may be deceived; but manipulation may be involved.

In many nations, there is increasing interest in "dark patterns" online, which can be seen as an assortment of manipulative strategies designed to alter people's choices and to take their money. Some dark patterns make second-order decisions for us. Indeed, that might be their central point. Dark patterns include prechecked boxes; automatic enrollment in certain programs or automatic purchase of certain products; shrouded attributes (such as poor energy efficiency, late fees, and overuse fees); and fine print with respect to important terms and conditions.[1] In some cases, dark patterns subvert people's decision-making processes. They can be seen as a form of theft.

With an emphasis on decisional autonomy, I will be exploring the possibility of *a right not to be manipulated*. I suggest that we should recognize such a moral right, running against private actors and also against the government. As we shall see, lies, manipulation, and coercion have a great deal in common. All of them deprive people of autonomy in making decisions; they are objectionable for that reason, even if we have different explanations of why that autonomy matters. An understanding of the importance of autonomy in making decisions, and of why people prize that autonomy, will form the foundation of the right not to be manipulated.

In the process of the discussion, I shall address four separate questions: (1) What is manipulation? (2) What is wrong with manipulation? (3) Should there be a moral right not to be manipulated? (4) Should there be a legal right not to be manipulated, and if so, what should it include?

What Is Manipulation?

A great deal of effort has been devoted to the definition of manipulation, almost exclusively within the philosophical literature. The definitional question has proved exceptionally difficult to answer; the term "manipulation" may cover a diverse assortment of words and actions that do not fall within a single definition, and that are not subject to a unitary set of necessary and sufficient conditions. Many of the definitional efforts focus on the effects of manipulation in undermining people's ability to engage in rational deliberation. Avishai Margalit urges that manipulation "subverts the capacity to act for a reason," which means that it undermines a condition for autonomy, which is

---

[1] *See* Jamie Luguri & Lior Strahilevitz, *Shining a Light on Dark Patterns*, 13 J. LEGAL ANALYSIS 43 (2021).

"the need to secure the right cognitive capacity for choosing."[2] In his view, "manipulation hinges on seduction," and so is unlike coercion, which "hinges on intimidation."[3] On Christian Coons and Michael Weber's account, manipulation "is a kind of influence that bypasses or subverts the target's rational capacities."[4] T. M. Wilkinson urges that manipulation "subverts and insults a person's autonomous decision making," in a way that treats its objects as "tools and fools."[5] He thinks that "manipulation is intentionally and successfully influencing someone using methods that pervert choice."[6]

In a related account, Ruth Faden and Tom Beauchamp define psychological manipulation as "any intentional act that successfully influences a person to belief or behavior by causing changes in mental processes *other than those involved in understanding*."[7] Joseph Raz suggests that "[m]anipulation, unlike coercion, does not interfere with a person's options. Instead it perverts the way that person reaches decisions, forms preferences or adopts goals."[8]

The idea of "perverting" choice, invoked by both Wilkinson and Raz, or of "perverting" people's way of reaching decisions or forming preferences, is not self-defining; it should be understood to refer to methods that do not appeal to, or produce, the right degree or kind of reflective deliberation ("the right cognitive capacity for choosing"). If so, a defining characteristic of manipulation is that it "infringes upon the autonomy of the victim by subverting and insulting their decision-making powers."[9] In certain circumstances (not all!), seduction can have that consequence. (Note that some forms of manipulation are not seductive, as when the manipulator is inducing sadness or fear, or when certain terms are hidden in fine print or in numerous, confusing, and complex terms.[10])

---

[2] Avishai Margalit, *Autonomy: Errors and Manipulation*, 14 JERUSALEM REV. LEGAL STUD. 102, 104 (2016).

[3] *Id.*

[4] Christian Coons & Michael Weber, *Manipulation: Investigating the Core Concept and Its Moral Status*, in MANIPULATION: THEORY AND PRACTICE 1, 11 (Christian Coons & Michael Weber eds., 2014).

[5] T. M. Wilkinson, *Nudging and Manipulation*, 61 POL. STUD. 341, 345 (2013).

[6] *Id.* at 347.

[7] RUTH R. FADEN & TOM L. BEAUCHAMP, A HISTORY AND THEORY OF INFORMED CONSENT 354–68 (1986).

[8] JOSEPH RAZ, THE MORALITY OF FREEDOM 377–78 (1986).

[9] *See* Wilkinson, *supra* note 5, at 351.

[10] *See* Petra Persson, *Attention Manipulation and Information Overload*, 2 BEHAV. PUB. POL'Y 78 (2018).

The challenge is to concretize the ideas of "subverting" and "insulting." To meet that challenge, we might suggest that a statement or action counts as manipulative *when it does not sufficiently engage or appeal to people's capacity for reflective and deliberative choice.*[11] Subliminal advertising is an unambiguous example. Marketing strategies that appeal to people's deepest hopes and fears, or that trigger identifiable biases (such as present bias, availability bias, or optimistic bias), might also be counted as manipulative. (To know for sure, we would need to consider the details in the relevant case.) It is important to see that manipulation is not the same as deception. Manipulators trick you; deceivers lie to you. Your mother or your lover might manipulate you without deceiving you, and the same is true of a marketing campaign for aspirin or for cold medicines – or for a head of state. (George Orwell's *1984* is, among other things, a series of case studies in the horrors of manipulation.)

In an illuminating discussion, with strong implications for how to think about decisional autonomy, Anne Barnhill defines manipulation as "directly influencing someone's beliefs, desires, or emotions, such that she falls short of ideals for belief, desire, or emotion in ways typically not in her self-interest or likely not in her self-interest in the present context."[12] The idea of "falling short of ideals" is exceedingly helpful, and it should be seen as an effort to capture the same idea as the word "sufficiently" in my earlier definition. Note that the standard here is best taken as objective, not subjective. The question is whether someone has, *in fact*, been influenced in a way that leads her to fall short of relevant ideals. One of the advantages of Barnhill's definition is that it includes cases in which people should not be and are not making reflective and deliberative choices, but are nonetheless being manipulated. You might be manipulated into falling in love with someone, even if we insist (as we should!) that falling in love is not really a matter of a reflective and deliberative choosing.

---

[11] *See* CASS R. SUNSTEIN, THE ETHICS OF INFLUENCE (2016). A powerful set of counterarguments, showing that this view is too narrow, can be found in Moti Gorin, *Do Manipulators Always Threaten Rationality?*, 51 AM. PHIL. Q. 51 (2014). Gorin shows that "good reasons and sound arguments" are and can be "used manipulatively." *Id.* at 59.

[12] Anne Barnhill, *What Is Manipulation?*, *in* MANIPULATION: THEORY AND PRACTICE, *supra* note 4, at 51, 72. Barnhill builds on Robert Noggle, *Manipulative Actions: A Conceptual and Moral Analysis*, 33 AM. PHIL. Q. 43 (1996).

Still, there are problems with Barnhill's definition. One is that it seems to include lies and deception, which are distinct from manipulation. Another is that it excludes, from the category of manipulation, influences that are in the self-interest of the chooser. Some acts of manipulation count as such even if they leave the chooser better off. You might be manipulated to go to a doctor when it is in your interest to do so; to go on a date that turns out to go shockingly well; or to purchase a car that you end up much enjoying. We might be willing to say that such acts are justified – but they are manipulative all the same. Plenty of manipulative acts are in the interest of choosers (a point to which I will return).

To understand manipulation in Barnhill's general way, it should not be necessary to make controversial claims about the nature of decision and choice, or the role of emotions. We should agree that many decisions are not reflective or deliberative, that they may be based on unconscious processing, and that people often lack a full sense of the wellsprings of their own choices.[13] Even if this is so, a manipulator might impose some kind of influence that leads people to fall short of ideals for belief, desire, or emotion. In ordinary language, the idea of manipulation is invoked by people who are not committed to controversial views about psychological or philosophical questions, and it is best to understand that idea in a way that brackets the relevant controversies.

What Is Wrong with Manipulation?

When is manipulation wrong, and what is wrong with it? To answer this question, we need an account of what makes something wrong. Kantian and welfarist approaches offer different answers to that question.

Kantians emphasize that people should be treated as ends rather than means – as subjects rather than objects. They focus on people's autonomy, independently of whether people choose or decide well. To Kantians, the central problem with manipulation is that it is disrespectful to choosers. It does not respect their capacity for agency; it offends their autonomy and their dignity. Human beings should be treated as adults, not as children, and if individuals or institutions do not sufficiently engage people's capacity for reflective choice, they are

---

[13] *See* Daniel Kahneman, Thinking, Fast and Slow (2011).

treating them without respect. Lying is not the same as manipulating, but it is wrong for the same reason. Kant explained: "By a lie a man throws away and, as it were, annihilates his dignity as a man."[14] That is a point about lying rather than about being lied to, but for the victims of lies, the Kantian problem is easy to identify. As Christine Korsgaard puts it, the problem with lying stems from "a pure moral claim: that a person has a right to run his own life because he is the person whose life it is."[15] Lying is a twin sibling to manipulation, and for Kantians, both are close cousins to coercion. Like coercion, manipulation takes away the agency of its objects and subjects them to the will of others.

As Margalit puts it, "coercion and manipulation upset autonomy differently, but both have one crucial dimension in common," having "to do with the subjugation of an agent's will to the will of others."[16] Raz takes a similar position, urging that "[c]oercion and manipulation subject the will of one person to that of another. That violates his independence and is inconsistent with his autonomy."[17] Coercion and manipulation "have acquired a symbolic meaning expressing disregard or even contempt for the coerced or manipulated people."[18] Thus Raz urges that the prohibition against coercion and manipulation has a "symbolic or expressive character," one that "transcends the severity of the actual consequences of those actions."[19]

Welfarists do not emphasize autonomy as such, and they do not focus on the expression of disregard or contempt. For them, actual consequences are what matter; they care about people's welfare. From the standpoint of welfare, a pervasive concern is that manipulators might be promoting their own interests rather than those of the chooser. Why – it might reasonably be asked – is it necessary to resort to manipulation, rather than to provide information and to engage

---

[14] This quotation comes from Kant's *Doctrine of Virtue*. It is quoted in SISSELA BOK, LYING: MORAL CHOICE IN PUBLIC AND PRIVATE LIFE 32 (2nd Vintage Books ed. 1999)

[15] Christine M. Korsgaard, *"It's for Your Own Good": Is There Moral Justification for Paternalistic Lies?*, ABC RELIGION & ETHICS, available at www.abc.net.au/religion/christine-korsgaard-is-there-moral-justification-for-paternalis/11950108 (updated June 13, 2022), available at www.abc.net.au/religion/christine-korsgaard-is-there-moral-justification-for-paternalis/11950108.

[16] Margalit, *supra* note 2, at 104.

[17] RAZ, *supra* note 8, at 378.

[18] *Id.*

[19] *Id.*

the chooser's reflective capacities? On this view, a serious problem with manipulators is that they lack relevant knowledge – about the chooser's situation, tastes, and values. Lacking that knowledge, they nonetheless subvert the process by which people make their own decisions about what is best for them. Things are in an important sense worse if manipulators are focused on their own interests rather than on those of the chooser's. It is in this respect that a self-interested manipulator can be said to be stealing from people – both limiting their agency and moving their opportunities and resources in the direction preferred by the manipulator. Paternalistic manipulators may or may not doing that, but they are assuming that they know best, and that is often false. Self-interested manipulators are thieves – of money, emotions, time and attention, or something else – and paternalistic manipulators are similar, even if their motives are entirely benign.

For these reasons, the welfarist objection to manipulation is rooted in the same concerns that underlie John Stuart Mill's Harm Principle.[20] Mill offers an assortment of arguments on behalf of that principle, including the importance of learning, experimentation, self-determination, and self-development. The argument from self-development might be his most heartfelt, but for present purposes, Mill's most important claim is *epistemic*. It points to what choosers know, and what outsiders do not know. Thus Mill insists that the individual "is the person most interested in his own well-being," and the "ordinary man or woman has means of knowledge immeasurably surpassing those that can be possessed by any one else."[21] When society seeks to overrule the individual's judgment, it does so on the basis of "general presumptions," and these "may be altogether wrong, and even if right, are as likely as not to be misapplied to individual cases."[22] If the goal is to ensure that people's lives go well, Mill concludes that the best solution is for public officials (and others) to allow people to find their own path. Consider, in the same vein, F. A. Hayek's remarkable suggestion that "the awareness of our irremediable ignorance of most of what is known to somebody [who is a chooser] is *the chief basis of the argument for liberty*."[23]

[20] *See* JOHN STUART MILL, ON LIBERTY (John Gray ed., 1991) (1859).
[21] *Id.* at 277.
[22] *Id.*
[23] F. A. HAYEK, *The Market and Other Orders, in* THE COLLECTED WORKS OF F. A. HAYEK 384 (Bruce Caldwell ed., 2014). Emphasis added.

These points can be applied to manipulators (emphatically including both friends and public officials) no less than to those who engage in coercion. The claim, in short, is that if you think that people are about to make a mistake, you should explain why you think so. You should tell them why they are wrong. You should inform them. You should not manipulate them. On welfarist grounds, the risk is that if you manipulate them to get them to do what you think is in their interest, you will miss something of crucial importance. With respect to the conduct of their own lives, we might insist that choosers usually know better than outsiders, emphatically including manipulators. If we follow Mill and Hayek, and believe that individuals are in the best position to make decisions for themselves, then we might fear that any effort to manipulate people will reduce their welfare, because it does not sufficiently allow them to make such decisions. The obligation of the adviser, or the outsider, is to put people in the position to make good decisions (by their own lights) – not to manipulate them. The reason – a follower of Mill and Hayek might claim – is that choosers have epistemic advantages over outsiders. On this view, manipulators threaten to reduce people's welfare because they find ways to ensure that they will choose in the way that manipulators want.

It is true and important that behavioral scientists have raised serious questions about Mill's argument.[24] If choosers suffer from some kind of bias, they might choose poorly. We have seen a number of examples; consider optimistic bias, present bias, and limited attention. On welfarist grounds, we cannot rule out the possibility that manipulation is justified as a way of helping people not to err.[25] It follows that the force of the welfarist objections to manipulation is contingent; it depends on the context and the circumstances. Someone might engage in manipulation to convince a chooser to stop drinking or smoking, or to pay attention to his weight. Like liars, manipulators might make people better off; they might even save lives. They need not be thieves; on welfarist assumptions, they might be saints. With respect to lying, Jeremy Bentham, founder of utilitarianism, emphasized the need to focus on consequences: "Falsehood, taken by itself, consider it as not

---

[24] *See* SARAH CONLY, AGAINST AUTONOMY: JUSTIFYING COERCIVE PATERNALISM (2012); Ryan Bubb & Richard H. Pildes, *How Behavioral Economics Trims Its Sails and Why*, 127 HARV. L. REV. 1593 (2014).

[25] *See* Jonathan Baron, *A Welfarist Approach to Manipulation*, 1 J. MKTG. BEHAV. 283 (2016).

being accompanied by any other material circumstances, can never, upon the principle of utility, constitute any offense at all."[26] Henry Sidgwick, also a utilitarian, spoke similarly: "But if the lawfulness of benevolent deception in any case be admitted, I do not see how we can decide when and how far it is admissible, except by considerations of expediency; that is, by weighing the gain of any particular deception against the imperilment of mutual confidence involved in all violations of the truth."[27]

These points help explain when and how welfarists might conclude that manipulation is justified. *First*, welfarists would insist on distinguishing between beneficial and harmful manipulation. It is fine to manipulate terrorists and kidnappers. If people are trying to kidnap you, you are within your rights to try to manipulate them. In ordinary life, welfarists are not likely to object if friends or family members manipulate people in order to save their lives or to prevent grievous harm, or even to have a little fun.

Second, manipulation might be part of an overall process or system that is unobjectionable. If parents manipulate their children, perhaps we have no cause for complaint; among friends or spouses, a little manipulation, and possibly a lot, can be fine (though lines can be crossed, depending partly on the consequences). If competition in the market is working well, and preventing significant abuses, the same might be said about advertisers and marketers of many different kinds.[28] At least relatively mild forms of manipulation might be an inevitable, and fully acceptable, part of competition itself.

Third, welfarists should acknowledge that some forms of manipulation are trivial or unimportant, and hardly a serious ethical wrong – and they would acknowledge that if the consequences of manipulation are very good and cross some (high) threshold, the presumption against it can be overcome. If a lawyer manipulates a client not to file a pointless lawsuit, perhaps we would not have serious reason for complaint. *Fourth*, welfarists would be open to the possibility that manipulation, like coercion, is an acceptable response to situations in which people are making a serious error because they lack important information

---

[26] JEREMY BENTHAM, AN INTRODUCTION TO THE PRINCIPLES OF MORALS AND LEGISLATION 233 (Dover Phil. Classics 2007) (1789).

[27] HENRY SIDGWICK, *The Classification of Duties: Veracity*, *in* THE METHODS OF ETHICS 316 (7th ed. 1962) (1874).

[28] For a sustained argument that the system of competition is not a sufficient safeguard here, *see* GEORGE A. AKERLOF & ROBERT J. SHILLER, PHISHING FOR PHOOLS (2015).

or are suffering from a behavioral bias. Even so, welfarists might well conclude that the best response is to provide information or to correct the bias, not to manipulate people.

Moral Rights, Legal Rights

We should be able to agree that a more-or-less identifiable category of actions counts as manipulation; that those actions do not respect people's capacity for agency; that those actions are often unacceptable for that reason; that those actions often lead people in directions that make their lives worse, perhaps because the manipulator is evil or self-serving, perhaps because the manipulator is at an epistemic disadvantage compared to the chooser. Manipulators try to seduce choosers to do as they wish, and they often succeed. In these circumstances, we should enthusiastically embrace a right not to be manipulated.

We should see that right as rooted in a principle of decisional autonomy, supported for different reasons by Kantians and welfarists, and operating against both private and public institutions. I have pointed to cases in which the right not to be manipulated might be defeasible. A terrorist, or someone engaged in domestic abuse, forfeits that right. But moral rights of all kinds are not absolute. A right not to be manipulated is especially important in the modern era, when the capacity to manipulate people, especially online, may be greater than ever before.

In this light, we should be very glad to have a social norm against manipulation, and we might want to fortify it, perhaps to protect against marketers or politicians.[29] We might also be tempted to think that manipulation falls into a category of actions properly promoted or discouraged by social norms, but generally unaccompanied by law or regulation. On the positive side, we might speak of kindness, considerateness,[30] civility, grace, or generosity. No law requires these things. On the negative side, we might speak of unkindness, incivility, gracelessness, or meanness. No law punishes these things.

The first reason to be reluctant to invoke law is vagueness. Many norms, including those that protect moral rights, are directed against conduct that is not and cannot be defined with sufficient precision for

[29] *See* ROBERT E. GOODIN, MANIPULATORY POLITICS (1980).
[30] *See* EDNA ULLMANN-MARGALIT, NORMAL RATIONALITY (Avishai Margalit & Cass R. Sunstein eds., 2017).

law. This problem raises serious concerns: People will not have fair notice about what they can and cannot do, and enforcement authorities will have undue discretion to pick and choose. In ordinary language, and even as elaborated by the most careful philosophers, manipulation cannot easily be the foundation for criminal law and regulation.

The second reason is overbreadth. Many categories of bad conduct include a large assortment of actions, some of which are not so bad as to warrant punishment, and some of which might not be bad at all in the circumstances. People also have a right to be bad (so long as they are not all that bad), which is one reason that unkindness, incivility, and inconsiderateness are not unlawful. As we have seen, that point certainly holds for manipulation. (A world without manipulation would be no fun. Who wants never to be seduced?) We might think that terms such as "fraud" and "assault" have similar problems, and that thought is not entirely wrong. Still, longstanding traditions are available to specify and to concretize such terms, greatly weakening concerns about vagueness and overbreadth. The same cannot be said of manipulation.

Still, there is a great deal that can be done, focusing on the worst cases. We have seen that in some such cases, manipulative behavior is a form of theft, and when that is so, it should be forbidden for that reason. (Compare lying, which is not forbidden, with libel, which is.) We do best by focusing on specific practices of manipulative behavior – those that are plainly harmful and very hard to defend on any ground.

Take, for example, a practice by the Donald Trump campaign in March 2020: People who donated to the campaign were directed to an online form which, amidst a lot of other fine print, contained a pre-filled check mark reading, "Make this a monthly recurring donation."[31] In June of the same year, the campaign used a similar strategy, called "the money bomb," to default people into making an additional donation for Trump's birthday.[32] And in September, the campaign changed "a monthly recurring donation," with that check mark, into "a weekly recurring donation."[33] As the campaign continued, the "weekly recurring

---

[31]   Shane Goldmacher, *How Trump Steered Supporters into Unwitting Donations*, N.Y. Times (updated August 7, 2021), www.nytimes.com/2021/04/03/us/politics/trump-donations.html; *see also* Nathaniel Posner et al., Dark Defaults: How Choice Architecture Steers Campaign Donations (October 29, 2022) (manuscript), https://papers.ssrn.com/sol3/papers.cfm?abstract_id=4258478.

[32]   Goldmacher, *supra* note 31.

[33]   *Id.*

donation" box was made less conspicuous and moved beneath other text.[34]

These strategies worked; they created a surge in donations, including a large number of unintended payments, which, in many cases, exceeded credit card limits, required people to pay overdraft fees to their banks, and led people to cancel their cards to avoid recurring payments. By one calculation, the use of "dark defaults," as they have been called, increased revenue by $42 million. Remarkably, most donors did not learn what was happening and change their behavior.[35]

When do prechecked boxes count as manipulation, and so as a form of theft? To answer those questions, we need to answer two further ones. (1) Are prechecked boxes entirely transparent and visible? (2) Are they in the interest of all or most who are affected by them? If the answer to both questions is "yes," we do not have manipulation, and we do not have a problem. If the answer to both questions is "no," we have manipulation, and we have a serious problem. Indeed, we should find manipulation if the answer to the first question is "no," even if the answer to the second question is "yes." If the answer to the first question is "yes," but the answer to the second question is "no," we do not have manipulation (even if we have another kind of problem).

It is important to see that by themselves, prechecked boxes are hardly manipulative, and they might be a terrific idea. A cellphone or a laptop has the equivalent of prechecked boxes, including default settings, and they are a blessing. If people are told explicitly that a company that sells an online service (such as Netflix, Apple, or Amazon) will automatically renew their subscription, it is not at all clear that the law should intervene. (To be sure, it matters whether most people, given the choice, would favor automatic renewal.) The most serious problems arise when people *are not given clarity that they are committing themselves to certain terms* – and when the relevant terms are highly unlikely to be what people would have chosen if they had known about the choice. As a general rule, there should be a prohibition on billing people in accordance with terms to which they did not actively consent, certainly in cases in which they would not do that if they had been asked. Here is one of the darkest of dark patterns, and it is a form of theft. It should be forbidden.

---

[34] *Id.*
[35] *See* Posner et al., *supra* note 31.

The underlying principle is one of decisional autonomy, which means that hidden fees and costs belong in a prohibited category. Regulators should take firm aim at those fees and costs. In a representative action, the Department of Transportation required US air carriers and online travel agents to alter their web interfaces to incorporate all ticket taxes in upfront, advertised fares. The goal was to allow consumers to make informed choices. Evidence suggests that this behaviorally informed intervention, designed to overcome shrouded prices, has been highly effective and thus saved consumers a great deal of money.[36]

By contrast, some "dark patterns," even if they are plausibly regarded as manipulative, are not easily seen as a form of theft, and as a general rule, they should not be forbidden by law. Suppose, for example, that people are repeatedly requested to do something ("wouldn't you like to buy this book?"); that consumers are told (truthfully) that supplies are limited; or that some kind of countdown timer is used to promote a sense of urgency ("only two hours left!"). It is much harder to see these practices as theft, and it is much harder to justify legal intervention.

In thinking about whether to proscribe manipulation, we do best to target and to build on the most egregious cases, and to draw up categories for regulation with close reference to them. Recall that lies, as such, are not a violation of the law; it is libel that is a violation of the law, and the same is true for perjury and false advertising. Where lies are prohibited, it is because they do serious damage; in some cases, they are a form of theft. They undermine or eliminate people's ability to make their own decisions. They take something from some people for the benefit of others. In some cases, manipulative practices have the same character. That is when, and why, the law should target them.

---

[36] *See* Sebastien Bradley & Naomi E. Feldman, *Hidden Baggage: Behavioral Responses to Changes in Airline Ticket Tax Disclosure*, 12 AM. ECON. J.: ECON. POL'Y 58 (2020).

EPILOGUE
"Get Drunk!"

A close friend of mine – let's call him David – has a minor heart condition, which increases the risk of stroke. To reduce that risk, David's doctor recommended that he take a daily medication. The medication was not without side effects; it would simultaneously increase the risk of bleeding. Even so, the doctor believed that David would be wise to take the medication. David decided not to do that. He reasoned that purely on the numbers, the decision was a pretty close call, and that he would not *like* taking the medication every day, or thinking about taking the medication every day. David's doctor told him that while he did not agree with him, he thought that the decision was not unreasonable. He added that in the medical profession, he had been taught to respect "patient autonomy." The reason? "It's *your* life, after all."

This book has been written within the liberal tradition. Whether we are speaking of the decision to opt, the decision to delegate, the decision to know, the decision to believe, or something else, the liberal idea of autonomy has been central throughout. To be sure, that idea has been chastened by the findings of behavioral science, which calls attention to human error. But decisions about decisions are made by individuals, and across a broad territory and when there is no harm to others, individuals ought to have the right to make those decisions for themselves. As we have seen, that right might be rooted in ideas about autonomy as such; it might be rooted in ideas about welfare. Choosing and knowing, for example, might be fun, rewarding, and meaningful, or they might be burdensome and painful. On that question, individuals will hardly know everything, but they will know a great deal, and often more than anyone else.

* * *

Does liberalism have poems? Are there liberal poets? John Stuart Mill, who loved Shelley, thought so: "Although a philosopher cannot, by culture, make himself, in the peculiar sense in which we now use the term, a poet, unless he have that peculiarity of nature which would probably have made poetry his earliest pursuit; a poet may always, by culture, make himself a philosopher."[1] But can a poet make himself a philosopher of liberalism?

Charles Baudelaire, a contemporary of Mill, died in 1867. In 1869, a collection of Baudelaire's prose poems was published under the title *Le Spleen de Paris*. Among them was *Enivrez-Vous*. Here it is, in full:

> One should always be drunk. That's all that matters; that's our one imperative need. So as not to feel Time's horrible burden that breaks your shoulders and bows you down, you must get drunk without ceasing.
>
> But what with? With wine, with poetry, or with virtue, as you choose. But get drunk.
>
> And if, at some time, on the steps of a palace, in the green grass of a ditch, in the bleak solitude of your room, you are waking up when drunkenness has already abated, ask the wind, the wave, a star, the clock, all that which flees, all that which groans, all that which rolls, all that which sings, all that which speaks, ask them what time it is; and the wind, the wave, the star, the bird, the clock will reply: 'It is time to get drunk! So that you may not be the martyred slaves of Time, get drunk; get drunk, and never pause for rest! With wine, with poetry, or with virtue, as you choose!'

Now that's a liberal poem. *Enivrez-Vous* is liberal in its celebration of autonomy; profoundly authoritarian, it offers a license to its readers. Getting drunk, and refusing to be a martyred slave of Time, is not a sin,

---

[1] JOHN STUART MILL, THOUGHTS ON POETRY AND ITS VARIETIES (1860), *reprinted in* COLLECTED WORKS OF JOHN STUART MILL: VOLUME I 343, 363 (John M. Robinson & Jack Stillinger eds., 1981).

an offense, a transgression, or a violation of anything. It's a right, but it's no mere right; it's an "imperative need," something that counteracts "Time's horrible burden." You might object that the poem is not so liberal after all, because what I am calling a license takes the form of an imperative, a kind of mandate: "One should always be drunk." But it is a poem, not a treatise, and a license would be far too grudging or qualified, and a lot less fun. "One may drink" would not have the right valence. (Note well: This is not a poem about, or an essay on, tolerance. It asks you to act, not to tolerate. It's about your attitude toward yourself, not your attitude toward others.)

The poem is also liberal in its recognition, at once mischievous and celebratory, of the diversity of preferences and tastes – of what gets one drunk. In his *Autobiography*, Mill said that *On Liberty* was meant as "a kind of philosophic text-book of a single truth," which is "the importance, to man and society, of a large variety of types of character, and of giving full freedom to human nature to expand itself in innumerable and conflicting directions."[2] That is a plea for decisional autonomy, and for respecting people's decisions about their decisions. For some, wine is best; for others, poetry; for others, virtue. (For many, it's all three.) The power of Baudelaire's poem comes, of course, from the oddity of the juxtaposition. It is a bit shocking, but not all that interesting, for a poet to celebrate getting drunk. It is far more interesting (and far more liberal) for a poet to link wine, poetry, and virtue, and to see them all as sources of inebriation. Part of the fun, and the clarity, of *Enivrez-Vous* is its insistence that poetry and virtue can get you drunk, too.

It is true that you might insist, with Mill and many other liberals, that some pleasures are higher than others, and that those of poetry and virtue are higher than those of wine. Even if that's true and important (and it is), let's not say it too loudly, or with too much earnestness, or with condemnation of the lower pleasures. Liberals insist on accepting divergent conceptions of the good.

Enivrez-Vous is quintessentially liberal as well in its insistence on human agency and on activity rather than passivity ("as you choose!"). The reader is instructed to "get" drunk, as well as to make the choice about exactly how. Different people can exercise their agency in different ways. If you decide to get drunk on poetry (as Baudelaire evidently

---

[2] JOHN STUART MILL, AUTOBIOGRAPHY 253 (4th ed. New York, Henry Holt & Co. 1874).

did), that is fine; so too if you get drunk on good works. And, of course, the listed options are merely illustrative. The reader is invited to think: What, exactly, gets me drunk? (That is an excellent question to ask.)

Mill himself was, of course, insistent on agency as well. In speaking of happiness, he urged that we mean "not a life of rapture, but moments of such, in an existence made up of few and transitory pains, many and various pleasures, with a decided predominance of the active over the passive."[3] Baudelaire was speaking of "a life of rapture," but he was a poet, and maybe he didn't entirely mean it.

Finally, the poem is liberal in its exuberance – its pleasure in its own edginess, its defiance, its sheer rebelliousness, its implicit laughter, its love of life and what it has to offer. It is the opposite of dutiful. Its middle finger is raised. It is far more exuberant than Mill's *On Liberty*, but it is exuberant in the same way. (It can easily be seen as a companion to that book. Consider Mill's embrace of "experiments of living"; Mill had his own ways of getting drunk. By the way, *Enivrez-Vous* was probably written in the same decade as *On Liberty*.) It celebrates activity and joy; Baudelaire found a way to combine those two celebrations, without the slightest sentimentality. Far from being desiccated and lifeless, the poem is fun (and funny). It exemplifies what it celebrates.

Here is Mill on Shelley, whom he preferred to Wordsworth: "He is a poet, not because he has ideas of any particular kind, but because the succession of his ideas is subordinate to the course of his emotions."[4] Here is William Blake on John Milton: "The reason Milton wrote in fetters when he wrote of Angels & God, and at liberty when of Devils & Hell, is because he was a true Poet and of the Devil's party without knowing it."[5] Baudelaire was not of the Devil's party, but he was a true poet, and he knew something about Hell.

Nothing about Baudelaire is simple, of course, and the same is true of liberalism. Baudelaire is often said to have been anti-republican and pro-aristocracy; he admired Joseph de Maistre (a true and complete horror, and an antiliberal). But he was not especially political. Still, *Enivrez-Vous* is unmistakably a product of a liberal imagination.

[3] JOHN STUART MILL, UTILITARIANISM 18 (7th ed. London, Longmans, Green, & Co. 1879).
[4] MILL, *supra* note 1, at 362.
[5] WILLIAM BLAKE, THE MARRIAGE OF HEAVEN AND HELL 10 (Boston, John W. Luce & Co. 1906) (1794).

We live in a period in which liberalism is under considerable pressure. On the left, "liberalism," or more specifically "neoliberalism," is said to be old and dead and boring and dull and exhausted, and to have failed dismally. Some people on the left hold it responsible for an assortment of social evils, including poverty, climate change, inequality, racism, sexism, the demise of labor unions, the rise of monopolies, technocracy, and a general sense of alienation and disempowerment. On the right, and particularly the religious right, "liberalism" is said to have ruined everything. It is allegedly responsible for much that is bad – a growth in out-of-wedlock childbirth, repudiation of traditions (religious and otherwise), a rise in populism, increased reliance on technocracy (the bane of both left and right), inequality, environmental degradation, sexual promiscuity, deterioration of civic associations, a diminution of civic virtue, political correctness on university campuses, and a general sense of alienation.

I have put liberalism in quotation marks, because the set of ideas that is under attack is not always specified, and because its connection to liberal political thought is not clear. Any list of liberal thinkers ought to include John Locke, Jeremy Bentham, Mill, Benjamin Constant, Mary Wollstonecraft, Immanuel Kant, Friedrich Hayek, Isaiah Berlin, John Rawls, Joseph Raz, Amartya Sen, Ronald Dworkin, Martha Nussbaum, Jeremy Waldron, and Christine Korsgaard. (Walt Whitman and Bob Dylan should be counted as liberals as well. Whitman, sounding a lot like Baudelaire, only more saccharine: "Do anything, but let it produce joy." Dylan, sounding a lot like Baudelaire, only more edgy: "Everybody must get stoned.") A lengthy book could easily be written about the differences between Bentham and Mill, and in important respects, Hayek and Dworkin are not on the same team.

Still, Baudelaire's poem captures something essential about the most appealing forms of liberalism (captured, in different ways, by Mill, Whitman, and Dylan as well): its celebration of freedom, the diversity of tastes and preferences, human agency, and a kind of exuberance. When thinking about decisions about decisions, it is a good idea to keep that celebration in mind.

ACKNOWLEDGMENTS

The origins of this book lie in some spirited discussions in 1989 with Edna Ullmann-Margalit, in which we began to explore the topic of second-order decisions. Those discussions led to a forerunner of Chapter 1 of this book. I was also privileged to collaborate with Ullmann-Margalit on two other essays, one of which became the foundation for Chapter 7. Ullmann-Margalit died far too young in 2010; I like to think that if she had lived, this book would have been coauthored (and I know that if that had happened, it would have been much better). Heartfelt and continuing thanks to her for the collaborations, and also to her widower and my friend, Avishai Margalit, for permission to draw on our joint work here.

I am grateful as well to Tali Sharot for many collaborations and in particular for joint work that led to Chapters 4 and 5. I have learned much from Sharot; I am especially grateful to her for her emphasis on the emotional impacts of decisions. I came late to that particular party, but I am grateful to be there. Thanks too to Sharot for permission to draw on joint work here.

Over the years, many friends and colleagues have discussed these issues with me, and commented on work that in one or another way found its way into these pages. I single out Jon Elster, Jack Goldsmith, Robert Goodin, Stephen Holmes, Martha Nussbaum, Eric Posner, Richard Posner, and Adrian Vermeule. Elster deserves special thanks for introducing me to a whole world of ideas in the 1980s; those ideas made a large mark on this book.

Special thanks to Ethan Judd – research assistant, adviser, and partner – who has shepherded this book to completion. Robert Dreeson was a terrific and careful editor, offering many superb suggestions. Special thanks also to Sarah Chalfant and Rebecca Nagel, extraordinary agents, who offered valuable advice and guidance throughout.

All of the chapters here have been significantly reworked, but I have drawn on the following, and I am grateful to the relevant journals for permission to do so here:

Chapter 1 draws from Cass R. Sunstein and Edna Ullmann-Margalit, *Second-Order Decisions*, 110 ETHICS 5 (1999).

Chapter 2 was written for this book but an overlapping essay, written shortly after, is *Big Decisions: "Opting," Psychological Richness, and Public Policy*, J. POLIT. PHIL. (2023), available at https://onlinelibrary.wiley.com/doi/abs/10.1111/jopp.12296

Chapter 3 draws from Cass R. Sunstein, *Ruining Popcorn: The Welfare Effects of Information*, 58 J. RISK AND UNCERTAINTY 121 (2019).

Chapter 4 draws from Cass R. Sunstein, Sebastian Bobadilla-Suarez, Stephanie C. Lazzaro, and Tali Sharot, *How People Update Beliefs About Climate Change*, 102 CORNELL LAW REVIEW 1431 (2017).

Chapter 5 draws from Tali Sharot, Max Rollwage, Stephen Fleming, and Cass R. Sunstein, *Why and When Beliefs Change*, Perspectives in Psychological Science (2022), available at https://journals.sagepub.com/doi/abs/10.1177/17456916221082967?journalCode=ppsa

Chapter 6 draws from Cass R. Sunstein, *On Preferring A to B, While Also Preferring B to A*, 30 RATIONALITY AND SOCIETY 305 (2018).

Chapter 7 draws from Cass R. Sunstein and Edna Ullmann-Margalit, *Solidarity Goods*, from 9 JOURNAL OF POLITICAL PHILOSOPHY 129 (2001).

Chapter 8 draws from Cass R. Sunstein *Valuing Facebook*, 4 BEHAVIOURAL PUBLIC POLICY 370 (2020).

Chapter 9 draws from Cass R. Sunstein, *Algorithms, Correcting Biases*, 86 SOCIAL RESEARCH 499 (2019).

Chapter 10 draws from *Manipulation As Theft*, 12 THE JOURNAL OF EUROPEAN PUBLIC POLICY 1959 (2022).

The Epilogue draws from Cass R. Sunstein, *Liberalism, Inebriated*, 2 LIBERTIES, ISSUE 1 (2022).

INDEX

Printed in the United States
by Baker & Taylor Publisher Services